AF796847

The Week of Atoning Sacrifice:

"For This Cause Came I Into the World"

Randal S. Chase

Compiled and Edited By
Michael D. Chase

The Week of Atoning Sacrifice:
"For This Cause Came I Into the World"
© 2014 Randal S. Chase

All rights reserved. No part of this book may be reproduced in any form or by any means without permission in writing from the publisher, Plain and Precious Publishing. This work is not an official publication of The Church of Jesus Christ of Latter-day Saints. The views expressed herein are the responsibility of the author and do not necessarily represent the position of the Church or Plain and Precious Publishing.

Send inquiries to:
Plain and Precious Publishing
3378 E. Sweetwater Springs Drive
Washington, UT 84780

Send e-mail: info@makingpreciousthingsplain.com

For more copies visit www.makingpreciousthingsplain.com

For a listing of all Plain and Precious Publishing products, visit www.makingpreciousthingsplain.com
or call 435–251–8520.

Printed in the United States of America

ISBN: 978-1-937901-16-5

Cover: "The Crucifixion" by Carl H. Bloch.

The Week of Atoning Sacrifice:

"For This Cause Came I Into the World"

Table of Contents

"THE CRUCIFIXION," CARL H. BLOCH

"FOR THIS CAUSE CAME I INTO THE WORLD"

Section One

The Week of Atoning Sacrifice

(March 27–April 2, A.D. 33)[1]

The events described in this section include those that occurred during the final week of Jesus' ministry.

The chapters in this section are:

1. Condemning Priesthood Hypocrisy
2. Signs of the Second Coming
3. Parables of the Latter-day Kingdom
4. The Last Supper and First Sacrament
5. The Holy Spirit and Jesus' Intercessory Prayer
6. The Atonement in Gethsemane
7. Jesus' Crucifixion and Death

The final week of Jesus' ministry is a study in contrasts. It began with His prophecy-fulfilling entry into Jerusalem riding upon an ass while the masses shouted praises to what they hoped would be their liberating King. But by the end of the week some of those same crowds would loudly demand His crucifixion and shout that they had no other king but Caesar.

The Savior's disciples swore their loyalty to Him, with Peter vowing that he would die for his Master. But within hours, Peter denied three times that he even knew Jesus and then wept bitterly over his failure. One of His disciples (Judas Iscariot) betrayed Him. All of them except John were absent at the time of His crucifixion. Two of the Sanhedrin, Joseph of Arimathaea and Nicodemus, carefully removed His lifeless body and buried it in haste.

Following is a chronological list of events that took place during this period and the scriptures from the four Gospels that tell the story.[2]

THE WEEK OF ATONING SACRIFICE

	Matt.	Mark	Luke	John
FIRST DAY (Sunday)				
Jerusalem and Bethany, Judea				
Triumphal Entry into Jerusalem	21:1–11	11:1–10	19:29–44	12:12–19
Certain Greeks Visit Christ—a Voice from Heaven				12:20–36
Return to Bethany		11:11		
SECOND DAY (Monday)				
Cursing of the Barren Fig Tree	21:18–`19	11:12–14		
Second Cleansing of the Temple	21:12–16	11:15–18	19:45–48	
Return to Bethany	21:17	11:19	21:37	
THIRD DAY (Tuesday)				
Discourse on Faith	21:19–22	11: 20–26	21:38	
Question of Authority	21:23–27	11:27–33	20:1–8	
Parable of the Two Sons	21:28–32			
Parable of the Wicked Husbandmen	21:33–46	12:1–12	20: 9–18	
Parable of the Royal Marriage Feast	22:1–14			
A Question about Tribute to Caesar	22:15–22	12:13–17	20:19–26	
Marriage after the Resurrection	22: 23–33	12:18–27	20: 27–40	
The Great Commandment	22:34–40	12:28–34		
"Who Is Christ's Father?"	22:41–46	12:35–37	20:41–44	
Scribes and Pharisees Condemned	23:1–36	12:38–40	20:45–47	
Jesus Laments over Jerusalem	23:37–39			
The Widow's Mite		12:41–44	21:1–4	
Christ Defines Purpose of His Mission				12:37–50
Olivet Discourse 24:1–51		13:1–37	21:5–36	
Parable of the Ten Virgins	25:1-13			
Parable of the Entrusted Talents	25:14–30			
The Inevitable and Final Judgment	25:31–46			
Jesus' Betrayal Foretold	26:1–2			

THE WEEK OF ATONING SACRIFICE

	Matt.	Mark	Luke	John
THIRD DAY (Tuesday) (Cont.d)				
The Plot Against Jesus	26: 3–5	14:1–2	22:1–2	
Judas Arranges Betrayal	26:14–16	14:10–11	22:3–6	
FOURTH DAY (Wednesday) (See explanation in footnotes) [3]				
Arrangements for the Passover Meal	26:17–19	14:12–16	22:7–13	
Strife over Precedence in the Passover Chamber	26:20	14:17	22:14; 24:30	
Jesus Washes the Apostles' Feet				13:1–20
Passover Meal—Introduction of the Sacrament	26:26–29	14:22–25	22:15–20	
Jesus Indicates the Betrayer	26:21–25	14:18–21	22:21–23	13:21–26
Judas Leaves the Chamber				13:27–30
Jesus Foretells His Own Death				13:31-35
Apostles Express Loyalty	26:31–35	I4:27–31	22:31–38	13:36–38
Discourse about the Comforter				14:1–31
They Sing a Hymn and Proceed to the Mt. of Olives	26:30	14:26	22:39	
Relationship to Christ & World; His Death Explained				15:1–27;16:1–33
High Priestly Prayer				17:1–26
Agony in Gethsemane	26:36–46	14:32–42	22:40–46	18:1–2
FIFTH DAY (Thursday)				
The Betrayal by Judas	26:47–50	14:43–45	22:47–48	18:2–9
The Arrest	26:51–56	14:46–52	22:49–53	18:10–12
Jesus Questioned by Annas			22:54–55	18:13,19–24
Examined Before Caiaphas	26:57–68	14:53–65	22:63–65	18:14–16,18
Peter Denies Knowing Jesus	26:69–75	14:66–72	22: 55–62	18:17,25–27
Formal Trial and Condemnation	27:1–2	15:1	22:66–71;23:1	
Judas Iscariot's Death	27:3–10		23:2–5	
Before Pilate, Then Herod	27:11–14	15:2–5	23:6–12	18:28–38
Again Before Pilate	27:15–23	15:6–14	23:13–23	18:39–40.
Barabbas Released	27:26–30	15:15–i9	23:25	19:1–3
Pilate Sentences Jesus	27:24–25	15:20–23,	23:24	19:4–16
The Way to Calvary	27:31–34,38	15:25,27,28	23:26–33	19:16–18
Superscription on the Cross	27:37	15:26	23:38	19:19–22
His First Utterance on the Cross			23:34	
Soldiers Divide His Clothing	27:35–36	15:24	23;34	19:23–24
Mocking and Scoffing	27:39–44	15:29–32	23:35–37	
Second Utterance from the Cross			23:39–43	
Third Utterance by the Savior				19:25–27
Darkness Covers the Earth	27:45	15:33	23:44–45	
Fourth Statement	27:46–47	15:34–35		
Fifth Statement, Sixth Utterance,	27:48–49	15:36		19:28–30
Final Utterance; Jesus Dies	27:50	15:37	23:46	19:30

THE WEEK OF ANOTNING SACRIFICE

	Matt.	Mark	Luke	John
FIFTH DAY (Thursday) (Cont'd.)				
Centurion's Testimony	27:51–56	15:38–41	23:45,47–49	
His Side Pierced	27:57–61	15:42–47	23:50–56	19:31–37
His Burial				19:38–42
Jesus' Ministry to the Spirit World	1 Peter 3:18–20; D&C 138:1–52			
SIXTH DAY (Friday)				
Guards Are Placed at the Tomb	27:62–66			

Notes

1. For an explanation of these and other precise dates that appear in this section, see John P. Pratt, "The Restoration of Priesthood Keys on Easter 1836, Part 1: Dating the First Easter," *Ensign*, June 1985, 59–68.

2. Adapted from *The Life and Teachings of Jesus and His Apostles* [1979], 138, 144, 150, 158, 164, 170, 178, 190.

3. **Leviticus 23:5** The Passover was an annual feast held on the 14th day of Nisan. In Israel, a new day began at sunset. Thus, at twilight, as the 14th day of Nisan was dawning, the Passover lambs were slain. Sunset of the following day initiated the first day of the Feast of Unleavened Bread. While Passover lasted only one day originally, the Feast of Unleavened Bread lasted a full seven days. Eventually, both festivals were combined into one, making the entire Passover period eight days in length.

   Leviticus 23:6–7 The Feast of Unleavened Bread at the time of Jesus had been combined with Passover, and so it began at Passover and continued for a week (v. 6). The first day after Passover was technically the first day of the week-long Feast of Unleavened Bread. It was considered a "high day," an additional non-Saturday Sabbath to be observed in addition to the normal Sabbath that occurs on Saturday.[4] Thus, during this final week of the Savior's life, Friday was considered a Sabbath day in addition to Saturday, and the crucifixion would have taken place on Thursday rather than Friday. This being true, the Savior did indeed remain in the tomb for three days and nights—Thursday, Friday, and Saturday—before raising on Sunday morning.

4. "The Feast of Unleavened Bread," http://endtimepilgrim.org/unleavened.htm

Chapter 1

Condemning Priesthood Hypocrisy

(Matthew 21–23; John 12:1–8)

INTRODUCTION

Jerusalem in an Uproar

- **John 11:55–57 Passover excitement is heightened by speculation concerning Jesus.** As they did every Passover, "many went out of the country up to Jerusalem before [prior to] the passover, to purify themselves" (v. 55). Jerusalem was abuzz with rumor and anticipation concerning Jesus. They "sought . . . for Jesus, and spake among themselves, as they stood in the temple, What think ye, that he will not come to the feast?" (v. 56). Meanwhile, the leaders of the Jews "had given a commandment, that, if any man knew where he were, he should shew it, that they might take him" (v. 57).

A. BIDA, 1874

- **John 11:53; 12:10–11 Jewish leaders take "counsel together . . . to put him to death."** The raising of Lazarus had enraged them. They feared the loss of their positions of prestige and power, and they plotted how to kill Jesus. They also plotted to kill Lazarus (12:10). His being raised from the dead caused "many of the Jews [to go] away, and believe . . . on Jesus" (12:11).

- **John 11:54 Faced with such animosity, Jesus retires for a short while.** He "walked no more openly among the Jews; but went thence unto a country near to the wilderness, into a city called Ephraim, and there continued with his disciples." They would soon be called upon to lead the Church and needed some final training.

A Brief Stay in Bethany

- **John 12:1, 9 Six days before Passover, Jesus visits Lazarus, Mary, and Martha** (v. 1). He spent the evening with them in Bethany, as He often did during His ministry whenever He visited Jerusalem. When they became aware that He was there, "much people" came to Bethany "not for Jesus' sake only, but that they might see Lazarus also, whom he had raised from the dead" (v. 9).

- **John 12:2–3 Mary anoints the Savior's feet with spikenard, a costly ointment.** Martha served them supper while Lazarus sat at the table with Jesus (v. 2). We must understand the word *sat* to understand what happened next. In those days, when people "sat" at a meal they actually reclined, with their feet outward from the table. And while Jesus was in this posture, "Mary [took] a pound of ointment of spikenard, very costly, and anointed the feet of Jesus, and wiped his feet with her hair: and the house was filled with the odour of the ointment" (v. 3).

  Elder James E. Talmage said: "To anoint the head of a guest with ordinary oil was to do him honor; to anoint his feet also was to show unusual and signal regard; but the anointing of head and feet with spikenard, and in such abundance, was an act of reverential homage rarely rendered even to kings. Mary's act was an expression of adoration; it was the fragrant outwelling of a heart overflowing with worship and affection."[1]

- **John 12:4–5 Mary's actions are criticized by Judas.** Already filled with the spirit of dissension, Judas asked, "Why was not this ointment sold for three hundred pence, and given to the poor?" (v. 5).

- **John 12:6 Judas is a hypocrite.** John hastens to add that Judas "cared [not] for the poor," but objected to the use of the money "because he was a thief, and had the bag, and bare what was put therein." The man obviously loved money and would eventually sell Jesus to enemies for 30 pieces of silver. John suggests here that he was also pilfering the funds used by the Twelve, over which he had supervisory responsibility.

PROVIDENCE LITHOGRAPHIC CO., 1906, #38

- **John 12:7–8 Jesus defends Mary's act of worship.** "Then said Jesus, Let her alone: against the day of my burying hath she kept this" (v. 7). It was common to anoint the dead with sweet-smelling ointment, which was what the women were planning to do when they came to Jesus' grave one week later (see Luke 24:1). Mary was doing the same for Him now, and Jesus appreciated her act of love. "The poor always ye have with you," He observed, "but me ye have not always" (v. 8).

THE FIRST DAY

(Sunday)[2]

Jesus Journeys to Jerusalem

- **John 12:12–13 The people assemble to shout praise for Jesus.** The Sabbath was now over, and Jesus planned to go into Jerusalem on the first day of His final week of life. On our calendar, it was a Sunday. And "when they heard that Jesus was coming to Jerusalem, [the people] took branches of palm trees, and went forth to meet him."

- **Matthew 21:1–7 Jesus stops at Bethphage.** On their way to Jerusalem, they passed through Bethphage on the slopes of the Mount of Olives (v. 1). From there, Jesus sent two disciples on an errand, "saying unto them, Go into the village over against you, and straightway ye shall find an ass tied, and a colt with her: loose them, and bring them unto me. And if any man say ought unto you, ye shall say, The Lord hath need of them; and straightway he will send them" (vv. 2–3). All this was done to fulfill the prophecy of Zechariah (vv. 4–5).

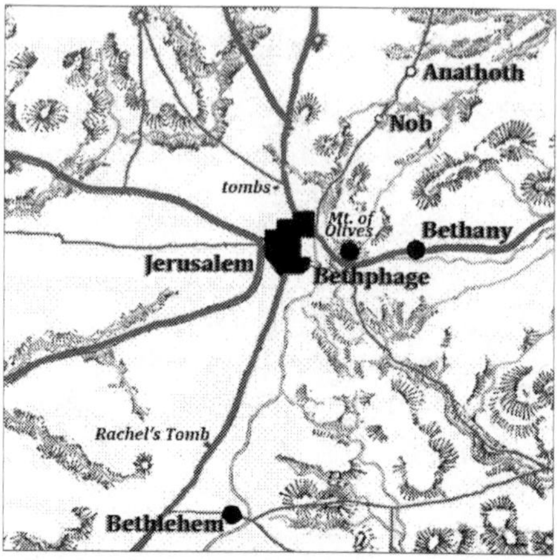

— **Zechariah 9:9** "Rejoice greatly, O daughter of Zion; shout, O daughter of Jerusalem: behold, thy King cometh unto thee: he is just, and having salvation; lowly, and riding upon an ass, and upon a colt the foal of an ass."

"And the disciples went, and did as Jesus commanded them, And brought the ass, and the colt, and put on them their clothes, and they set him thereon" (vv. 6–7).

Elder James E. Talmage said:

> It was no meaningless pageantry; but the actual advent of the King into His royal city, and His entry into the temple, the house of the King of kings. He came riding on an ass, in token of peace, acclaimed by the Hosanna shouts of multitudes; not on a caparisoned steed with the panoply of combat and the accompaniment of bugle blasts and fanfare of trumpets.
>
> That the joyous occasion was in no sense suggestive of physical hostility or of seditious disturbance is sufficiently demonstrated by the indulgent unconcern with which it was viewed by the Roman officials, who were usually prompt to send their legionnaires swooping down from the fortress of Antonia at the first evidence of an outbreak; and they were particularly vigilant in suppressing all Messianic pretenders, for false Messiahs had arisen already, and much blood had been shed in the forcible dispelling of their delusive claims.[3]

Jesus Enters Jerusalem

PROVIDENCE LITHOGRAPHIC CO, 1904, #42

- **Luke 19:37–38 The multitude is filled with gratitude for Jesus' miracles.** The praise began as soon as Jesus began the descent from the Mount of Olives down into the Kidron Valley. "The whole multitude of the disciples began to rejoice and praise God with a loud voice for all the mighty works that they had seen" (v. 37).

- **Matthew 21:8–11 The multitude shouts "Hosanna" as He enters Jerusalem.** "And a very great multitude spread their garments in the way; others cut down branches from the trees, and strawed them in the way. And the multitudes that went before, and that followed, cried, saying, Hosanna to the Son of David: Blessed is he that cometh in the name of the Lord; Hosanna in the highest" (vv. 8–9). John records their praise as "Hosanna: Blessed is the King of Israel that cometh in the name of the Lord" (John 12:13). Luke records it as "Blessed be the King that cometh in the name of the Lord: peace in heaven, and glory in the highest"—very similar praise to that sung by the angels at His birth (Luke 19:38; 2:13–14). It was an amazing scene—one that moved the entire city to wonder, "Who is this?" (v. 10). "And the multitude said, This is Jesus the prophet of Nazareth of Galilee" (v. 11).

  — **Hosanna Shout:** An English version of the Greek translation of the Aramaic—the word *hosanna* is actually a prayer, an appeal that means "help" or "save, I pray." It had been shouted at temple dedications in ancient Israel and also perhaps by Joshua's army as they brought down the walls of Jericho. But always, it was used to praise the Lord Jehovah. Its use by the multitude showed they recognized that Jesus was the Savior.

Elder Bruce R. McConkie said: "As we see our Lord's triumphal entry into Jerusalem, amid waving palm branches, riding over the [carefully] placed clothing of the people, and accepting their acclamations of praise and divinity, it is as though Zechariah had viewed the scene and written, not prophecy, but history. Every detail of this unique episode joined in testifying of the identity of the central figure in the picture. It was as though Jesus had said: '. . . Now I come unto you as the King of Israel in the very way that the prophet of old said I would; and your participation in this event is itself a witness that I am He who should come to redeem my people.'"[4]

PROVIDENCE LITHOGRAPHIC CO., 1904, #36

Elder James E. Talmage said: "The Romans saw nothing to fear, perhaps much to smile at, in the spectacle of a King mounted upon an ass, and attended by subjects, who, though numerous, brandished no weapons but waved instead palm branches and myrtle sprigs. The ass has been designated in literature as 'the ancient symbol of Jewish royalty,' and one riding upon an ass as the type of peaceful progress. . . . The manner of His entry should have appealed to the learned teachers of the law and the prophets; for Zechariah's impressive forecast . . . was frequently cited among them [see Zechariah 9:9]."[5]

- **Luke 19:39–40 The Pharisees are offended by the praise for Jesus.** "And some of the Pharisees from among the multitude said unto him, Master, rebuke thy disciples. And he answered and said unto them, I tell you that, if these should hold their peace, the stones would immediately cry out."

Jesus Blesses His Disciples

- **Mark 11:11 Jesus goes directly to the temple.** This was His usual practice whenever He entered Jerusalem (see John 8:1–2).

On this occasion, He "entered into Jerusalem, and into the temple: and when he had looked round about upon all things, and . . . the eventide was come, he went [back] out unto Bethany with the twelve."

- **JST Mark 11:13 Jesus "blesse[s] the disciples" before departing the temple.** While the above passage from the King James Version of the Bible records that Jesus went to the temple, it does not reveal all that He did while there. The Joseph Smith Translation (JST) makes it clear that He spent significant time alone with His disciples. JST Mark 11:13 (which corresponds to KJV Mark 11:11) adds the following:

> "And Jesus entered into Jerusalem, and into the temple. And when he looked round about upon all things, *and blessed the disciples*, the eventide was come; and he went out unto Bethany with the twelve" (emphasis added).

Elder Bruce R. McConkie said: "Though Jerusalem, as a whole, was to be desolated and scourged as few cities have ever been, yet the faithful within her walls were to be saved, preserved, and blessed."[6]

THE SECOND DAY
(Monday)

Cursing the Fig Tree

THE HOLMAN BIBLE, 1890, #54

- **Matthew 21:18–19 Jesus curses a barren fig tree.** The following morning, on the way back to Jerusalem, being hungry, the Lord and His disciples came upon a fig tree that was full of leaves—normally a signal that it would also be full of fruit (vv. 18–19). But the tree was barren, and Jesus cursed it (see also Mark 11:12–14, 20–24).

"And when he saw a fig tree in the way, he came to it, and found nothing thereon, but leaves only, and said unto it, Let no fruit grow on thee henceforward for ever. And presently the fig tree withered away" (v. 19). This cursing of the fig tree is the only recorded instance in which the Lord used His divine power to destroy.

- **Matthew 21:20–22 The power of faith.** "And when the disciples saw it, they marvelled, saying, How soon is the fig tree withered away!" (v. 20). And as always, Jesus used the incident as a teaching moment. "Jesus answered and said unto them, Verily I say unto you, If ye have faith, and doubt not, ye shall not only do this which is done to the fig tree, but also if ye shall say unto this mountain, Be thou removed, and be thou cast into the sea; it shall be done. And all things, whatsoever ye shall ask in prayer, believing, ye shall receive."

- **The barren fig tree symbolized apostate Jewish religion.** Among the rabbis, the fig tree was a symbol of the Jewish religion. This tree was covered with foliage, but it was deceptively barren. Judaism was like the fruitless tree—claiming to be the true religion, but bearing no fruit.

  Elder James E. Talmage said: "[The tree] was made the object of the curse and the subject of the Lord's instructive discourse, because, having leaves, it was deceptively barren. Were it reasonable to regard the tree as possessed of moral agency, we would have to pronounce it a hypocrite; its utter barrenness coupled with its abundance of foliage made of it a type of human hypocrisy."[7]

The Second Cleansing of the Temple

- **Matthew 21:12–13 The Lord visits and cleanses the temple** (see also Mark 11:15–17). On this second day of His final week (Monday), "Jesus went into the temple of God, and cast out all them that sold and bought in the temple, and overthrew the tables of the moneychangers, and the seats of them that sold doves, And said unto them, It is written, My house shall be called the house of prayer; but ye have made it a den of thieves."

- **John 2:13–16 He had done this before—three years earlier**, almost to the day. Like bookends on His ministry, the cleansing of the temple symbolized both the corruption of its present occupants and the sacredness of its purpose. On the first occasion, Jesus "made a scourge of small cords, [and] he drove them all out of the temple, and the sheep, and the oxen; and poured out the changers' money, and overthrew the tables; And said unto them that sold doves, Take these things hence; make not my Father's house an house of merchandise."

C. H. BLOCH

  We should take note that in the first cleansing Jesus called the temple "my Father's house" (John 2:16), while in this later instance He called it "my house" (Matthew 21:13).

- **Matthew 21:14–16 The chief priests and scribes are offended by the shouts of praise for Jesus.** No longer performing His miracles in private settings, "the blind and the lame came to him in the temple; and he healed them" (v. 14). "And when the chief priests and scribes saw the wonderful things that he did" and heard the shouts of "hosanna," they were offended (v. 15). They asked Jesus, "Hearest thou what these say? And Jesus saith unto them, Yea; have ye never read, Out of the mouth of babes and sucklings thou hast perfected praise?" (v. 16). This was a quote from Psalm 8:2 (see also Matthew 11:25; 1 Corinthians 1:27).

PROVIDENCE LITHOGRAPHIC CO., 1906, #38

Elder Bruce R. McConkie said: "Not children in the sense of infants as the King James Version has it, but disciples, members of the Church, those who had testimonies of Jesus' divinity. From these adult 'children of the kingdom,' these members of the Church who through repentance and baptism had become 'newborn babes' in Christ (1 Peter 2:2), came 'perfected praise.' How could such come from any except those who had knowledge and who were subject to the dictates of the Holy Spirit?"[8]

"The chief priests were the guardians of the temple and, in fact, guardians (as they supposed) of the whole structure of Jewish religion. They glutted themselves on the profits from temple business, and so the temple was not just the source of their favored social position (which they coveted so jealously) but also the source of their incomes—more, their fortunes.

"Jesus had come within the confines of their sacred stewardship before, early in His ministry, and on that occasion He had called the temple 'my Father's house' (John 2:16). Though His claim on that occasion offended the priests (because He claimed to be the Son of God, whose temple it was), still the claim itself declared that the temple belonged to God, and with that, at least, the chief priests agreed.

"But now, near the end of His ministry, He openly declared His messiahship, and those 'children of the kingdom' heard Him call the temple 'my house' (Matthew 21:13). Apparently His followers understood this claim by Jesus, for they began to sing and praise Him as the long-awaited Messiah. When the wrath and violence of the temple purging was over, Jesus' followers gathered around Him to receive what He might give them, for it was His house, and no one had a more perfect right to minister there than He."[9]

Elder James E. Talmage said: "His wrath of indignation was followed by the calmness of gentle ministry; there in the cleared courts of His house, blind and lame folk came limping and groping about Him, and He healed them. The anger of the chief priests and scribes was raging against Him; but it was impotent. They had decreed His death, and had made repeated efforts to take Him, and there He sat within the very area over which they claimed supreme jurisdiction, and they were afraid to touch Him because of the common people, whom they professed to despise yet heartily feared—'for all the people were very attentive to hear him.'"[10]

The Necessity of Jesus' Death and Resurrection

- **John 12:20–26 Jesus teaches the Greeks that it is necessary for Him to die.** Among those who had come to Jerusalem for the Passover were "certain Greeks"—either gentile converts or Jews who lived in Greece (v. 20). They immediately sought out "Philip, which was of Bethsaida of Galilee, and desired him, saying, Sir, we would see Jesus. Philip cometh and telleth Andrew: and again Andrew and Philip tell Jesus" (vv. 21–22). And unto these faithful souls Jesus bore witness of His coming death and resurrection.

  "The hour is come, that the Son of man should be glorified," He testified (v. 23). But before that could be accomplished He must first die. "Verily, verily, I say unto you [a figure of speech that means "I testify unto you"], except a corn of wheat fall into the ground and die, it abideth alone: but if it die, it bringeth forth much fruit" (v. 24).

  Speaking of His disciples, Jesus also suggested that they might have to sacrifice their worldly lifestyles (if not their very lives) in order to obtain the kingdom of God. "He that loveth his life shall lose it; and he that hateth his life in this world shall keep it unto life eternal. If any man serve me, let him follow me; and where I am, there shall also my servant be: if any man serve me, him will my Father honour" (vv. 25–26).

  The Prophet Joseph Smith said: "After the testimony of the Scriptures on this point, the assurance is given by the Holy Ghost, bearing witness to those who obey Him, that Christ Himself has assuredly risen from the dead; and if He has risen from the dead, He will, by His power, bring all men to stand before Him: for if He has risen from the dead the bands of the temporal death are broken that the grave has no victory. If then, the grave has no victory, those who keep the sayings of Jesus and obey His teachings have not only a promise of a resurrection from the dead, but an assurance of being admitted into His glorious kingdom; for, He Himself says, 'Where I am there also shall my servant be' [see John 12:26]."[11]

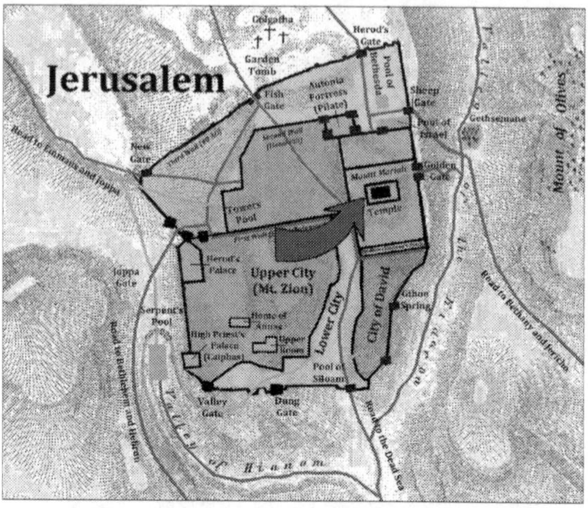

All these events occurred at the temple

- **John 12:27–30 God speaks out of heaven.** Aware of what was coming, Jesus admitted that His "soul [was] troubled," but what could He say? He could plead, "Father, save me from this hour," but He knew that "for this cause came I unto this hour" (v. 27). He bravely prayed, "Father, glorify thy name," and "then came there a voice from heaven, saying, I have both glorified it, and will glorify it again" (v. 28). A few people who stood nearby heard it and said that the voice "thundered," while others said, "An angel spake to him" (v. 29). Jesus confirmed that they had heard God's voice, but that it "came not because of me, but for your sakes" (v. 30).

Elder Harold B. Lee said: "In the Gospel of John is related a[n] . . . experience in the Master's ministry showing how, out of a multitude, only a few—or none—may hear God when He speaks. . . . Only the Master, apparently, knew that God had spoken. So often today, men and women are living so far apart from things spiritual that when the Lord is speaking to their physical hearing, to their minds with no audible sound, or to them through His authorized servants who, when directed by the Spirit, are as His own voice, they hear only a noise as did they at Jerusalem. Likewise, they receive no inspired wisdom, nor inward assurance, that the mind of the Lord has spoken through His prophet leaders."[12]

The voice of God is consistently described in the scriptures as a "still, small voice." God does not shout. He does not need to shout. His voice, though gentle, pierces mortals to their very souls. Indeed, the voice is perceived by our spirits rather than by our ears. Thus, it seems that His voice is penetrating to the core and emanates from within.

— **1 Kings 19:11–13** The Lord comforted Elijah on Mount Horeb, speaking to him through a "still small voice."

— **1 Nephi 17:45** God's voice is similarly described in the Book of Mormon. "Ye are swift to do iniquity but slow to remember the Lord your God. Ye have seen an angel, and he spake unto you; yea, ye have heard his voice from time to time; and he hath spoken unto you in a still small voice, but ye were past feeling, that ye could not feel his words; wherefore, he has spoken unto you like unto the voice of thunder, which did cause the earth to shake as if it were to divide asunder."

— **3 Nephi 11:3** When Jesus descended onto the American continent, the voice of God was also heard. "And it came to pass that while they were thus conversing one with another, they heard a voice as if it came out of heaven; and they cast their eyes round about, for they understood not the voice which they heard; and it was not a harsh voice, neither was it a loud voice; nevertheless, and notwithstanding it being a small voice it did pierce them that did hear to the center, insomuch that there was no part of their frame that it did not cause to quake; yea, it did pierce them to the very soul, and did cause their hearts to burn."

Elder Boyd K. Packer said: "Inspiration comes more easily in peaceful settings. Such words as *quiet, still, peaceable, Comforter* abound in the scriptures: 'Be *still*, and know that I am God' (Psalm 46:10; emphasis added). And the promise, 'You shall receive my Spirit, the Holy Ghost, even the Comforter, which shall teach you the *peaceable* things of the kingdom' (D&C 36:2; emphasis added). Elijah felt a great wind, an earthquake, a fire. The Lord was not in any of them; then came 'a still small voice' (1 Kings 19:12)."[13]

President Ezra Taft Benson said: "Do you take time to listen to the promptings of the Spirit? Answers to prayer come most often by a still voice and are discerned by our deepest, innermost *feelings*. I tell you that you can know the will of God concerning yourselves if you will take the time to pray and to listen."[14]

President Gordon B. Hinckley said: "Now, let me just say, categorically, that the things of God are understood by the Spirit of God, and one must have and seek and cultivate that Spirit, and there comes understanding and it is real. I can give testimony of that. . . . I think the best way I could describe the process is to liken it to the experience of Elijah as set forth in the book of First Kings. Elijah spoke to the Lord, and there was a wind, a great wind, and the Lord was not in the wind. And there was an earthquake, and the Lord was not in the earthquake. And there was a fire, and the Lord was not in the fire. And after the fire a still, small voice, which I describe as the whisperings of the Spirit (see 1 Kings 19:9–12)."[15]

- **John 12:31–36 Jesus testifies of the manner of His death—that He will be "lifted up" (on the cross).** Jesus boldly proclaimed that "the prince of this world [Satan, shall] be cast out" (v. 31). And He, the Savior of all humankind, will be "lifted up from the earth" in order that he might "draw all men unto me" (v. 32). He said this, "signifying what death he should die" (v. 33)—that He would be crucified.

  The people had heard Him proclaim that He was the Christ, and said, "We have heard out of the law that Christ abideth for ever: and how sayest thou, The Son of man must be lifted up? who is this Son of man?" (v. 34). The phrase "Son of Man" is a shortened version of the name-title "Son of the Man of Holiness," which Man of Holiness is God the Father. How then, they reasoned, could the Christ ever be put to death? And if He was saying that He would be crucified, how could He be the Christ? Obviously, they under-stood only certain parts of the scriptures, because they plainly teach that the Savior would suffer and die (see Isaiah 53).

  Jesus warned them, "Yet a little while is the light with you. Walk while ye have the light, lest darkness come upon you: for he that walketh in darkness knoweth not whither he goeth" (v. 35). His mortal life would last only four more days. "While ye have light, believe in the light, that ye may be the children of light," He continued (v. 36). And then He departed and hid Himself from them.

Reasons Why People Rejected the Savior

Given such dramatic witnesses of the Savior's divinity, how is it possible that most of the people rejected Him? The scriptures provide a number of explanations.

- **2 Nephi 10:3 No other people would have crucified Jesus.** Jerusalem possessed "those who [were] the more wicked part of the world [who would] crucify him . . . and there [was] none other nation on earth that would crucify their God."

- **John 12:42–43 They loved the praise of men more than the praise of God.** There were, even among the "chief rulers," many who "believed on him; but because of the Pharisees they did not confess him, lest they should be put out of the synagogue: For they loved the praise of men more than the praise of God."

- **John 5:45–47 They didn't believe the words of the prophets.** Jesus did not need to "accuse [them] to the Father: there is one that accuseth you, even Moses, in whom ye trust. For had ye believed Moses, ye would have believed me: for he wrote of me. But if ye believe not his writings, how shall ye believe my words?"

- **Matthew 13:13–15 Some were spiritually unperceptive**—"walking in darkness at noon-day" (D&C 95:6). This was the reason Jesus taught with parables, "because they seeing see not; and hearing they hear not, neither do they understand" (v. 13). In this regard, they fulfilled the prophecy of Isaiah (v. 14). "For this people's heart is waxed gross, and their ears are dull of hearing, and their eyes they have closed; lest at any time they should see with their eyes, and hear with their ears, and should understand with their heart, and should be converted, and I should heal them" (v. 15).

- **Jacob 4:14 Many looked beyond the mark.** The Book of Mormon prophet Jacob described the Jews as "a stiffnecked people [who] despised the words of plainness, and killed the prophets, and sought for things that they could not understand. Wherefore, because of their blindness, which blindness came by looking beyond the mark, they must needs fall; for God hath taken away his plainness from them, and delivered unto them many things which they cannot understand, because they desired it. And because they desired it God hath done it, that they may stumble."

- **2 Nephi 10:5 Some were engaged in priestcraft and iniquity.** Jacob testified that they were guilty of "priestcrafts and iniquities," which caused them to "stiffen their necks against him, that he be crucified." Nephi defined priestcraft as "men preach[ing] and set[ting] themselves up for a light unto the world, that they may get gain and praise of the world" rather than seeking "the welfare of Zion" (2 Nephi 26:29).[16]

- **Matthew 12:39 Some were immoral and could not receive the Spirit.** In speaking of the disbelievers of His day, Jesus noted that "an evil and adulterous generation seeketh after a sign; and there shall no sign be given to it, but the sign of the prophet Jonas."

  Elder Bruce R. McConkie said:

  > Those who seek signs—either to create faith or to feed their egos—whether in or out of the Church, shall fail in their search for divine approval. "He that seeketh signs shall see signs, but not unto salvation. . . . Faith cometh not by signs, but signs follow those that believe. Yea, signs come by faith, not by the will of men, nor as they please, but by the will of God. Yea, signs come by faith, unto mighty works, for without faith no man pleaseth God; and with whom God is angry he is not well pleased; wherefore, unto such he showeth no signs, only in wrath unto their condemnation" (D&C 63:7–11).
  >
  > For the scribes and Pharisees of all generations; for the wicked and ungodly in every age; for those without faith, who walk in worldly paths, there is only one sign, one alone, to prove Christ's divinity, and that is the sign of the prophet Jonas. That sign is that Jesus was crucified, died, and rose again the third day in glorious immortality. It is that as Jonah of old spent three days and three nights in the belly of a whale, so shall the Son of Man spend a like period in an earthly tomb. It is that as the whale vomited Jonah from the blackness of a living tomb, so Jesus comes forth in a newness of life from a grave that cannot hold Him. It is that the Son of Man—the Son of God—burst the bands

> of death, became the firstfruits of them that sleep, and ever liveth in immortal glory. The resurrection proves that Jesus is the Messiah; it is the sign, given of God, to all men of the truth and divinity of His work. . . .
>
> What sign does He give that Christ is the Son of God? . . . To the Saints there are many, but to the scribes and Pharisees of the world there is only one—the fact of resurrection. Christ is the Redeemer, and His redemption from death establishes His divinity. How could there be a resurrection without a Redeemer? Truly the resurrection bears witness of the Redeemer. . . .
>
> Such are the signs—and there are none others—that God gives to the wicked and ungodly. If they believe and repent, if they are baptized and receive the Holy Ghost, if they walk uprightly before the Lord—then signs without end, miracles unceasing, wonders beyond mortal comprehension, all these flow unto them forever and ever. Such is the law that governs signs.[17]

- **Luke 14:15–20 Some were caught up in the cares of this world.** They were so busy with their daily lives that they had no time for the Savior and His message. Jesus told a parable about this problem—the parable of the great supper. This supper represented the Lord's invitation to receive exaltation, and yet all those who were invited "with one consent began to make excuse. The first said unto him, I have bought a piece of ground, and I must needs go and see it: I pray thee have me excused. And another said, I have bought five yoke of oxen, and I go to prove them: I pray thee have me excused. And another said, I have married a wife, and therefore I cannot come."

THE THIRD DAY

(Tuesday)

Religious Leaders Challenge Him

- **Matthew 21:23–27 The next morning angry religious rulers challenge the Lord's authority** (see also Mark 11:27–33). Jesus again returned to the temple and began to teach when "the chief priests and the elders of the people came unto him as he was teaching, and said, By what authority doest thou these things? and who gave thee this authority?" (v. 23). It was a trick question and Jesus had no intention of arguing with them. He responded, "I also will ask you one thing, which if ye tell me, I in like wise will tell you by what authority I do these things. The baptism of John, whence was it? from heaven, or of men?" (vv. 24–25). "And they reasoned with themselves, saying, If we shall say, From heaven; he will say unto us, Why did ye not then believe him? But if we shall say, Of men; we fear the people; for all hold John as a prophet. And they answered Jesus, and said, We cannot tell" (vv. 25–27). Since they refused to acknowledge the authority of God in John the Baptist's case, He said unto them, "Neither tell I you by what authority I do these things" (v. 27).

Jesus then proceeded to tell them four parables which illustrated their wickedness and hypocrisy as religious leaders.

The Parable of the Two Sons

- **Matthew 21:28–32 One son says he will not go, but then does; the other says he will go, but then does not.** The parable was about "a certain man [who] had two sons; and he came to the first, and said, Son, go work to day in my vineyard. He answered and said, I will not: but afterward he repented, and went. And he came to the second, and said likewise. And he answered and said, I go, sir: and went not" (vv. 28–30). The chief priests, scribes, and Pharisees were represented by the second son who said he would go, but did not. The people they despised—the publicans—were represented by the first son who said he would not labor but later repented and went (see also JST Matthew 21:32–34).

Jesus rebuked Sadducees & Pharisees

Jesus asked them, "Whether of them twain did the will of his father?" and they answered correctly, "The first" (v. 31). Jesus then explained that the parable applied to these false religious leaders by saying, "Verily I say unto you, That the publicans and the harlots go into the kingdom of God before you" (v. 31). "For John came unto you in the way of righteousness, and ye believed him not: but the publicans and the harlots believed him: and ye, when ye had seen it, repented not afterward, that ye might believe him" (v. 32).

The Parable of the Wicked Husbandmen

- **Matthew 21:33–41 The wicked husbandmen slay the master's son.** This parable involved "a certain householder, which planted a vineyard, and hedged it round about, and digged a winepress in it, and built a tower, and let it out to husbandmen, and went into a far country" (v. 33). This householder represents God the Father. "And when the time of the fruit drew near, he sent his servants to the husbandmen, that they might receive the fruits of it. And the husbandmen took his servants, and beat one, and killed another, and stoned another. Again, he sent other servants more than the first: and they did unto them likewise" (vv. 34–36). These servants represent the prophets that God sent to the children of Israel. Then, "last of all he sent unto them his son, saying, They will reverence my son. But when the husbandmen saw the son, they said among themselves, This is the heir; come, let us kill him, and let us seize on his inheritance. And they caught him, and cast him out of the vineyard, and slew him" (vv. 37–39). This "son," of course, represents the Savior.

  Jesus then asked the chief priests and Pharisees, "When the lord . . . of the vineyard cometh, what will he do unto those husbandmen?" (v. 40). And they answered, "He will miserably destroy those wicked men, and will let out his vineyard unto other husbandmen, which shall render him the fruits in their seasons" (v. 41). That was correct, and by their own words the chief priests and Pharisees therefore judged and condemned themselves (see also Mark 12:1–9).

The Parable of the Rejected Stone

- **Matthew 21:42–44 "The stone which the builders rejected" is Jesus Christ.** Jesus asked the supposedly learned scribes and

Pharisees, "Did ye never read in the scriptures, The stone which the builders rejected, the same is become the head of the corner: this is the Lord's doing, and it is marvellous in our eyes?" (v. 42; see Psalm 118:22–23). This cornerstone is Jesus Christ. "Therefore say I unto you, The kingdom of God shall be taken from you, and given to a nation bringing forth the fruits thereof. And whosoever shall fall on this stone shall be broken: but on whomsoever it shall fall, it will grind him to powder" (vv. 43–44). Thus, the builders who reject this stone (the scribes and Pharisees) will lose their inheritance to others who will accept the Lord.

— **Acts 4:10–12** Peter testified that Jesus is the fulfillment of the cornerstone prophecy. "Be it known unto you all, and to all the people of Israel, that by the name of Jesus Christ of Nazareth, whom ye crucified, whom God raised from the dead, even by him doth this man stand here before you whole. This is the stone which was set at nought of you builders, which is become the head of the corner. Neither is there salvation in any other: for there is none other name under heaven given among men, whereby we must be saved."

- **Matthew 21:45–46 The chief priests and Pharisees are angry but do not dare seize Him.** They realized that He was talking about them in these parables, but they did not seize Him for fear of the multitude, "because they took him for a prophet."

The Parable of the Marriage of the King's Son

- **Matthew 22:1–14** This parable has important similarities to the parable of the great supper, which Jesus spoke earlier (see Luke 14:15–24), but with some important differences. In this parable Jesus compared the kingdom of heaven to "a certain king, which made a marriage for his son, And sent forth his servants to call them that were bidden to the wedding: and they would not come" (vv. 2–3).

  As with the earlier parable, the supper represents exaltation, but in this case the king is God the Father and the son is Jesus Christ. The king "sent forth other servants [the prophets], saying, Tell them which are bidden, Behold, I have prepared my dinner . . . , and all things are ready: come unto the marriage. But they made light of it, and went their ways, one to his farm, another to his merchandise: And the [rest] took his servants, and entreated them spitefully, and slew them" (vv. 4–6).

ARTIST UNKNOWN, ILLUSTRATOR OF THE CHILDREN'S BIBLE

When the king heard what they had done to his servants, "he was wroth: and he sent forth his armies, and destroyed those murderers, and burned up their city" (v. 7). This represents the destruction that would fall on apostate Jewry under the hand of the Romans in a few years (A.D. 70).

"Then saith he to his servants, The wedding is ready, but they which were bidden were not worthy. Go ye therefore into the highways, and as many as ye shall find, bid to the marriage" (vv. 8–9). These strangers represent the gentiles to whom the gospel message would be taken. "So those servants went out into the highways, and gathered together all as many as they found, both bad and good: and the wedding was furnished with guests" (v. 10).

P. PRIOLO, THE BIBLE & ITS STORY, 1908

But there remained a problem at this supper. "When the king came in to see the guests, he saw there a man which had not on a wedding garment: And he saith unto him, Friend, how camest thou in hither not having a wedding garment? And he was speechless. Then said the king to the servants, Bind him hand and foot, and take him away, and cast him into outer darkness; there shall be weeping and gnashing of teeth. For many are called, but few are chosen" (vv. 11–14).

The guest the king saw without a wedding garment was one who had come into the Church but had not kept the commandments and therefore did not wear the robes of righteousness.

The Prophet Joseph Smith said: "That this son was the Messiah will not be disputed, since it was the kingdom of heaven that was represented in the parable; and that the Saints, or those who are found faithful to the Lord, are the individuals who will be found worthy to inherit a seat at the marriage supper, is evident from the sayings of John in the Revelation where he represents the sound which he heard in heaven to be like 'a great multitude,' or like 'the voice of mighty thunderings, saying, the Lord God Omnipotent reigneth. Let us be glad and rejoice, and give honor to Him; for the marriage of the Lamb is come, and His wife hath made herself ready. And to her was granted that she should be arrayed in fine linen, clean and white: For the fine linen is the righteousness of Saints' [Revelation 19:6–8]."[18]

Elder Bruce R. McConkie said:

> In this Parable of the Marriage of the King's Son, sometimes called the Parable of the Royal Marriage Feast, Jesus teaches these truths: (1) His own divine Sonship; (2) the impending destruction of Jerusalem; (3) the rejection of the Jewish remnant of the covenant race; (4) the gospel call to the Gentiles; and (5) that those who answer the gospel call will not be chosen for salvation unless they put on the robes of righteousness (compare Luke 14:16–24).
>
> Deity Himself is the king in the parable; Jesus, His offspring and heir, is the king's son; and those first invited to "the marriage of the Lamb" (D&C 58:11) are the chosen and favored hosts of Israel to whom the gospel had been offered in ages past. "The remnant" who rejected the later invitation with violence and murder were Jewish descendants of ancient Israel; and it was their city, Jerusalem, which was violently destroyed.
>
> This glorious event [the king's marriage for his son; see Matthew 22:2], still future, has reference to the ushering in of Messiah's millennial reign, the day when He shall reign in triumph and glory over all the earth. By their preaching in this present dispensation, the "servants" of the King are inviting guests to come to the marriage supper of the Lamb. "For this cause I have sent you," the Lord says to His modern missionaries, "that a feast of fat things might be prepared for the

poor; yea, a feast of fat things, of wine on the lees well refined, that the earth may know that the mouths of the prophets shall not fail; Yea, a supper of the house of the Lord, well prepared, unto which all nations shall be invited." . . . (D&C 58:6–11; 65:3).

That a royal marriage feast would signal the beginning of the Messiah's triumphant reign had been revealed to the prophets of old (see Zephaniah 1:7–8). Among the Jews of Jesus' day, however, the doctrine had been diluted and distorted. According to rabbinical tradition, only the seed of Abraham would be invited while the Gentile peoples would remain hungry and unfed.[19]

— **D&C 58:8–11 All nations will be invited.** The wise, learned, noble, and rich will be invited first. Then the poor and blind and lame and deaf will be invited. Missionaries, commissioned and with authority, go forth today to invite all to come to the feast of righteousness found in the restored gospel. Those who put material things before the gospel cannot have the blessings of the feast. Those who commit murder and persecute will be destroyed.

— **Revelation 19:7–9 The righteous Saints are the Lord's "wife"** who is arrayed in glorious white at this great feast, representing their righteousness (vv. 7–8). And "blessed are they which are called unto the marriage supper of the Lamb" (v. 9).

Challenges from Various Factions

- **Matthew 22:15 The Pharisees conspire with others to try to entangle Jesus in His talk.** By now it was obvious that they could not dissuade Jesus from His teaching and healing in the temple. They therefore entered into conspiracies with some of their own enemies to try to cause Jesus to say something offensive.

- **The Herodians.** First, the Pharisees (who despised the Romans) collaborated with the Herodians (a faction which upheld Roman rule) in questioning the Savior.

GUSTAVE DORÉ, 1896

  — **Matthew 22:16–17 The Herodians test Jesus' loyalty to Rome** in an effort to tempt Him into a subversive state-ment or act. First they made a phony statement of admiration: "Master, we know that thou art true, and teachest the way of God in truth, neither carest thou for any man: for thou regardest not the person of men" (v. 16). "Tell us therefore, What thinkest thou? Is it lawful to give tribute unto Cæsar, or not?" (v. 17).

  — **Matthew 22:18–22 Jesus uses a coin to show what our relationship toward government should be** (see also Articles of Faith 1:12). He said, "Why tempt ye me, ye hypocrites? Shew me the tribute money" (vv. 18–19). They quickly "brought unto him a penny," and, showing them the face of it, He asked, "Whose is this image and superscription?" (vv. 19–20).

  The Herodians responded that the image was Caesar's (v. 21). Then Jesus said to them, "Render therefore unto Cæsar the things which are Cæsar's; and unto God the things that are God's" (v. 21). And "when they had heard these words, they marvelled, and left him, and went their way" (v. 22).

- **The Sadducees.** The Sadducees controlled the temple and its ceremonies. But they were worldly and unbelieving. They had become caught up in Greek philosophy and lifestyles during the centuries of apostasy between Malachi and John the Baptist. They did not believe in life after death, nor did they believe in a physical resurrection. So it is interesting that they sought to trap Jesus with a question about marriage after death.

- **Matthew 22:23–28 The Sadducees ask about marriage after the resurrection.** They said to Jesus, "Master, Moses said, If a man die, having no children, his brother shall marry his wife, and raise up seed unto his brother" (v. 24). So, they asked, if a series of seven brothers, each of whom marries the same woman in turn until all the brothers are dead, and, last of all, the woman also dies, "therefore in the resurrection whose wife shall she be of the seven? for they all had her" (v. 28).
- **Matthew 22:29–33 Jesus says the Sadducees understand neither the scriptures nor the power of the priesthood,** which they held and used in the temple (v. 29). Jesus taught them that "in the resurrection they neither marry, nor are given in marriage, but are as the angels of God in heaven" (v. 30). Like baptism, marriage is an ordinance that must be performed in this life, and interestingly enough, it must be performed in the temple to have any effect in the hereafter. How ironic it is that these pompous priests who controlled the temple did not understand this doctrine!

Jesus was not finished correcting them. Knowing that they didn't believe in the resurrection, He asked, "As touching the resurrection of the dead, have ye not read that which was spoken unto you by God, saying, I am the God of Abraham, and the God of Isaac, and the God of Jacob? God is not the God of the dead, but of the living" (vv. 31–32). And again, when they heard this, "they were astonished at his doctrine" (v. 33).

Elder James E. Talmage said:

> Jesus stopped not, however, to question the elements of the problem as presented to Him; whether the case was assumed or real mattered not, since the question "Whose wife shall she be?" was based on an utterly erroneous conception. "Jesus answered and said unto them, Ye do err, not knowing the scriptures, nor the power of God. For in the resurrection they neither marry, nor are given in marriage, but are as the angels of God in heaven."

The Lord's meaning was clear, that in the resurrected state there can be no question among the seven brothers as to whose wife for eternity the woman shall be, since all except the first had married her for the duration of mortal life only, and primarily for the purpose of perpetuating in mortality the name and family of the brother who first died.

Luke records the Lord's words as follows in part: "But they which shall be accounted worthy to obtain that world, and the resurrection from the dead, neither marry, nor are given in marriage: Neither can they die any more: for they are equal unto the angels; and are the children of God, being the children of the resurrection." In the resurrection there will be no marrying nor giving in marriage; for all questions of marital status must be settled before that time, under the authority of the Holy Priesthood, which holds the power to seal in marriage for both time and eternity.[20]

— **D&C 132:15–16, 19 clarifies Jesus' words to the Sadducees.** Those who do not make and keep the covenants of temple marriage will be single in heaven. For those who do make and keep these covenants, marriage will last for eternity.

- **The Pharisees.** The Pharisees were the supposed scriptorians among the Jews, along with the scribes. They were "doctors of the law" who boasted that their own teachings about the law of Moses were more important than the scriptures themselves. And they boldly attacked anyone who questioned their teachings.

JAMES J. TISSOT, 1904

— **Matthew 22:34–40 The Pharisees question Jesus about the "greatest commandments" in the law.** Neither the Herodians nor the Saddu- cees had been able to trap Jesus in His words. So now the Pharisees took their turn. One of them, a lawyer, asked Jesus, "Master, which is the great commandment in the law?" (v. 36).

Jesus answered that the greatest commandment is to "love the Lord thy God with all thy heart, and with all thy soul, and with all thy mind" (vv. 37–38). And the second greatest commandment "is like unto it, Thou shalt love thy neighbour as thyself" (v. 39). Literally all other commandments and teachings of the prophets can be kept by faithfully doing these two things (v. 40).

Elder Howard W. Hunter said: "He loves the Lord with all his heart who . . . is ready to give up, do, or suffer anything in order to please and glorify Him. He loves God with all his soul . . . who is ready to give up life for His sake and to be deprived of the comforts of the world to glorify Him. He loves God with all his strength who exerts all the powers of his body and soul in the service of God. He loves God with all his mind who applies himself only to know God and His will, who sees God in all things and acknowledges Him in all ways."[21]

- **Matthew 22:41–46 Jesus asks the Pharisees a question they cannot answer.** First He asked them concerning the Christ: "Whose son is he?" and they said unto Him, "The Son of David" (v. 42). This was correct. But how, Jesus asked, could Christ be David's descendant if David called Christ his "Lord"? (vv. 43–45). This they could not answer, and "neither durst any man from that day forth ask him any more questions" (v. 46).

Jesus Condemns Rabbinical Hypocrisy

- **Matthew 23:1–3 Jesus teaches respect for Rabbinical priesthood, but not to follow their behavior.** Having exposed the hypocrisy of the Pharisees, Jesus turned to His disciples and taught them. "The scribes and the Pharisees sit in Moses' seat: All therefore whatsoever they bid you observe, that observe and do; but do not ye after their works: for they say, and do not" (vv. 2–3). They were to respect their priesthood but not their behavior.

- **Matthew 23:4–12 The hypocrisy of the Pharisees.** They "bind heavy burdens and grievous to be borne, and lay them on men's shoulders; but they themselves will not move them with one of their fingers" (v. 4). They make a great show of their works in order to "be seen of men" —making their phylacteries larger than other men's, and enlarging "the borders of their garments"

(v. 5). They "love the uppermost rooms at feasts, and the chief seats in the synagogues, and greetings in the markets, and to be called of men, Rabbi, Rabbi" (vv. 6–7).

A. BIDA, 1874

"But be not ye called Rabbi," Jesus taught His disciples, "for one is your Master, even Christ; and all ye are brethren" (v. 8). "And call no man your father upon the earth: for one is your Father, which is in heaven" (v. 9). What does this suggest about priests of today who are regularly addressed as "Father"? And finally, "neither be ye called masters: for one is your Master, even Christ," and "he that is greatest among you shall be your servant" (vv. 10–11). "And whosoever shall exalt himself shall be abased; and he that shall humble himself shall be exalted" (v. 12).

JAMES J. TISSOT, 1904

- **Matthew 23:13–33 Jesus pronounces eight woes upon these hypocritical leaders.** Turning back to the Pharisees, Jesus boldly cried out eight withering accusations that must have caused all who heard them to cringe. The word *hypocrite*, translated from Greek, means an actor or pretender. And the word *woe* means suffering, affliction, grief, calamity, or misfortune. All of these were the legacy of Judah's misguided religious leaders of all sects.

“Woe unto you, scribes and Pharisees, hypocrites! for ye shut up the kingdom of heaven against men: for ye neither go in yourselves, neither suffer ye them that are entering to go in” (v. 13). This was the first of eight specific woes or warnings He issued against them in the temple that day.

“Woe unto you, scribes and Pharisees, hypocrites! for ye devour widows’ houses, and for a pretence make long prayer: therefore ye shall receive the greater damnation” (v. 14).

“Woe unto you, scribes and Pharisees, hypocrites! for ye compass sea and land to make one proselyte, and when he is made, ye make him twofold more the child of hell than yourselves” (v. 15).

“Woe unto you, ye blind guides, which say, Whosoever shall swear by the temple, it is nothing; but whosoever shall swear by the gold of the temple, he is a debtor!” (v. 16). Which is greater, He asked, “the gold, or the temple that sanctifieth the gold?” (v. 17). The Pharisees were teaching ways to avoid having to keep covenants by saying things like “whosoever shall swear by the altar, it is nothing; but whosoever sweareth by the gift that is upon it, he is guilty. Ye fools and blind: for whether is greater, the gift, or the altar that sanctifieth the gift?” (vv. 18–19). An oath or covenant made upon an altar applies to both the altar and everything upon it (v. 20). And the same is true about oaths and covenants in the temple and in the name of God (vv. 21–22). All were to be kept with exactness, not excused by some technicality about how they were made.

“Woe unto you, scribes and Pharisees, hypocrites! for ye pay tithe of mint and anise and cummin, and have omitted the weightier matters of the law, judgment, mercy, and faith: these ought ye to have done, and not to leave the other undone. Ye blind guides, which strain at a gnat, and swallow a camel” (vv. 23–24).

“Woe unto you, scribes and Pharisees, hypocrites! for ye make clean the outside of the cup and of the platter, but within they are full of extortion and excess. Thou blind Pharisee, cleanse first that which is within the cup and platter, that the outside of them may be clean also” (vv. 25–26).

> "Woe unto you, scribes and Pharisees, hypocrites! for ye are like unto whited sepulchres, which indeed appear beautiful outward, but are within full of dead men's bones, and of all uncleanness. Even so ye also outwardly appear righteous unto men, but within ye are full of hypocrisy and iniquity" (vv. 27–28).
>
> "Woe unto you, scribes and Pharisees, hypocrites! because ye build the tombs of the prophets, and garnish the sepulchres of the righteous, And say, If we had been in the days of our fathers, we would not have been partakers with them in the blood of the prophets. Wherefore ye be witnesses unto yourselves, that ye are the children of them which killed the prophets. Fill ye up then the measure of your fathers" (vv. 29–32).
>
> "Ye serpents, ye generation of vipers, how can ye escape the damnation of hell?" (v. 33).

- **Matthew 23:34–36 That particular generation will be held accountable for murder.** This same Jesus, as the Lord Jehovah, had sent unto the Jews "prophets, and wise men, and scribes," but these servants of God were killed and crucified, scourged in the synagogues, and persecuted from city to city (v. 34). Therefore, the wicked Pharisees would be held responsible for "all the righteous blood shed upon the earth, from the blood of righteous Abel unto the blood of Zacharias son of Barachias, whom ye slew between the temple and the altar" (v. 35). None of this would be forgotten in the day of judgment, but "all these things shall come upon this generation" (v. 36).

The Widow's Mites

Before leaving the temple for the last time, Jesus observed a tender scene, described here by Elder Alexander B. Morrison:

> Jesus, the Master Teacher, repeatedly taught eternal truths drawn from common experiences of life. One such lesson deals with the need to be generous in our giving—to give with the spirit of sacrifice and devout intent to bless those less fortunate than ourselves. Luke records that as Jesus sat in the temple He observed those who cast their contributions into the treasure chests therein. Some deposited their gifts with devoutness and sincerity of purpose, but others,

though they gave great sums of silver and gold, did so ostentatiously, primarily to be seen of men.

Among the long lines of contributors was a poor widow, who cast into the treasure chest all that she had, two small bronze coins, known as mites. Taken together they amounted to less than half a cent in American money. Noting the disparity between what she gave and the much greater contributions of some others, Jesus proclaimed, "Of a truth I say unto you, that this poor widow hath cast in more than they all." Though the rich had given from their abundance, "she of her penury hath cast in all the living that she had" (Luke 21:1–4; see also Mark 12:41–44). Jesus knew it is not the amount we give that matters. In the arithmetic of heaven, value is determined not by quantity but by quality. It is the intent of the willing heart and mind that is acceptable to God (see 2 Corinthians 8:12).[22]

Notes

1. *Jesus the Christ,* 3rd ed. [1916], 512.
2. For an explanation of this and other precise dates that appear in this chapter, see John P. Pratt, "The Restoration of Priesthood Keys on Easter 1836, Part 1: Dating the First Easter," *Ensign*, June 1985, 59–68. See also *The Life and Teachings of Jesus and His Apostles* [1979], 135–36, 138, 144.
3. *Jesus the Christ*, 516–17.
4. *Doctrinal New Testament Commentary*, 3 vols. [1965–73], 1:577–78.
5. *Jesus the Christ*, 517.
6. *Doctrinal New Testament Commentary*, 1:579.
7. *Jesus the Christ*, 527.
8. *Doctrinal New Testament Commentary*, 1:585.
9. *The Life and Teachings of Jesus and His Apostles* [1979], 143.
10. *Jesus the Christ*, 528–29.
11. *History of the Church*, 2:19.

12. In Conference Report, Oct. 1966, 115, 116; or *Improvement Era*, Dec. 1966, 1142.

13. In Conference Report, Oct. 1991, 27; or *Ensign*, Nov. 1991, 21.

14. In Conference Report, Oct. 1977, 46; or *Ensign*, Nov. 1977, 32.

15. In Conference Report, Oct. 1996, 71; or *Ensign*, Nov. 1996, 51.

16. See Topical Guide, "Priestcraft," 387.

17. *The Mortal Messiah: From Bethlehem to Calvary*, 4 vols. [1979–81], 2:223–24, 225.

18. *History of the Church*, 2:19.

19. *Doctrinal New Testament Commentary*, 1:597.

20. *Jesus the Christ*, 548.

21. In Conference Report, Apr. 1965, 58; or *Improvement Era*, June 1965, 512.

22. In Conference Report, Oct. 1999, 32; or *Ensign*, Nov. 1999, 26–27.

CHAPTER 2

SIGNS OF THE SECOND COMING

(JOSEPH SMITH—MATTHEW; MATTHEW 24)

THE THIRD DAY

(Tuesday)[1]

INTRODUCTION

- **JS–Matthew 1:1 Jesus leaves the temple for the last time.** At the conclusion of His denunciation of the scribes and Pharisees for their hypocrisy, Jesus left the temple with these parting words:

  "I say unto you, that ye shall not see me henceforth and know that I am he of whom it is written by the prophets, until ye shall say: Blessed is he who cometh in the name of the Lord, in the clouds of heaven, and all the holy angels with him."

A. BIDA, 1874

- **JS–Matthew 1:2–3 Not one stone of the temple will be left upon another.** As Jesus and His disciples passed by the buildings of the temple He made a startling prophetic statement. The disciples asked Him to "show us concerning the buildings of the temple, as thou hast said—They shall be thrown down, and left unto you desolate" (v. 2). He marveled that they had seen so much and yet did not understand His plain words of prophecy. “Verily I say unto you, there shall not be left here, upon this temple, one stone upon another that shall not be thrown down” (v. 3).

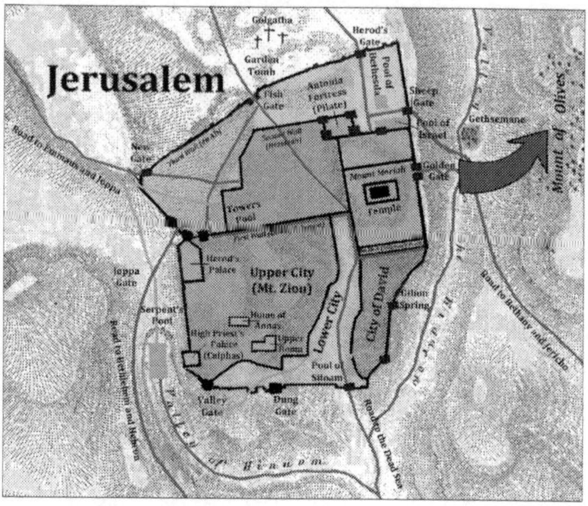

Jesus’ disciples then came to Him at the Mount of Olives, and, at their request, He explained further what was to come both in their day and in the latter days (see Matthew 24:3–51; JS—Matthew 1:4–55). Jesus’ teachings and prophecies in this setting are known as the “Olivet Discourse.”

God’s Foreknowledge of Events

One of God’s powers enables Him to know the end from the beginning (see Abraham 2:8). And knowing all that is coming, He is able to use this knowledge to help those of His children who are willing to listen to Him (see Words of Mormon 1:7).

The Prophet Joseph Smith said: “The great Jehovah contemplated the whole of the events connected with the earth, pertaining to the plan of salvation, before it rolled into existence . . . ; the past, the present, and the future were and are, with Him, one eternal ‘now;’ He knew of the Fall of Adam, the iniquities of the antediluvians, of the depth of iniquity that would be connected with the human family, their weakness and strength, their power and glory, apostasies, their crimes, their righteousness and iniquity; He comprehended the Fall of man, and his redemption; He knew the plan of salvation and pointed it out; He was acquainted with the situation of all nations and with their destiny.”[2]

- **Matthew 24:42–44 Man does not know when Christ shall come again.** This has a purpose. As Jesus said, "Watch therefore: for ye know not what hour your Lord doth come" (v. 42). This keeps us ever on alert, always preparing ourselves for the great day of the Lord. For "if the goodman of the house had known in what watch the thief would come, he would have watched, and would not have suffered his house to be broken up" (v. 43). We are commanded to be "ready: for in such an hour as ye think not the Son of man cometh" (v. 44).

Why the Lord Provides Signs of His Coming

- **D&C 45:35–39 Signs give us hope.** We are expressly advised to "be not troubled, for, when all these things shall come to pass, ye may know that the promises which have been made unto you shall be fulfilled" (v. 35). They should be cause for rejoicing that the Lord's promises will not fail. "When they shall see all these things, then shall they know that the hour is nigh. And it shall come to pass that he that feareth me shall be looking forth for the great day of the Lord to come, even for the signs of the coming of the Son of Man" (vv. 38–39).

- **Helaman 16:5 Signs cause us to remember the prophecies and repent.** In Book of Mormon times, the Lord's prophets told the Nephites "of things which must shortly come, that they might know and remember at the time of their coming that they had been made known unto them beforehand." The purpose was so that "they might believe [and] as many as believed on the words of [the prophets] went forth . . . to be baptized, . . . repenting and confessing their sins."

- **2 Nephi 11:8 Signs cause us to rejoice in the midst of difficulties.** Jacob read the words of Isaiah to his people so that they might "lift up their hearts and rejoice for all men" as they likened the prophet's teachings to themselves "and unto all men."

- **John 16:19–22 Signs help us to see beyond our suffering.** Jesus warned His disciples that "ye shall weep and lament, but the world shall rejoice: and ye shall be sorrowful, but your sorrow shall be turned into joy" (v. 20). He compared their troubles to a woman in the travail of childbirth, who experiences "sorrow, because her hour is come: but as soon as she is delivered of the child, she remembereth no more the anguish, for joy that a man is born into the world" (v. 21). His disciples would certainly "have sorrow: but I will see you again, and your heart shall rejoice, and your joy no man taketh from you" (v. 22).

Jesus Laments over Jerusalem

JAMES J. TISSOT, 1904

According to tradition, Jesus was on the Mount of Olives when He said these things and uttered these prophecies. He was directly opposite, across the Kidron Valley, from a point in the wall surrounding Jerusalem that was just a few yards south of the Gate Beautiful. From this spot, a beautiful panoramic view of that historic city unfolds.

- **Matthew 23:37–39 Jesus laments what could have been for Jerusalem.** Said He, "O Jerusalem, Jerusalem, thou that killest the prophets, and stonest them which are sent unto thee, how often would I have gathered thy children together, even as a hen gathereth her chickens under her wings, and ye would not!" (v. 37). Not only now, but in centuries past, the Lord Jehovah had tried multiple times to redeem the city and its people, only to have them reject and kill His messengers. Now, "behold, your house is left unto you desolate" (v. 38). And they would not see their King again until the day when they would cry out, "Blessed is he that cometh in the name of the Lord!" (see also Luke 13:34–35).

  Elder Bruce R. McConkie explains why Jesus wept for Jerusalem:

- — Jerusalem was a city of depravity—a "spiritual Sodom" and like "Egypt" (Revelation 11:8).
- — Jerusalem was doomed spiritually and would soon be desolated (Luke 19:41–44).
- — Jerusalem was the site of the temple, home of the prophets, and the city of our Lord's ministry.
- — Jerusalem crucified the Son of God—"the more wicked part of the world," for "there is none other nation on earth that would crucify their God" (2 Nephi 10:3).
- — Jerusalem is the future world capital and the center from which "the word of the Lord" shall go unto all people (Isaiah 2:3).

Truly Jerusalem's history is like that of no other place; and truly Jesus, with cause, wept because of the rebellion of her children.[3]

- **JS–Matthew 1:4 The disciples ask Jesus two questions** concerning His prophecies. They are the same two questions we still ask today.

1. "Tell us when shall these things be?"
2. "What [shall be] the sign of thy coming, and of the end of the world?"

Jesus' answers were specific and unveiled by metaphor. What He said would happen is precisely what will happen, and we need not attempt to "spiritualize" His words by assuming they are simply figurative.

The Prophet Joseph Smith said:

> Now men cannot have any possible grounds to say that this is figurative, or that it does not mean what it says: for He is now explaining what He had previously spoken in parables; and according to this language, the end of the world is the destruction of the wicked, the harvest and the end of the world have an allusion directly to the human family in the last days, instead of the earth, as many have imagined; and that which shall precede the coming of the Son of Man, and the restitution of all things spoken of by the mouth of all the holy prophets since the world began; and the angels are to have something to do in this great work, for they are the reapers.

As, therefore, the tares are gathered and burned in the fire, so shall it be in the end of the world; that is, as the servants of God go forth warning the nations, both priests and people, and as they harden their hearts and reject the light of truth, these first being delivered over to the buffetings of Satan, and the law and the testimony being closed up, as it was in the case of the Jews, they are left in darkness, and delivered over unto the day of burning; thus being bound up by their creeds, and their bands being made strong by their priests, are prepared for the fulfillment of the saying of the Savior—"The Son of Man shall send forth His angels, and gather out of His Kingdom all things that offend, and them which do iniquity, and shall cast them into a furnace of fire, there shall be wailing and gnashing of teeth" [see Matthew 13:41–42].

We understand that the work of gathering together of the wheat into barns, or garners, is to take place while the tares are being bound over, and preparing for the day of burning . . . [A]fter the day of burnings, the righteous shall shine forth like the sun, in the Kingdom of their Father. Who hath ears to hear, let him hear.[4]

Modern Clarifications of Jesus' Answers

- **D&C 45:60–61 The Joseph Smith Translation (JST) of the Bible.** In 1830, the Lord directed Joseph Smith to make a new translation of the Bible (see also D&C 35:18–20; 42:56–58; 45:72–73). The Lord said to him, "And now, behold, I say unto you, it shall not be given unto you to know any further concerning this chapter, until the New Testament be translated, and in it all these things shall be made known; Wherefore I give unto you that ye may now translate it, that ye may be prepared for the things to come."

  His inspired revision of Matthew 24, once known as Joseph Smith 1, is now known as Joseph Smith—Matthew and abbreviated as JS—Matthew. It provides details and clarifications that are missing from the Gospel of Matthew and will be our primary source for the discussion of Jesus' prophecies in this chapter.

- **D&C 45 A revelation that repeats and clarifies prophecies given to the ancient disciples.** This revelation was given as part of the Prophet Joseph Smith's new translation of the Bible which he received by revelation. It adds details that do not appear in Matthew 24 or in JS—Matthew.

We will refer to both of these modern sources (JS—Matthew and D&C 45) for clarifications as we discuss Jesus' prophecies of the latter days and of His Second Coming.

EVENTS IN THE APOSTLES' LIFETIMES

One of the weaknesses of Matthew 24 in the King James Bible is that it does not distinguish between prophecies Jesus made concerning events to come in the Apostles' lifetimes and prophecies that will be fulfilled in the latter days. JS—Matthew restores these distinctions with clarity. It deals first with events to come in the Apostles' lifetimes.

Prophecies of Deceit, Persecution, and Iniquity

THE HOLMAN BIBLE, 1890, #54

- **JS–Matthew 1:5–6, 9 False prophets and messiahs.** Jesus warned His disciples to "take heed that no man deceive you" (v. 5). He predicted that after His departure, "many shall come in my name, saying—I am Christ— and shall deceive many" (v. 6). This can be interpreted to mean that men would arise claiming to be Christ Himself who had come back to earth. It can also be interpreted to mean that some would rise up and proclaim that Jesus is the Christ and yet "shall deceive many" (v. 9). Both would be true.

  In the years that followed there were indeed false Christs—Simon Magus, Menander, Dositheus, and others--and false teachers preaching damnable heresies. The epistles in the New Testament are full of warnings concerning deceivers who had already arisen while the Apostles were still alive. These false Christs and false teachers led many of the early Saints to apostatize from the faith.

- **JS–Matthew 1:7 Persecution.** Jesus warned the Apostles that "they [will] deliver you up to be afflicted, and shall kill you, and ye shall be hated of all nations, for my name's sake." In the years ahead, Apostles were put in prison (see Acts 5:18); Stephen was stoned (see Acts 7:54–60); and Herod Agrippa I ordered James (the son of Zebedee) killed (see Acts 12:1–2). The Jews not only persecuted those who believed in Christ, but also zealously tried to influence the Romans to oppose the Christian movement. Eventually, most, if not all, of the Apostles were martyred. Only John the Beloved remained.

- **JS–Matthew 1:8 Disloyalty.** In the midst of doctrinal confusion and strife, Jesus said that "many [would become] offended, and shall betray one another, and shall hate one another." Though He had taught that His disciples were to love one another, the battles of doctrine and positions of power turned ugly and bloody and caused many divisions among the followers of Christ.

- **JS–Matthew 1:10 Abundant iniquity.** Jesus said that "iniquity shall abound" both outside and inside the Church. The Apostolic Fathers—those who wrote from about A.D. 50 to A.D. 150—bear ample witness to the iniquity that filled the Apostle-less Church. Greed, avarice, covetousness, and even adultery were known among the heads of the various sects that arose in the absence of revelation.[5]

- **JS–Matthew 1:10–11 Human compassion will fail as love waxes cold.** Jesus said that "because iniquity shall abound, the love of many shall wax cold" (v. 10). People became disillusioned and disbelieving because of the bad behavior of their leaders. Feelings of brotherly love and compassion were replaced with suspicion and competition and false claims of authority. Nevertheless, Jesus promised, "He that remaineth steadfast and is not overcome, the same shall be saved" (v. 11).

Prophecies of Jerusalem's Destruction

FRANCESCO HAYES, 1867

- **JS–Matthew 1:12 The abomination of desolation will come upon Jerusalem.** In A.D. 70, the Romans destroyed the besieged city. People suffered inexpressible horrors of starvation, cannibal-ism, and wanton bloodshed. The prophet Daniel predicted that it would happen, and Jesus now assured them that Daniel's words were true. "When you, therefore, shall see the abomination of desolation, spoken of by Daniel the prophet, concerning the destruction of Jerusalem, then you shall stand in the holy place."

The Lord has given similar counsel in our day:

— **D&C 87:8 We are to stand in holy places and "be not moved."** What are these holy places? They are our homes, our chapels, our temples, and other gatherings of the righteous who are preparing for the Lord's coming. Some will not endure the calamities to come because they will abandon the very places that would keep them safe.

— **D&C 101:22 We are to gather together in prayer and worship.** In those same holy places mentioned above, we are to assemble with other Saints for the purpose of worship and prayer.

— **D&C 133:14–15 We are to leave "Babylon."** Instead of clinging to the world, we are to abandon its wicked practices and stand apart from the blood and sins of our generation. We are to be a holy people and a royal priesthood. But this gathering is not to be "in haste" or without preparation. It must be orderly (v. 15).

President Ezra Taft Benson said: "Holy men and holy women stand in holy places, and these holy places include our temples, our chapels, our homes, and the stakes of Zion, which are, as the Lord declares, 'for a defense, and for a refuge from the storm, and from wrath when it shall be poured out without mixture upon the whole earth' (D&C 115:6)."[6]

THEBIBLEREVIVAL.COM, #29

- **JS–Matthew 1:13–17 The people will need to abandon the city.** Speaking of the days ahead in the Apostles' lifetimes, the Lord said, "Let them who are in Judea flee into the mountains; Let him who is on the housetop flee, and not return to take anything out of his house; Neither let him who is in the field return back to take his clothes" (vv. 13–15).

When the Romans came in upon them they had no time for such things, and when the warning came to them from their inspired leaders, they were to immediately go and not look back. The Lord specifically mentioned the difficulty that would arise for those "with child, and unto them that give suck," and told them to "pray ye the Lord that your flight be not in the winter, neither on the Sabbath day," when their travel would be greatly inhibited (vv. 16–17).

Although many Jews did not believe their great city and temple could be destroyed, the Lord's prophecies were fulfilled in A.D. 70. Believing that the Messiah would come and help them in battle, the Jews revolted against the Romans in A.D. 66. Four years later the Romans destroyed the entire city. Those who listened to the Savior and fled into the mountains were spared. Those who didn't were scattered or destroyed.

Eusebius, an early Christian historian, said that the Christians living in Jerusalem were advised by revelation to flee from the city and go to Pella, a city across the Jordan River and up toward the Sea of Galilee (see map on next page).[7]

Elder Marion G. Romney said: "You all know the sequel, how the Jews carried through their awful plot and crucified the Son of God, and how thereafter they continued to fight against His gospel. You remember, too, the price they paid, how in 70 A.D. the city fell into the hands of the Romans as the climax of a siege in which the historian Josephus tells us there were a million one hundred thousand people killed and tens of thousands were taken captive, to be afterwards sold into slavery, or to be slain by wild beasts, or in gladiatorial combat for the amusement of Roman spectators. All of this destruction and the dispersion of the Jews would have been avoided had the people accepted the gospel of Jesus Christ and had their hearts changed by it."[8]

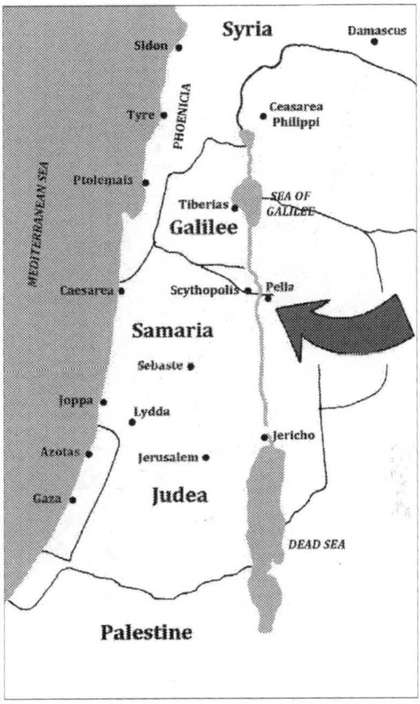

B. RIVIERE, 1890

Elder Bruce R. McConkie said: "Jesus specified the destruction would come in the days of the disciples. And come it did, in ven- geance, without restraint. Hunger exceeded human endurance; blood flowed in the streets; destruction made desolate the temple; 1,100,000 Jews were slaughtered; Jerusalem was ploughed as a field; and a remnant of a once mighty nation was scattered to the ends of the earth. The Jewish nation died, impaled on Roman spears, at the hands of Gentile overlords."[9] All of this terrible destruction fulfilled Jesus' prophecy. How different it could have been if the people had only listened and obeyed.

Daniel's Prophecies Concerning These Events

- **Daniel 9:26–27 The Messiah's death and the city's desolation.** Daniel predicted that the "Messiah [shall] be cut off"—not for His own sake but for ours. Then, "the people of the prince" (Roman soldiers in the service of Caesar) shall "come [and] destroy the city and the sanctuary" (v. 26). This attack will be like a flood in its swiftness and violence, and at the end thereof "desolations are determined" (v. 26).

  With the destruction of the temple, "sacrifice and . . . oblation [will] cease," and the "overspreading of abominations" will "make [Jerusalem] desolate," ending in its complete consummation, which "shall be poured upon the desolate" (v. 27).

- **Daniel 11:31 The destruction of the temple.** With the force of arms, "they shall pollute the sanctuary . . . and shall take away the daily sacrifice," replacing it with an "abomination that maketh desolate." This is the abomination of desolation that Jesus was referring to in His prophecies (see JS—Matthew 1:12).

- **Daniel 12:11 A long period of apostasy without a temple.** From the time that Jerusalem and the temple are destroyed there will be a long period of apostasy. Daniel characterizes it as "a thousand two hundred and ninety days," but his "days" are symbolic and not literal. We know from history there were 1,766 years before another temple of the Lord would grace the earth (when the Kirtland Temple was dedicated in 1836).

- **JS–Matthew 1:18–20 The Lord's characterization of these difficulties.** Jesus told His disciples that in their day "shall be great tribulation on the Jews, and upon the inhabitants of Jerusalem, such as was not before sent upon Israel, of God, since the beginning of their kingdom until this time; no, nor ever shall be sent again upon Israel" (v. 18). But the destruction of Jerusalem would only be "the beginning of the sorrows which shall come upon them [the Jews]" (v. 19). "And except those days [the days of their suffering] should be shortened, there should none of their flesh be saved; but for the elect's sake, according to the covenant, those days shall be shortened" (v. 20).

EVENTS IN THE LATTER DAYS

Signs to Precede the Lord's Coming

JS–Matthew 1:21 provides a transition between events predicted for the Apostles' lifetimes and events in the latter days before the Second Coming. Repeatedly the Lord says, "And again . . ." to indicate a recurring sign—one that would occur in both eras. "Behold, these things I have spoken unto you concerning the Jews," Jesus said, followed by "and again [in] those days" (meaning in the latter days).

Many false prophets and religious movements sprang up in the early 1800s

- **JS–Matthew 1:21–22 False Christs and false prophets.** "And again, after the tribulation of those days which shall come upon Jerusalem, if any man shall say unto you, Lo, here is Christ, or there, believe him not; For in those days there shall also arise false Christs, and false prophets, and shall show great signs and wonders, insomuch, that, if possible, they shall deceive the very elect, who are the elect according to the covenant."

  We have seen a solid stream of false prophets and Christs since the 1800s, and some of them have been persuasive enough to hold an ongoing following even today. Even some Latter-day Saints have been caught up in their claims. The most popular in recent years have been supposed self-help groups who, in the name of self-improvement, have persuaded men and women to leave their families in pursuit of utopian lifestyles. All such movements are anti-Christ, meaning that they offer a substitute for faith in Jesus Christ and His Church, and as such they will lead only to damnation.

- **Matthew 7:15–20 How we can avoid being deceived by false prophets.** Jesus warned against such false prophets, "which come to you in sheep's clothing, but inwardly they are ravening wolves" (v. 15). And He counseled that we can "know them by their fruits" (v. 16). That which leads to the destruction of faith or family can never be from God. "Do men gather grapes of thorns, or figs of thistles? Even so every good tree bringeth forth good fruit; but a corrupt tree bringeth forth evil fruit. A good tree cannot bring forth evil fruit, neither can a corrupt tree bring forth good fruit" (vv. 16–18). And "every tree that bringeth not forth good fruit is hewn down, and cast into the fire" (v. 19). Then Jesus said again by way of emphasis, "By their fruits ye shall know them" (v. 20).
    - **D&C 45:57 Those who are not deceived.** The Lord declared in our own dispensation that "they that are wise and have received the truth, and have taken the Holy Spirit for their guide, . . . have not been deceived." These faithful followers of Christ "shall not be hewn down and cast into the fire, but shall abide the day."
    - **D&C 46:7–8 Obedience and prayer are the key.** The Lord said, "Ye are commanded in all things to ask of God, who giveth liberally; and that which the Spirit testifies unto you even so I would that ye should do in all holiness of heart, walking uprightly before me, considering the end of your salvation, doing all things with prayer and thanksgiving" (v. 7). By doing these things we can avoid being "seduced by evil spirits, or doctrines of devils, or the commandments of men; for some are of men, and others of devils" (v. 7). "Wherefore, beware lest ye are deceived" (v. 8).

Elder Harold B. Lee said: "The Prophet Joseph Smith, in his inspired version of . . . [Matthew 24:24], added these significant words: 'who are the elect, according to the covenant' [Joseph Smith—Matthew 1:22]. This is what has been said, in effect, in this conference: Unless every member of this Church gains for himself an unshakable testimony of the divinity of this Church, he will be among those who will be deceived in this day when the 'elect according to the covenant' are going to be tried and tested. Only those will survive who have gained for themselves that testimony."[10]

President Joseph F. Smith said: "The greatest achievement mankind can make in this world is to familiarize themselves with divine truth, so thoroughly, so perfectly, that the example or conduct of no creature living in the world can ever turn them away from the knowledge that they have obtained. 'In the footsteps of the Master,' the greatest of all the teachers that this world has ever received, is the safest and surest course to pursue that I know of in the world. We can absorb the precepts, the doctrines, and the divine word of the Master, without any fear that the Exemplar will fail of carrying out and executing His own precepts and fulfilling His own doctrines and requirements."[11]

- **JS–Matthew 1:23, 28–29 "Wars . . . and rumors [news] of wars."** Jesus provided this sign "for the elect's sake" (v. 23), which means the members of His Church. "You also shall hear of wars, and rumors of wars; see that ye be not troubled, for all I have told you must come to pass; but the end is not yet" (v. 23). He repeats this sign in verse 28, followed by this prediction: "Nation shall rise against nation, and kingdom against kingdom" (v. 29).

  — **D&C 6:34 "Be not troubled" by wars and rumors of wars.** Especially in the most recent years, it seems as if warfare will never cease. Terrorists, like Gadianton robbers, infest every land and even control some governments. It can all be quite worrisome. But the Lord has counseled, "Fear not, little flock; do good; let earth and hell combine against you, for if ye are built upon my rock, they cannot prevail."

  I had reason to reflect upon this promise in a high priests group meeting one Sunday morning. The brethren were speaking of the continual bloodshed that terrorist groups visit upon even the most innocent civilians. They also noted that the "war on terror" had turned into the longest-lasting war in American history and still was not over. There was an air of pessimism in the discussion, as if nothing could ever solve it.

I felt compelled to say to them, "Brethren, those terrorists are doomed. We already know how it will all turn out. The Lord has spoken it. And He has also counseled us not to fear. We just need to 'do good' in our personal and collective lives and then wait upon the Lord for His decisive overthrow of all such wickedness."

— **D&C 45:34–35 These continual wars are a sign that Christ's coming is near.** When Jesus shared these prophecies with His Apostles, "they were troubled" (v. 34). But He said to them, "Be not troubled, for, when all these things shall come to pass, ye may know that the promises which have been made unto you shall be fulfilled" (v. 35).

Elder Bruce R. McConkie prophesied: "Bands of Gadianton robbers will infest every nation, immorality and murder and crime will increase, and it will seem as though every man's hand is against his brother. We need not dwell more upon these things. We are commanded to search the scriptures where they are recounted with force and fervor, and they shall surely come to pass. . . . It may be, for instance, that nothing except the power of faith and the authority of the priesthood can save individuals and congregations from the atomic holocausts that surely shall be. And so we raise the warning voice and say: Take heed; prepare; watch and be ready. There is no security in any course except the course of obedience and conformity and righteousness."[12]

Elder McConkie also prophesied: "This war will be a religious war, a war in which the servants of Satan assail the servants of the Lord and those allied with them. The great and abominable church will wage war against everything that is decent in the world and will then be thrown down by devouring fire. . . . We repeat: It is a religious war. The forces of antichrist are seeking to destroy freedom and liberty and right; they seek to deny men the right to worship the Lord; they are the enemies of God. The one-third who remain in the land of Israel are the Lord's people. They believe in Christ and accept Joseph Smith as His prophet and revealer for the last days."[13]

Elder M. Russell Ballard said:

> Although the prophecies tell us that these things are to take place, more and more people are expressing great alarm at what appears to be an acceleration of worldwide calamity. . . . Admittedly, we have ample reason to be deeply concerned because we see no immediate answers to the seemingly unsolvable problems confronting the human family. But regardless of this dark picture, which will ulti-mately get worse, we must never allow ourselves to give up hope! . . .
>
> . . . The Lord is in control. He knows the end from the beginning. He has given us adequate instruction that, if followed, will see us safely through any crisis. His purposes will be fulfilled, and someday we will understand the eternal reasons for all of these events. Therefore, today we must be careful not to overreact, nor should we be caught up in extreme preparations, but what we must do is keep the commandments of God and never lose hope!
>
> But where do we find hope in the midst of such turmoil and catastrophe? Quite simply, our one hope for spiritual safety during these turbulent times is to turn our minds and our hearts to Jesus Christ. . . . Armed with the shield of faith, we can overcome many of our daily challenges and overpower our greatest weaknesses and fears, knowing that if we do our best to keep the commandments of God, come what may, we will be all right.[14]

- **JS–Matthew 1:24–26 False rumors about Christ's coming.** Even those who believe in Christ may be deceived. A sister in my CES class recently approached me about a neighbor who had become caught up in a group that was supposedly preparing for Christ's coming. Their leader had counseled them to sell their homes, pool their resources, and live in tents outside the cities. As with all such cults, this will only end in financial and spiritual poverty for all who are involved. The

Lord declared plainly, "If they shall say unto you: Behold, he is in the desert; go not forth: [or] Behold, he is in the secret chambers; believe it not" (v. 25). We cannot prepare for His coming in convents, retreats, or any other form of isolation. The Lord does not work in such ways. "For as the light of the morning cometh out of the east, and shineth even unto the west, and covereth the whole earth, so shall also the coming of the Son of Man be" (v. 26).

- **JS–Matthew 1:27 Israel gathered in from all over the earth.** Jesus used the metaphor of a carcass and eagles to illustrate His point. "And now I show unto you a parable. Behold, wheresoever the carcass is, there will the eagles be gathered together; so likewise shall mine elect be gathered from the four quarters of the earth." These prophecies are being fulfilled today. Missionary work is increasing, and the gospel is being taught and accepted in more and more places across the world.

- **JS–Matthew 1:31 A witness to "all nations."** "And again, . . . [notice how this is a repeating sign] this Gospel of the Kingdom shall be preached in all the world, for a witness unto all nations, and then shall the end come, or the destruction of the wicked."

PHOTO COURTESY OF FEMA, 1980

- **JS–Matthew 1:29 Natural disasters, affecting even the righteous.** "There shall be famines, and pestilences, and earthquakes, in divers places." I recently heard a scientist on television make the claim that there is no increase in natural disasters—only an increase in our awareness of them. This provided an opportunity for him to criticize religious people who he claimed were emotional rather than rational. I thought to myself, "And I'll bet your name is Korihor" (see Alma 30).

How vain are the learned in our day! If they say something is so, then we are expected to believe them without question. Yet, when I checked the record for myself, I found that there has indeed been an increase in earthquake, volcanic, and tornado activity in the past 100 years. Jesus declared that it would be so, and it is so.

— **D&C 63:34 "The saints also shall hardly escape."** We are not immune to the ravishes of nature. The Lord causes it to rain upon both the wicked and the righteous (see Matthew 5:45). "Nevertheless, I, the Lord, am with them, and will come down in heaven from the presence of my Father and consume the wicked with unquenchable fire." The righteous will be spared such total destruction, but may nevertheless suffer for a time.

Elder Bruce R. McConkie said: "There will be earthquakes and floods and famines. The waves of the sea shall heave themselves beyond their bounds, the clouds shall withhold their rain, and the crops of the earth shall wither and die. There will be plagues and pestilence and disease and death. An overflowing scourge shall cover the earth and a desolating sickness shall sweep the land. Flies shall take hold of the inhabitants of the earth, and maggots shall come in upon them (see D&C 29:14–20). 'Their flesh shall fall from off their bones, and their eyes from their sockets' (D&C 29:19)."[15]

The Prophet Joseph Smith said: "[I] explained concerning the coming of the Son of Man; also that it is a false idea that the Saints will escape all the judgments, whilst the wicked suffer; for all flesh is subject to suffer, and 'the righteous shall hardly escape' [see D&C 63:34]; still many of the Saints will escape, for the just shall live by faith; yet many of the righteous shall fall a prey to disease, to pestilence, etc., by reason of the weakness of the flesh, and yet be saved in the Kingdom of God. So that it is an unhallowed principle to say that such and such have transgressed because they have been preyed upon by disease or death, for all flesh is subject to death; and the Savior has said, 'Judge not, lest ye be judged' [see Matthew 7:1]."[16]

- **JS–Matthew 1:30, 42 Moral degeneration, as in the days of Noah.** As in former days, "iniquity shall abound [and] the love of men shall wax cold; but he that shall not be overcome, the same shall be saved" (v. 30). And "it shall be with them, as it was in the days which were before the flood; for until the day that Noah entered into the ark they were eating and drinking, marrying and giving in marriage" (v. 42). Do we not see this all around us? The wicked relish in their wickedness and perversions, hurling insults and threats at anyone who dares to question them. They party and march and make lewd displays. And they will continue to do so until the Lord comes and puts an end to all such foolishness.

- **JS–Matthew 1:32 Another abomination of desolation in Jerusalem.** "And again shall the abomination of desolation, spoken of by Daniel the prophet, be fulfilled." This happened when the Roman army overran Jerusalem in A.D. 70. It will happen yet again in the latter days.

  Elder Bruce R. McConkie said: "All the desolation and waste which attended the former destruction of Jerusalem is but prelude to the coming siege. Titus and his legions slaughtered 1,100,000 Jews, destroyed the temple, and ploughed the city. In the coming reenactment of this 'abomination of desolation,' the whole world will be at war, Jerusalem will be the center of the conflict, every modern weapon will be used, and in the midst of the siege the Son of Man shall come, setting His foot upon the Mount of Olives and fighting the battle of His Saints (see Zechariah 12:1–9)."[17]

  Elder McConkie also said: "In the coming day—a dire, dread, damning day—woes without measure will fall upon men. Pestilence, plagues, and death will stalk the earth. The kings of the earth and of the whole world will gather to fight the battle of that great day of God Almighty. Their command center will be at Armageddon, overlooking the valley of Megiddo. All nations will be gathered against Jerusalem. Two hundred thousand thousand warriors and more—two hundred million men of arms and more—shall come forth to conquer or die on the plains of Esdraelon and in all the nations of the earth. At the height of this war, the Lord Jesus will put His foot on the Mount of Olives and save His ancient covenant people. Of all this we are aware."[18]

- **JS–Matthew 1:33 Darkening of the sun and moon.** The Lord said that "immediately after the tribulation of those days," or perhaps as a result of the pollutions and warfare that will overtake all the earth, "the sun shall be darkened, and the moon shall not give her light, and the stars shall fall from heaven, and the powers of heaven shall be shaken." The idea of stars falling from heaven is particularly interesting given the recent emphasis on the danger from asteroids. Just one such impact, similar to the one that carved out the Gulf of Mexico, would darken the sky with its debris, darkening the sun and killing off much of the earth's plant and animal life. The earth will be "burned" at Christ's coming, but that burning may occur from natural causes.

- **JS–Matthew 1:34–35 Every word of prophecy will be fulfilled.** The Lord declared that "this generation, in which these things shall be shown forth, shall not pass away until all I have told you shall be fulfilled" (v. 34). The word "generation" here means "dispensation," and the promise is that all of these things will occur in the dispensation of the fulness of times. And, "although, the days will come, that heaven and earth shall pass away; yet my words shall not pass away, but all shall be fulfilled" (v. 35). We may count on these signs to be shown, and when they are, we may know that His coming is nigh—even at our doors.

  The Prophet Joseph Smith said:

  > The coming of the Son of Man never will be—never can be till the judgments spoken of for this hour are poured out: which judgments are commenced. Paul says, "Ye are the children of the light, and not of the darkness, that that day should overtake you as a thief in the night." [See 1 Thessalonians 5:2, 4–5; D&C 106:4–5.] It is not the design of the Almighty to come upon the earth and crush it and grind it to powder, but He will reveal it to His servants the prophets.
  >
  > Judah must return, Jerusalem must be rebuilt, and the temple, and water come out from under the temple, and the waters of the Dead Sea be healed. It will take some time to rebuild the walls of the city and the temple, . . . and all this must be done before the Son of Man will make His appearance. There will be wars and rumors of wars, signs in the heavens above and on

the earth beneath, the sun turned into darkness and the moon to blood, earthquakes in divers places, the seas heaving beyond their bounds.[19]

- **JS–Matthew 1:36 The sign of the Son of Man will be seen by all people.** "After the tribulation of those days, and the powers of the heavens shall be shaken, then shall appear the sign of the Son of Man in heaven, and then shall all the tribes of the earth mourn; and they shall see the Son of Man coming in the clouds of heaven, with power and great glory." What is this sign? It is the same one that appeared in the sky at His birth and the same one that the Nephites saw (see 3 Nephi 1). It will appear again as "a great sign in heaven, and all the people shall see it together" (D&C 88:93).

PHOTO COURTESY OF NASA

The Prophet Joseph Smith said: "Then will appear one grand sign of the Son of Man in heaven. But what will the world do? They will say it is a planet, a comet, etc. But the Son of Man will come as the sign of the coming of the Son of Man, which will be as the light of the morning cometh out of the east."[20]

- **JS–Matthew 1:37 "Whoso treasureth up my word, shall not be deceived."** If we "treasure up" His word, "the Son of Man shall come, and he shall send his angels before him with the great sound of a trumpet, and they shall gather together the remainder of his elect from the four winds, from one end of heaven to the other." Those who are casual about their scripture study will not be prepared for all that will occur prior to His coming. They will be deceived or frightened away, and, like the five foolish virgins, will find themselves without sufficient spiritual strength to abide the day of His coming.

President Harold B. Lee said:

> There are among us many loose writings predicting the calamities which are about to overtake us. Some of these have been publicized as though they were necessary to wake up the world to the horrors about to overtake us. Many of these are from sources upon which there cannot be unquestioned reliance. Are you . . . aware of the fact that we need no such publications to be forewarned, if we were only conversant with what the scriptures have already spoken to us in plainness? [See Matthew 24; Joseph Smith—Matthew; D&C 38; 45; 101; 133.] . . .
>
> . . . These are some of the writings with which you should concern yourselves, rather than commentaries that may come from those whose information may not be the most reliable and whose motives may be subject to question. And may I say, parenthetically, most of such writers are not handicapped by having any authentic information on their writings. . . .
>
> If our people want to be safely guided during these troublous times of deceit and false rumors, they must follow their leaders and seek for the guidance of the Spirit of the Lord in order to avoid falling prey to clever manipulators who, with cunning sophistry, seek to draw attention and gain a following to serve their own notions and sometimes sinister motives.[21]

No Man Knows the Precise Hour

- **JS–Matthew 1:37 He comes!** We can know for certain that "the Son of Man shall come, and he shall send his angels before him with the great sound of a trumpet, and they shall gather together the remainder of his elect from the four winds, from one end of heaven to the other." While the world mocks those who believe in a great Second Coming of Christ, the faithful watch for the signs that will precede and accompany it.

- **JS–Matthew 1:38–39 The parable of the fig tree** is helpful in knowing when His coming is near. The fig tree puts forth its leaves before every other tree and is a reliable indicator of the approach of summer. Thus, "when its branches are yet tender, and it begins to put forth leaves, you know that summer is nigh at hand" (v. 38). In the same manner, "mine elect, when they shall see all these things, they shall know that he is near, even at the doors" (v. 39).

- **JS–Matthew 1:40–43 Most people will be surprised and unprepared**, as in the days of Noah. The Lord repeats for emphasis, "But of that day, and hour, no one knoweth; no, not the angels of God in heaven, but my Father only" (v. 40). Any man or group who claims to have figured it out is mistaken. "But as it was in the days of Noah, so it shall be also at the coming of the Son of Man; . . . for until the day that Noah entered into the ark they were eating and drinking, marrying and giving in marriage; And knew not until the flood came, and took them all away; so shall also the coming of the Son of Man be."

- **JS–Matthew 1:44–46 "You know not at what hour your Lord doth come."** It will be so sudden that "in the last days, two shall be in the field, the one shall be taken, and the other left; Two shall be grinding at the mill, the one shall be taken, and the other left" (vv. 44–45). This reminds me of a joke I heard about the city of Enoch. There was a man who, though otherwise righteous, decided to take a Sunday off and go fishing. He went, but when he returned he found the city empty and a note on his door that read, "Sorry we missed you. Enoch." We must always be ready, with oil in our spiritual lamps, so that when the Bridegroom comes we will be prepared to be with Him. "And what I say unto one, I say unto all men; watch, therefore, for you know not at what hour your Lord doth come" (v. 46).

- **JS–Matthew 1:47–48 "Be ye . . . ready."** As discussed at the beginning of this chapter, the Lord knows that if we knew when He will come, we might become complacent until the last minute. Instead, like a wise house owner, we should guard against a "thief in the night" by watching and being prepared. "Therefore be ye also ready, for in such an hour as ye think not, the Son of Man cometh."

- **JS–Matthew 1:49–54 The parable of the faithful servant.** Jesus compared those in the latter days who would be preparing for Christ's coming to "a faithful and wise servant, whom his lord hath made ruler over his household, to give them meat in due season" (v. 49). If, when the Lord comes, He finds His servant managing things well, "he shall make him ruler over all his goods" (v. 50). "But if that evil servant shall say in his heart: My lord delayeth his coming, And shall begin to smite his fellow-servants, and to eat and drink with the drunken, The lord of that servant shall come in a day when he looketh not for him, and in an hour that he is not aware of, And shall cut him asunder, and shall appoint him his portion with the hypocrites; there shall be weeping and gnashing of teeth."

- **1 Thessalonians 4:16–17 The righteous will be "caught up . . . in the clouds" when the Savior comes.** Paul said that "the Lord himself shall descend from heaven with a shout, with the voice of the archangel, and with the trump of God: and the dead in Christ shall rise first" (v. 16). These, along with those who "are alive and remain shall be caught up together with them in the clouds, to meet the Lord in the air" (v. 17).

  — **D&C 88:96–98 The first fruits of the resurrection.** "The saints that are upon the earth, who are alive, shall be quickened and be caught up to meet him. And they who have slept in their graves shall come forth, for their graves shall be opened; and they also shall be caught up to meet him in the midst of the pillar of heaven—They are Christ's, the first fruits, they who shall descend with him first, and they who are on the earth and in their graves." All these will be "caught up to meet him; and all this by the voice of the sounding of the trump of the angel of God."

Elder Bruce R. McConkie said:

> Those who shall abide the day, who shall remain on the earth when it is transfigured (see D&C 63:20–21), are those who are honest and upright and who are living at least that law which would take them to a terrestrial kingdom of glory in the resurrection. Anyone living by telestial standards can no longer remain on earth and so cannot abide the day.
>
> Hence we find Malachi listing among those who shall not abide the day the following: sorcerers; adulterers; false swearers; those who oppress the hireling, the widow, and the fatherless in their wages; those who lead men away from the truth; those who do not fear God; members of the true Church who do not pay an honest tithing; they that work wickedness; and the proud. All these, he says, shall be as stubble when the day

comes that shall burn as an oven (see Malachi 3; 4; D&C 64:23–25).[22]

THE COMING OF THE LORD

The Lord's Appearance on the Mount of Olives

- **Zechariah 14:4–7 Christ will fight against the enemies of Israel.** The Jews will lie on the brink of disaster—their city surrounded by millions of enemies, everyone starving and many of them wounded. Much of the city will have been taken captive. The two prophets who were sent to them by the Lord will lie dead in the streets. All will seem hopeless. And then the Lord will come.

  As soon as "his feet shall stand . . . upon the mount of Olives, which is before Jerusalem on the east, . . . the mount of Olives shall cleave in the midst thereof . . . and there shall be a very great valley; and half of the mountain shall remove toward the north, and half of it toward the south" (v. 4). This will provide a pathway for escape and the Jews will "flee to the valley of the mountains" for safety (v. 5).

  As was the case among the Nephites when Jesus was born, "the light shall not be clear, nor dark"—"one day" will be more than a day and a night because "at evening time it shall be light" (vv. 6–7). Thus, there will be a day and a night and another day with no darkness.

  Elder Bruce R. McConkie said: "Speaking of these final battles which shall accompany His return, the Lord says: 'I will gather all nations against Jerusalem to battle; and the city shall be taken, and the houses rifled, and the women ravished; and half of the city shall go forth into captivity, and the residue of the people shall not be cut off from the city' [Zechariah 14:2]. However, the final end of the conflict shall be different this time than it was anciently. 'Then shall the Lord go forth,' the prophetic record says, 'and fight against those nations, as when he fought in the day of battle. And his feet shall stand in that day upon the mount of Olives, . . . and the Lord shall be king over all the earth' [Zechariah 14:3–4, 9]."[23]

- **Revelation 16:14–21 Great natural disasters will devastate the enemies of Israel.** John called the enemies of Israel "the spirits of devils, working miracles, which go forth unto the kings of the earth and of the whole world, to gather them to the battle of that great day of God Almighty" (v. 14). They will gather "into a place called in the Hebrew tongue Armageddon" (v. 16). This is the army that will threaten to destroy Jerusalem. But as they seem about ready to conquer, "a great voice out of the temple of heaven, from the throne" will say, "It is done" (v. 17). Then there will be "voices, and thunders, and lightnings; and . . . a great earthquake, such as was not since men were upon the earth, so mighty an earthquake, and so great" (v. 18).

THEBIBLEREVIVAL.COM, #23

  Jerusalem will be divided into three parts while "the cities of the nations [fall]" and "Babylon [comes] in remembrance before God, to give unto her the cup of the wine of the fierceness of his wrath" (v. 19). The entire landscape will be changed (v. 20). And then the Lord will pour out upon the enemy army "a great hail out of heaven, every stone about the weight of a talent [approximately 34.3 kilograms or 75.6 pounds]: and men blasphemed God because of the plague of the hail [which] was exceeding great" (v. 21).

- **Zechariah 12:8–10 "They shall look upon me whom they have pierced."** "In that day shall the Lord defend the inhabitants of Jerusalem," wrote Zechariah (v. 8), and He will also "seek to destroy all the nations that come against Jerusalem" (v. 9). He will "pour upon the house of David, and upon the inhabitants of Jerusalem, the spirit of grace and of supplications: and *they shall look upon me whom they have* *pierced*, and they shall mourn for [me], as one mourneth for his only son, and shall be in bitterness for [me], as one that is in bitterness for his firstborn" (v. 10; emphasis added).

- **D&C 45:40–45 "Behold, I will come."** The battle for Jerusalem will involve "signs and wonders . . . in the heavens above, and in the earth beneath. And they shall behold blood, and fire, and vapors of smoke" (vv. 40–41). The remnant of the Jews will have gathered at Jerusalem (v. 43), and in their hour of great need "they shall look for me, and, behold, I will come; and they shall see me in the clouds of heaven, clothed with power and great glory; with all the holy angels; and he that watches not for [believes not in] me shall be cut off" (v. 44).

- **D&C 45:48–50 The wicked will mourn.** When the Lord sets His foot upon the Mount of Olives, "it shall cleave in twain, and the earth shall tremble, and reel to and fro, and the heavens also shall shake. And the Lord shall utter his voice, and all the ends of the earth shall hear it; and the nations of the earth shall mourn, and they that have laughed shall see their folly. And calamity shall cover the mocker, and the scorner shall be consumed; and they that have watched for iniquity shall be hewn down and cast into the fire." This is the "Second Coming" about which the wicked have scoffed, and when it is suddenly upon them they will realize their fate.

- **D&C 45:51–53 "What are these wounds in thine hands and in thy feet?"** Gazing upon their long-awaited Messiah who will have saved them from certain destruction, the Jews at Jerusalem will ask, "What are these wounds in thine hands and in thy feet?" (v. 51). And the Lord will answer, "These wounds are the wounds with which I was wounded in the house of my friends. I am he who was lifted up. I am Jesus that was crucified. I am the Son of God" (v. 52). "And then shall they weep because of their iniquities; then shall they lament because they persecuted their king" (v. 53). (See also Zechariah 13:6.)

  Elder Parley P. Pratt said:

  > The Lord shall come at the very time of the overthrow of that army; yes, in fact, even while they are in the act of taking

Jerusalem, and have already succeeded in taking one-half the city, spoiling their houses, and ravishing their women.

Then, behold their long-expected Messiah, suddenly appearing, shall stand upon the Mount of Olives, a little east of Jerusalem, to fight against those nations and deliver the Jews. Zechariah says the Mount of Olives shall cleave in twain, from east to west, and one-half of the mountain shall remove to the north, while the other half falls off to the south, suddenly forming a very great valley into which the Jews shall flee for protection from their enemies as they fled from the earthquake in the days of Uzziah, king of Judah; while the Lord cometh and all the Saints with Him.

Then will the Jews behold that long, long-expected Messiah, coming in power to their deliverance, as they always looked for Him. He will destroy their enemies, and deliver them from trouble at the very time they are in the utmost consternation, and about to be swallowed up by their enemies. But what will be their astonishment when they are about to fall at the feet of their Deliverer and acknowledge Him their Messiah! They discover the wounds which were once made in His hands, feet, and side; and on inquiry, at once recognize Jesus of Nazareth, the King of the Jews, the man so long rejected.[24]

- **Zechariah 12:11–14 "In that day shall there be a great mourning in Jerusalem"** for three reasons:

(1) Many Jews will have been slain by the besieging armies.
(2) Families will be scattered and unable to contact one another.
(3) The saved Jews will realize that He whom they have long rejected and whom their forefathers persecuted and killed is truly the Messiah.

President Joseph Fielding Smith said: "Then they will accept Him as their Redeemer, which they have never been willing to do. Then is the time as spoken of in this passage from Zechariah when every family will go and mourn apart; the house of David, the house of Nathan, the Jews [see Zechariah 12:10–14]. They will fall down. They will rend their garments, and they will mourn and they will weep because they were not willing to accept the Son of God but accepted the teachings of their fathers and rejected their Redeemer and Messiah. Then they will fall down at His feet and worship Him."[25]

Notes

1. For an explanation of this precise date, see John P. Pratt, "The Restoration of Priesthood Keys on Easter 1836, Part 1: Dating the First Easter," *Ensign*, June 1985, 59–68. See also *The Life and Teachings of Jesus and His Apostles* [1979], 144, 150.

2. *History of the Church*, 4:597.

3. See *Doctrinal New Testament Commentary*, 3 vols. [1965–73], 1:626.

4. *History of the Church*, 2:271.

5. See Tad R. Callister's book *The Inevitable Apostasy and the Promised Restoration* [2006]. This is one of the finest and most comprehensive works ever written concerning the conditions of apostasy after the deaths of the Apostles. I highly recommend it to anyone who wants to understand what happened and why.

6. "Prepare Yourselves for the Great Day of the Lord," in *BYU 1981 Fireside and Devotional Speeches* [1982], 68.

7. See *Doctrinal New Testament Commentary*, 1:644–45.

8. In Conference Report, Oct. 1948, 76–77; or *Improvement Era*, Nov. 1948, 751.

9. *Doctrinal New Testament Commentary*, 1:644.

10. In Conference Report, Oct. 1950, 129; or *Improvement Era*, Dec. 1950, 1006.

11. *Gospel Doctrine*, 5th ed. [1939], 3–4.

12. In Conference Report, Apr. 1979, 131, 133; or *Ensign*, May 1979, 93.

13. *The Millennial Messiah: The Second Coming of the Son of Man* [1982], 476, 465–66.

14. In Conference Report, Oct. 1992, 41, 42–43; or *Ensign*, Nov. 1992, 31, 32.

15. In Conference Report, Apr. 1979, 131; or *Ensign*, May 1979, 93.

16. *History of the Church*, 4:11.

17. *Doctrinal New Testament Commentary*, 1:659.

18. *The Millennial Messiah: The Second Coming of the Son of Man*, 476.

19. *History of the Church*, 5:336–37.

20. *History of the Church*, 5:337.

21. In Conference Report, Oct. 1972, 128, 126; or *Ensign*, Jan. 1973, 105–6.

22. *Doctrinal New Testament Commentary*, 1:669.

23. *Doctrinal New Testament Commentary*, 1:659–60.

24. *Key to the Science of Theology; A Voice of Warning* [1978], 32–33.

25. *The Signs of the Times* [1954], 171–72.

CHAPTER 3

PARABLES OF THE LATTER-DAY KINGDOM

(MATTHEW 25)

THE THIRD DAY

(Tuesday)[1]

INTRODUCTION

The Nature of Parables

P. VERONESE

The word *parable* comes from the Greek word *parabole*, which means "placing beside" or "together," a comparison, an illustration of one subject by another. A parable is an earthly story with a heavenly message. It is a "divine truth . . . presented by comparison with material things."[2]

Elder James E. Talmage said: "[Parables are] designed to convey some great spiritual truth. . . . [A parable is] a brief narrative or descriptive allegory founded on real scenes or events such as occur in nature and human life, and usually with a moral or religious application."[3]

Elder Talmage also said: "Let it not be forgotten that a parable is but a sketch, not a picture finished in detail; and that the expressed or implied similitude in parabolic teaching cannot logically and consistently be carried beyond the limits of the illustrative story. . . . The parable is to be studied in the spirit of its purpose; and strained inferences or extensions are unwarranted. A strong metaphor, a striking simile, or any other expressive figure of speech, is of service only when rationally applied; if carried beyond the bounds of reasonable intent, the best of such may become meaningless or even absurd."[4]

Thus, we must use caution in interpreting parables, making sure that we do not expand the meaning of a parable beyond that which the Savior intended. The safest course is to:

— Always interpret parables in the simplest terms, not in the most complex.
— If provided, always use the interpretation given by the Savior or His prophets.
— Interpret the parable's meaning within the context in which it was given.

The Prophet Joseph Smith said: "I have a key by which I understand the scriptures. I [i]nquire, what was the question which drew out the answer, or caused Jesus to utter the parable? . . . To ascertain its meaning, we must dig up the root and ascertain what it was that drew the saying out of Jesus."[5] In other words, look at the reason why the parable was given in the first place in order to understand the meaning of the story itself.

The Doctrine and Covenants is a valuable resource for understanding parables, as it relates and interprets a number of parables from the New Testament.

— D&C 35:16; 45:36–38	The fig tree.
— D&C 45:56–57; 63:54	The ten virgins.
— D&C 86:1–7; 101:64–67	The wheat and the tares.
— D&C 101:81–91	The importuning widow and the unjust judge.

We will use some of these latter-day scriptures to better understand the parables discussed in this chapter.

THREE PARABLES ABOUT THE LAST DAYS

Having just finished relating His prophecies concerning the future of Jerusalem and the last days, Jesus then shared three parables with His disciples that all had to do with the Church in the last days. While these were given to His earliest disciples, they are primarily about us in our latter-day dispensation. We will do well to consider them carefully.

The Parable of the Ten Virgins

19th Century Jewish Wedding Ceremony

The parable of the ten virgins is based on Jewish wedding customs in Jesus' day. Traditionally, the bridegroom and his friends escorted the bride from her home to the home of the bridegroom. Along the way, the friends of the bride waited to join them. When they arrived at the bridegroom's home, they went inside for the wedding. These weddings usually took place in the evening, so those waiting for the bride and bridegroom carried small lamps fueled by oil.

- **Matthew 25:1–13 A parable about the readiness of Church members to be summoned to the marriage feast at the end of the world.** Speaking of the Church in the latter days, the Lord spoke the parable of the ten virgins, saying, "The kingdom of heaven [shall] be likened unto ten virgins, which took their lamps, and went forth to meet the bridegroom. And five of them were wise, and five were foolish" (vv. 1–2). Thus, we may conclude that one-half of the members of the Church will be unwise and ill-prepared when the Lord comes.

The five virgins that were foolish “took their lamps, [but] took no oil with them” (v. 3). The five wise virgins “took oil in their vessels with their lamps” (v. 4). Then, as they all waited for “the bridegroom” to come, “they all slumbered and slept” (v. 5).

PROVIDENCE LITHOGRAPHIC CO., 1906, #38

Finally, “at midnight there was a cry made, Behold, the bride-groom cometh; go ye out to meet him” (v. 6). The great day had come, and “all those virgins arose, and trimmed their lamps” (v. 7). But the unwise could not light their lamps because they lacked sufficient oil by that time. They said to the wise, “Give us of your oil; for our lamps are gone out. But the wise answered, saying, Not so; lest there be not enough for us and you: but go ye . . . to them that sell, and buy for yourselves” (vv. 8–9).

A. BIDA, 1874

While the five foolish virgins were out trying to obtain oil, “the bridegroom came; and they that were ready went in with him to the marriage: and the door was shut” (v. 10). It was too late for the foolish virgins; they had missed His coming. They knocked on the door and cried out, “Lord, Lord, open to us. But he answered and said, Verily I say unto you, I know you not” (vv. 11–12). “Watch therefore,” Jesus said to His disciples, “for ye know neither the day nor the hour wherein the Son of man cometh” (v. 13).

— **D&C 45:56–59** provides a modern-day interpretation of this parable. The Lord says that "they that are wise and have received the truth, and have taken the Holy Spirit for their guide, and have not been deceived—verily I say unto you, they shall not be hewn down and cast into the fire, but shall abide the day" (v. 57). Thus, the "oil" is spiritual preparation. And if they are found worthy at the time of the Lord's coming, "the earth shall be given unto them for an inheritance; and they shall multiply and wax strong, and their children shall grow up without sin unto salvation. For the Lord shall be in their midst, and his glory shall be upon them, and he will be their king and their lawgiver" (vv. 58–59).

President Spencer W. Kimball said:

> I believe that the Ten Virgins represent the people of the Church of Jesus Christ and not the rank and file of the world. All of the virgins, wise and foolish, had accepted the invitation to the wedding supper; they had knowledge of the program and had been warned of the important day to come. They were not the gentiles or the heathens or the pagans, nor were they necessarily corrupt and reprobate, but they were knowing people who were foolishly unprepared for the vital happenings that were to affect their eternal lives.
>
> They had the saving, exalting gospel, but it had not been made the center of their lives. They knew the way but gave only a small measure of loyalty and devotion. I ask you: What value is a car without an engine, a cup without water, a table without food, a lamp without oil?
>
> Rushing for their lamps to light their way through the blackness, half of them found them empty. They had cheated themselves. They were fools, these five unprepared virgins. Apparently, the bridegroom had tarried for reasons that were sufficient and good. Time had passed, and He had not come. They had heard of His coming for so long, so many times, that the statement seemingly became meaningless to them. Would He ever come? So long had it been since they began expecting Him that they were rationalizing that He would never appear. Perhaps it was a myth.
>
> Hundreds of thousands of us today are in this position. Confidence has been dulled and patience worn thin. It is so hard to wait and be prepared always. But we cannot allow

ourselves to slumber. The Lord has given us this parable as a special warning.[6]

Elder Wilford Woodruff said: "The parable of the ten virgins is intended to represent the Second Coming of the Son of Man, the coming of the Bridegroom to meet the bride, the Church . . . ; and I expect that the Savior was about right when He said, in reference to the members of the Church, that five of them were wise and five were foolish; . . . if He finds one-half of those professing to be members of His Church prepared for salvation, it will be as many as can be expected, judging by the course that many are pursuing."[7]

— **D&C 45:56–59 How and when the wise virgins will be blessed.** President Spencer W. Kimball said: "In the parable, oil can be purchased at the market. In our lives the oil of preparedness is accumulated drop by drop in righteous living. Attendance at sacrament meetings adds oil to our lamps, drop by drop over the years. Fasting, family prayer, home teaching, control of bodily appetites, preaching the gospel, studying the scriptures—each act of dedication and obedience is a drop added to our store. Deeds of kindness, payment of offerings and tithes, chaste thoughts and actions, marriage in the covenant for eternity—these, too, contribute importantly to the oil with which we can at midnight refuel our exhausted lamps."[8]

The Parable of the Talents

- **Matthew 25:14–30** In New Testament times, a talent was a sum of money.[9] Jesus used the image of a talent to represent a sacred trust, upon which a servant was expected to improve. He told the story of "a man travelling into a far country, who called his own servants, and delivered unto them his goods. And unto one he gave five talents, to another two, and to another one; to every man according to his several ability; and straightway took his journey" (v. 15). Note that the amount entrusted to each servant was determined by each person's abilities. Unto whom much was given, much was expected in return. Unto others, less was entrusted and less was expected, although everyone was expected to make the most of whatever they had been given.

The man who "received the five talents went and traded with the same, and made them other five talents. And likewise he that had received two, he also gained other two. But he that had received one went and digged in the earth, and hid his lord's money" (vv. 16–18). To each of the first two servants, who had doubled their inheritance through wise choices, the Lord promised an entry into "the joy of thy lord" (vv. 19–23).

THE HOLMAN BIBLE, 1890, #59

Last of all came the man to whom only one talent had been entrusted. He said to his lord, "I knew thee that thou art an hard man, reaping where thou hast not sown, and gathering where thou hast not strawed: And I was afraid, and went and hid thy talent in the earth: lo, there thou hast that is thine" (vv. 24–25). There are two problems with this response. (1) The man had made no effort to improve upon his trust, and (2) he sought to blame his lord for his failure. Neither was acceptable.

His lord condemned him, calling him "wicked and slothful" (v. 26). He knew that his lord expected him to put his talent to good use and to improve upon it so that at his lord's coming "[the lord] should have received [his] own with usury [interest]" (v. 27). He commanded, "Take therefore the talent from him, and give it unto him which hath ten talents. For unto every one that hath shall be given, and he shall have abundance: but from him that hath not shall be taken away even that which he hath. And cast ye the unprofitable servant into outer darkness: there shall be weeping and gnashing of teeth" (vv. 28–30).

In this parable, the man traveling to a far country represents the Lord. The servants represent each of us. The talents represent gifts and talents given us from God. Despite differing talents, we are all expected to serve with all diligence. Note that the amount entrusted and the amount earned were not the point. Each who made the most of his trust was given the same reward. Only he who had buried his talent was condemned. And because he had neglected his stewardship it was taken from him and given to another who could be trusted.

— **D&C 46:11–12 Every person has been given at least one gift from God; some are more visible than others.** "For all have not every gift given unto them; for there are many gifts, and to every man is given a gift by the Spirit of God. To some is given one, and to some is given another, that all may be profited thereby." We should note that the reason for these gifts is so that "all may be profited thereby." We are given our gifts so that we can share them with others. When we come together into our ward and stake congregations, all of the gifts of the Spirit are present. Nobody has all of them, but by meeting with and blessing each other with our gifts we *all* can receive the benefit of *all* of the gifts of God.

The Parable of the Sheep and the Goats

- **Matthew 25:31–46 We will be judged by whether we have served our fellow men.** Jesus compared the Second Coming and the final judgment to the division of sheep and goats.

  "When the Son of man shall come in his glory, and all the holy angels with him, then shall he sit upon the throne of his glory: And before him shall be gathered all nations: and he shall separate them one from another, as a shepherd divideth his sheep from the goats: And he shall set the sheep on his right hand, but the goats on the left" (vv. 31–33).

J. C. WEIGEL, 1695

Jesus will divide sheep from goats

The "sheep" who are found on the Lord's right hand will be told, "Come, ye blessed of my Father, inherit the kingdom prepared for you from the foundation of the world" (v. 34). And how will they get there on His right hand? He will answer, "I was an hungred, and ye gave me meat: I was thirsty, and ye gave me drink: I was a stranger, and ye took me in: Naked, and ye clothed me: I was sick, and ye visited me: I was in prison, and ye came unto me" (vv. 35–36). And how will they have done these things unto the Lord? He will answer, "Inasmuch as ye have done it unto one of the least of these my brethren, ye have done it unto me" (vv. 37–40).

To the "goats" on the Lord's left hand, He will say, "Depart from me, ye cursed, into everlasting fire, prepared for the devil and his angels" (v. 41). And why? Because "I was an hungred, and ye gave me no meat: I was thirsty, and ye gave me no drink: I was a stranger, and ye took me not in: naked, and ye clothed me not: sick, and in prison, and ye visited me not" (vv. 42–43). And when they protest, asking when they failed to do these things for the Lord, He will answer, "Inasmuch as ye did it not to one of the least of these, ye did it not to me" (vv. 44–45). And these—those who have neglected their fellow beings—"shall go away into everlasting punishment: but the righteous into life eternal" (v. 46).

Elder Marion D. Hanks said: "Jesus taught His followers the parable of the sheep and the goats, representing the judgment to come, in which He clearly identified those who will inherit 'life eternal' and those who will 'go away into everlasting punishment' (Matthew 25:46). The key difference was that those who should inherit the kingdom with Him had developed the habit of helping, had experienced the joy of giving, and the satisfaction of serving—they had responded to the needs of the hungry, thirsty, homeless, the naked, the sick, and those in prison. . . . Nothing would seem more clear than the high premium the Savior put upon selfless service to others as an indispensable element of Christian conduct and of salvation."[10]

Notes

1. For an explanation of this precise date, see John P. Pratt, "The Restoration of Priesthood Keys on Easter 1836, Part 1: Dating the First Easter," *Ensign*, June 1985, 59–68. See also *The Life and Teachings of Jesus and His Apostles* [1979], 150.

2. See Bible Dictionary, "Parables," 740–41.

3. *Jesus the Christ,* 3rd ed. [1916], 298, 304.

4. *Jesus the Christ,* 285–86.

5. *History of the Church*, 5:261.

6. *Faith Precedes the Miracle* [1972], 253–54.

7. In *Journal of Discourses*, 18:110.

8. *Faith Precedes the Miracle*, 256.

9. See Bible Dictionary, "Money," 733–34.

10. In Conference Report, Apr. 1992, 10; or *Ensign*, May 1992, 9.

CHAPTER 4

THE LAST SUPPER AND FIRST SACRAMENT

(MATTHEW 26; LUKE 22; JOHN 13)

INTRODUCTION

Jesus observed the last Passover of His earthly life only hours before His Atonement and crucifixion. For hundreds of years faithful Jews had offered a Passover lamb each spring. This yearly ritual reminded them of the first Passover at the time Moses led Israel out of Egypt. It symbolized the Lord's mercy in saving the lives of their firstborn sons at that time. The time was now at hand when He who was the Lamb of God would, in fulfilling His Atonement, become the great and last sacrifice of all.

THE THIRD DAY

(Tuesday)[1]

An Illegal Conspiracy to Kill Jesus

- **Matthew 26:1–2 Jesus foretells His betrayal and death.** Jesus said to His disciples, "After two days is the feast of the passover, and the Son of man is betrayed to be crucified" (v. 2). By this we know that it was the third day of His final week, two days before the Thursday evening on which He would be betrayed.

- **Matthew 26:3–5 The leaders of the Jews plot to kill Him.** "Then assembled together the chief priests, and the scribes, and the elders of the people, unto the palace of the high priest, who was called Caiaphas, And consulted that they might take Jesus by subtilty, and kill him" (vv. 3–4). This murderous conspiracy was absolutely in violation of their own religious laws and also the laws of the ruling Romans. But they cared not a whit about what was legal; they feared the loss of their influence and power and would do anything to protect it. Jesus had to go. But they did not dare kill Him "on the feast day, lest there be an uproar among the people" (v. 5).

  Elder James E. Talmage said: "The rulers feared especially an outbreak by the Galileans, who had a provincial pride in the prominence of Jesus as one of their countrymen, and many of whom were then in Jerusalem. It was further concluded and for the same reasons, that the Jewish custom of making impressive examples of notable offenders by executing public punishment upon them at times of great general assemblages, be set aside in the case of Jesus; therefore the conspirators said: 'Not on the feast day, lest there be an uproar among the people.'"[2]

Judas Iscariot Joins the Conspiracy

- **Matthew 26:14–16 Judas betrays Jesus for 30 pieces of silver.** We do not know all his motivations for betraying Jesus. Certainly one of them was greed because he accepted a bribe for the deed. But for whatever reasons he had, Judas "went unto the chief priests, And said unto them, What will ye give me, and I will deliver him unto you? And they covenanted with him for thirty pieces of silver. And from that time he sought opportunity to betray him."

  This act was significant for a number of reasons. First, Jesus had predicted it. Second, it was the price of a slave under Jewish law (see Exodus 21:28–32). And third, it had been prophesied anciently by the prophet Zechariah.

  — **Zechariah 11:12–13 Jesus will be sold for 30 pieces of silver.** Zechariah foretold Judas Iscariot's betrayal of Jesus: "If ye think good, give me my price; and if not, forbear. So they weighed for my price thirty pieces of silver. And the Lord said unto me, Cast it unto the potter: a goodly price that I was prised at of them. And I took the thirty pieces of silver, and cast them to the potter in the house of the Lord." All of these elements of the prophecy were literally fulfilled.

Judas sold Jesus for 30 silver pieces

Elder Bruce R. McConkie said: "Thirty pieces of silver! Such would they pay for the life of their God—no more and no less. And by so doing all men ever after would know that they esteemed [Christ] as the basest of men. And thus, also, even their attempts to debase and insult would fulfill, in literal detail, the Messianic prophecy of Zechariah which had foretold their evil conspiracy. 'If ye think good, give me my price; and if not, forbear,' the Lord says of the sum for which He will be sold. 'So they weighed for my price thirty pieces of silver' (Zechariah 11:12)."[3]

- **Luke 22:3–6 Satan "entered . . . into" Judas Iscariot.** Luke says that Satan "entered . . . into Judas . . . Iscariot, being of the number of the twelve. And he went his way, and communed with the chief priests and captains, how he might betray him unto them. And they were glad, and covenanted to give him money. And he promised, and sought opportunity to betray him unto them in the absence of the multitude."

We cannot help but wonder how Judas could do it. Surely he had been with the Master when He healed the sick, calmed the storms, and raised the dead. He had heard for himself the Savior's prophecies of His betrayal and death. Did Judas simply not "connect the dots" and realize he was becoming party to Jesus' death? Those who wish to be kind struggle for explanations. I have heard members of the Church claim that "the devil made him do it" because of this scripture, that he was possessed and not in his right mind. We cannot know his state of mind for certain. But I am not one to believe that Satan can make an otherwise rational man do *anything* contrary to his agency. He has to want to do it and choose to do it. And judging by Judas's reaction after the fact, it would seem that he knew exactly what he was doing.

Still, there are instances where evil spirits take possession of the bodies of men. Elder Bruce R. McConkie said: "Satan is a spirit man, a being who was born the offspring of God in [the premortal existence], and who was cast out of heaven for rebellion. He and his spirit followers have power in some cases to enter the bodies of men; they are, also, sometimes cast out of these illegally entered habitations by the power of the priesthood (see Mark 1:21–28)."[4]

Elder McConkie continued: "[Even] if the body of Judas was not possessed literally by Satan, still this traitorous member of the Twelve was totally submissive to the will of the devil."[5] And Elder James E. Talmage said: "Before Judas sold Christ to the Jews, he had sold himself to the devil; he had become Satan's serf, and did his master's bidding."[6]

THE FOURTH DAY
(Wednesday)

Arranging for the Final Passover Meal

- **Leviticus 23:5 The Passover** was an annual feast held at sunset on the 14th day of Nisan. In Israel, a new day began at sunset. Thus, before sunset, on the 14th day of Nisan, the Passover lambs were slain in preparation for the Passover feast. Ever since the first Passover just before the Israelites' exodus from Egypt, countless Paschal lambs had been slain each year for some 1,500 years to usher in Passover, in similitude of the ultimate sacrifice of the true Lamb of God—Jesus Christ—whose sacrifice was now fast approaching. Like these lambs, Jesus would also be sacrificed on 14 Nisan.[7] Then, at sunset, the 15th day of Nisan would begin—the first day of the Feast of Unleavened Bread. While Passover lasted only one day originally, the Feast of Unleavened Bread lasted a full seven days. Eventually, both festivals were combined into one, making the entire Passover period eight days in length.

- **Leviticus 23:6–7 The Feast of Unleavened Bread** at the time of Jesus had previously been combined with Passover, and so it began at Passover and continued for a week (v. 6). The first day after Passover (15 Nisan) was technically the first day of the week-long Feast of Unleavened Bread. Whenever 15 Nisan occurred on a Saturday, it was considered a "high day"—made doubly sacred because it was a feast day as well as the weekly Sabbath day.[8] When 15 Nisan did not fall on a Saturday, it was considered a non-Saturday Sabbath, to be observed in addition to the normal Sabbath that occurs on Saturday.[9]

  Thus, during this final week of the Savior's life, Friday was considered a Sabbath day in addition to Saturday, and the crucifixion would have taken place on Thursday rather than Friday. This being true, the Savior did indeed remain in the tomb for three days and nights—Thursday, Friday, and Saturday—before raising on Sunday morning.

  During this week-long feast, the children of Israel ate unleavened bread. Leaven (yeast), was considered a symbol of sin, and during this feast it had to be removed from all Israelite dwellings. All bread was made without yeast during the seven days of this feast—rendering a flat bread that was generally fried in pans or baked.

  This custom was initiated at the time the Israelites left Egypt "in haste" (Exodus 12:11). Because of the limited time before they would have to depart, they would not have sufficient time to permit their bread to rise as was the custom. Instead they were commanded to bake it in haste and vacate their homes as quickly as possible. The Passover meal and the Feast of Unleavened Bread were held to commemorate this fact.

- **Matthew 26:17 Preparing for Jesus' final Passover.** On "the first day of the feast of unleavened bread [actually on the day of Passover] the disciples came to Jesus, saying unto him, Where wilt thou that we prepare for thee to eat the passover?"

- **Matthew 26:18–19 The location of the feast.** In preparation for His last Passover meal, Jesus made arrangements to meet in the upper room of a faithful woman disciple's home in

Jerusalem. He said to His disciples, "Go into the city to such a man, and say unto him, The Master saith, My time is at hand; I will keep the passover at thy house with my disciples" (v. 18). Tradition says that this was the Gospel writer Mark's home, and the woman was his mother. "And the disciples did as Jesus had appointed them; and they made ready the passover" (v. 19).

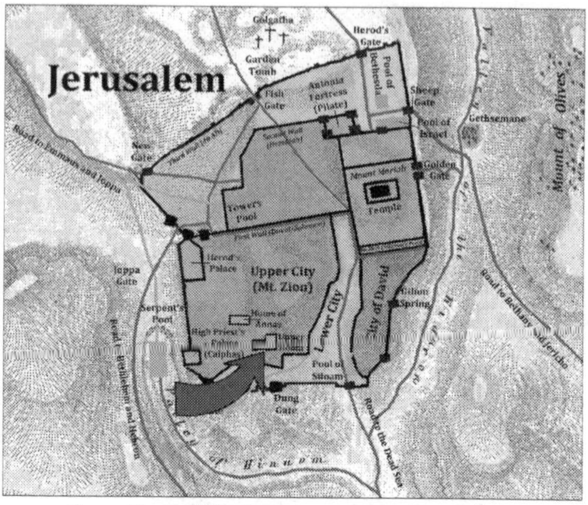

Location of the upper room in Jerusalem

JESUS INTRODUCES THE SACRAMENT

The final Passover was, in reality, two events rather than one: a formal celebration of the annual Passover supper and the first observance of the Lord's Supper in commemoration of the Atonement of Jesus Christ.

- **Matthew 26:26 Jesus introduces the ordinance of the sacrament bread** (see also Luke 22:19). It would have been customary to eat unleavened bread at the Passover feast. There was nothing unusual about eating bread. But "as they were eating" (note that the meal had already begun; this was not a blessing on the food in general), "Jesus took bread,

RUBENS, 1631–32

and blessed it, and brake it, and gave it to the disciples, and said, Take, eat; this is my body" (v. 26). He thus introduced a new symbolic ordinance: eating bread in remembrance of His body.

Why should we celebrate His body? Because He laid it down and then raised it up again to conquer death, thereby providing us with the gift of the resurrection. This is the first gift of the Atonement and it is given to all the children of God by a merciful Savior. When we partake of the sacrament bread we should be contemplating this gift and thanking God for it. Because of it, we and all of our loved ones will rise from our vile graves, alive again and forever because of Jesus Christ.

As an ordinance, this act would have included a covenant. All ordinances of salvation include covenants. We can therefore assume that the "blessing" Jesus offered contained that covenant. They were to eat bread—that is clear. But the Bible account does not tell us the nature of the covenant associated with this act. For this, we are dependent on the Book of Mormon and the Doctrine and Covenants.

— **D&C 20:77 The prayer on the bread** has been specified in latter-day revelation. It is this: "O God, the Eternal Father, we ask thee in the name of thy Son, Jesus Christ, to bless and sanctify this bread to the souls of all those who partake of it, that they may eat in remembrance of the body of thy Son, and witness unto thee, O God, the Eternal Father, that they are willing to take upon them the name of thy Son, and always remember him and keep his commandments which he has given them; that they may always have his Spirit to be with them. Amen." This same prayer is found in Moroni 4:3.

— We are thus covenanting to (1) take Jesus' name upon ourselves, (2) always remember Him, and (3) keep His commandments. That is our part of the covenant. And in return, He promises that we will "always have his Spirit" to be with us.

- **Matthew 26:27–28 Jesus introduces the ordinance of the sacrament wine** (see also Luke 22:20). Jesus next "took the cup, and gave thanks, and gave it to them, saying, Drink ye all of it; For this is my blood of the new testament, which is shed for many for the remission of sins." It would also have been customary to drink wine at the Passover feast. There was nothing unusual about drinking wine. But Jesus makes it clear that the wine they were about to drink was to be a symbol of His "blood . . . , which is shed for many for the remission of sins." He thus introduced a new symbolic ordinance: drinking wine in remembrance of His blood.

Why should we celebrate His blood? Because He shed it freely in Gethsemane and again several times along the way to Calvary, where He was nailed to a cross. That precious blood, like the blood of sacrificial lambs for many centuries, symbolically washes us clean from our sins. This is the second gift of the Atonement and it is given to all those who repent and come unto Christ for salvation. When we partake of the sacrament water we should be contemplating this gift and thanking God for it. Because of it, we and all of our loved ones can be washed clean and made worthy to enter into the celestial presence of the Father. Without this gift it would be simply impossible to have all the eternal blessings, both personal and family, that we hold so dear.

As an ordinance, this act would also have included a covenant. We can therefore assume that the "blessing" Jesus offered on the wine contained that covenant. They were to drink wine—that is clear. But the Bible account does not tell us the full nature of the covenant associated with this act. For this, we are again dependent on the Book of Mormon and the Doctrine and Covenants.

— **D&C 20:79 The prayer on the wine (or water)** has also been specified in latter-day revelation. It is this: "O God, the Eternal Father, we ask thee in the name of thy Son, Jesus Christ, to bless and sanctify this wine [water] to the souls of all those who drink of it, that they may do it in remembrance of the blood of thy Son, which was shed for them; that they may witness unto thee, O God, the Eternal Father, that they do always remember him, that they may have his Spirit to be with them. Amen." This same prayer is found in Moroni 5:2.

— We are thus covenanting to always remember Him, and in return, He promises that we will "always have his Spirit" to be with us. And since the sacramental ordinances are always done together—bread and water—we can assume that the enumerated promises of the prayer on the bread also apply to the water.

Elder James E. Talmage said: "While Jesus with the Twelve still sat at table, He took a loaf or cake of bread, and having reverently given thanks and by blessing sanctified it, He gave a portion to each of the Apostles, saying: 'Take, eat; this is my body'; or, according to the more extended account, 'This is my body which is given for you: this do in remembrance of me.' Then, taking a cup of wine, He gave thanks and blessed it, and gave it unto them with the command: 'Drink ye all of it; for this is my blood of the new testament, which is shed for many for the remission of sins. But I say unto you, I will not drink henceforth of this fruit of the vine, until that day when I drink it new with you in my Father's kingdom.' In this simple but impressive manner was instituted the ordinance, since known as the Sacrament of the Lord's Supper. The bread and wine, duly consecrated by prayer, become emblems of the Lord's body and blood, to be eaten and drunk reverently, and in remembrance of Him."[10]

Elder Jeffrey R. Holland said: "Since that upper room experience on the eve of Gethsemane and Golgotha, children of the promise have been under covenant to remember Christ's sacrifice in this newer, higher, more holy and personal way. . . . If remembering is the principal task before us, what might come to our memory when those plain and precious emblems are offered to us?"[11]

Elder Holland then suggested what we should remember about the Savior:[12]

— His love and strength in the Grand Council of Heaven.

- That He is the Creator of heaven and earth.
- All that He did in His premortal life as Jehovah.
- The simple grandeur of His birth.
- His teachings.
- His miracles and healings.
- That "all things which are good cometh of Christ" (Moroni 7:24).
- The unkind treatment, rejection, and injustice He endured.
- That He descended below all things in order to rise above them.
- That He made His sacrifices and endured His sorrows for each of us.

Performing Ordinances with Exactness

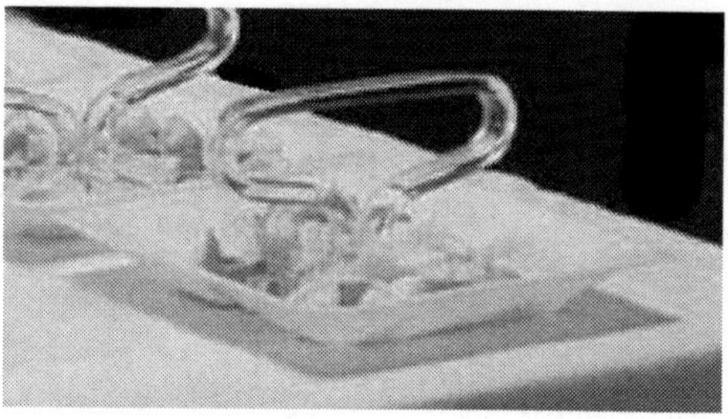

These prayers, given by the Lord Himself, contain specific terms of a covenant we are making with Him when we partake of these emblems. Along with the baptismal prayer and the words of the temple endowment ceremonies, these prayers are expected to be *word perfect* in their execution. This is done to ensure that the covenant we are making is *precisely* the one which the Lord wants us to make, and not some modification thereof. The performance of the ordinance is also expected to follow certain guidelines to ensure that it does not become either more or less than what the Lord intended and to be sure that we do not get overly focused on the pageantry at the expense of the promises.

Elder Matthew Cowley said: "The administration of the sacrament as a component of religious worship is so essential that the words in the prayer of sanctification have been given by direct revelation from God for this specific purpose. . . . In the blessing pronounced upon the sacred emblems of the Master's great sacrifice, the priest repeats God's own words—words which carry inspiration to the heart and soul of every participant in this holy ritual."[13]

Elder Delbert L. Stapley said:

> Now my brothers and sisters—there are only three prayers that the Lord has revealed to the Church, and two of them have to do with the ordinance of the sacrament, the blessing of the bread and the blessing of the water. These prayers are found in the fourth and fifth chapters of Moroni in the Book of Mormon and also in the 20th Section of the Doctrine and Covenants. While I will not attempt to repeat the sacramental prayers for you, I should like to point out [several] important considerations to remember in the revealed sacramental prayers. First, we partake of the sacrament in remembrance of the broken body and spilled blood of Christ.
>
> Then we witness unto the Father, and I think we should take note of that, first, that we will take upon us the name of His Son. . . . If we take upon us the name of Christ, even as we pledge to do—when we partake of the emblems of His body and blood, we agree to keep all the commandments until the end of our days.
>
> Second, we witness or pledge that we will always remember Him. As President McKay said, "Always remember Him in the home, in business, in society," and I would assume wherever else we might be.
>
> Third, we pledge to keep the commandments which He has given unto us, and last, we have a promise that if we do these things, and it is assumed that we do so worthily, that we shall always have His spirit to be with us.[14]

The Tokens of the Sacrament

- **D&C 27 Water instead of wine.** To understand why we use water instead of wine for the sacrament ordinance today, we can turn to D&C 27, which was received by the Prophet Joseph Smith in August and September of 1830 at Harmony, Pennsylvania. In early August, Newel Knight and his wife visited the Smiths in Harmony, Pennsylvania. Neither Sister Knight nor Emma Smith had yet been confirmed, so they decided to do this, and partake of the sacrament, before the Knights returned to their home in New York. Joseph went to obtain some wine for use in the sacrament. He said he "had gone only a short distance when I was met by a heavenly messenger, and received the following revelation [D&C 27]."[15]

- **D&C 27:3–4 Wine should be "made new among you."** The Lord commands "that you shall not purchase wine neither strong drink of your enemies; Wherefore, you shall partake of none except it is made new among you; yea, in this my Father's kingdom which shall be built up on the earth."

  This should not be interpreted to mean that we can never use wine for the sacrament. Rather, it says we are not to purchase wine from our enemies and are to use only "new wine of our own make" (see D&C 89:6), meaning essentially grape juice. This has reference to Joseph making sure the wine was pure and not tampered with by the enemies of the Church. In obedience to the revelation, they prepared wine of their "own make" and held their meeting.

  Some have interpreted this as a commandment to use only grape juice rather than fermented wine for the sacrament, but this cannot be correct, because the Church continued to use fermented sacramental wine both in Kirtland and in Nauvoo. It wasn't until 1906 that the Church adopted water as the standard liquid for this ordinance.

- **D&C 27:2 "It mattereth not."** Because the emblems of the sacra-ment are symbolic rather than mystically connected to the physical body and blood of the Lord, any food or liquid may, with permission from priesthood leaders, be used as the emblems by which we remember Him. During World War II, for example, when bread was not readily available in Europe, some congrega-tions used potato peelings in place of broken bread. However, unless required by extraordinary circumstances and approved by proper priesthood authority, we use bread and water for the sacrament emblems today.

Some Christians believe that the bread and the wine actually become the body and blood of Christ, which the believers then really eat and drink. This is the doctrine of transubstantiation, which the Church does not accept. In the Latter-day Saint view, after the emblems have been blessed, the bread is still bread and the water is still water, although they have been consecrated for a particular use as symbols of Christ's flesh and blood, and in that capacity they are treated with respect.

The Elements of All Ordinances

- **Every ordinance in the Church has three elements.** The sacramental ordinance is an excellent example of how the Lord teaches us through very simple but profound symbolic means.

  1. A physical act we must "perform" in order to show our agreement with its terms. In the case of the sacrament, it is the eating and drinking of the sacramental emblems. In the case of baptism, it is to go down into the water and be immersed. And temple ordinances have similar "performances" that are done as we make those covenants.

  2. Symbolic tokens that are used in the performance of the ordinance. These are things which are simply figurative, but which stand for mighty truths. In the case of the sacrament, they are the pieces of bread and the little cups of water. They are not literally the flesh and blood of Christ, but they *represent* those things. Baptism and temple ordinances also have their tokens, and in order to make the associated covenants we must use those tokens as instructed. One important principle about tokens is that they *always* have something to do with Christ, with whom we are making our covenants.

     Elder John A. Widtsoe spoke of the importance of understanding the symbolic meaning of tokens in order to properly make our covenants with the Lord. Though he was speaking specifically of the symbolism found in the temple endowment, the same principles apply to baptism and to the sacrament also.

"[Participating in sacred ordinances] implies a great effort of mind and concentration if we are to understand the mighty symbols that pass in review before us. Everything must be arranged to attune our hearts, our minds, and our souls to the work. Everything about us must contribute to the peace of mind that enables us to study and to understand the mysteries, if you choose, that are unfolded before us .... [For example,] no man or woman can come out of the temple endowed as he should be, unless he has seen, beyond the symbol, the mighty realities for which the symbols stand."[16]

3. Associated covenants (promises), which we are making with the Lord as we use the tokens to perform the ordinance. These mutual promises are often compared by the Lord to marriage vows, because He considers His relationship to us to be as sacred and binding as a marriage. For example, on a number of occasions He called Himself the Bridegroom, and compared His Second Coming to a wedding feast. When His people are unfaithful to Him, He says they are like an unfaithful wife who has gone "whoring" after other gods. He takes these covenants very seriously, and expects us to do the same. God always keeps His covenants. When we keep ours, He blesses us (see D&C 82:10).

Frequent Repetition of the Sacrament Ordinance

- **D&C 20:75 We are to partake of the sacrament often.** Because of our need to renew our covenants regularly, we are told that it is "expedient that the Church meet together often to partake of bread and wine in the remembrance of the Lord Jesus."

  Elder Matthew Cowley said:

  The Lord, being aware of man's tendency to transgress the law, and that "it is human to err" has enjoined His Church to "meet together often" and partake of the emblems of His redeeming sacrifice, and to offer up their sacraments that they may more fully keep themselves unspotted from the world. . . .

The Sabbath is the day appointed for sacrament service. In the religious worship of this day every member of the Church is expected to present himself before the sacrament board and renew his covenants with his Redeemer. For those who neglect this duty, there is no covenant renewal, and the Lord will not hold them blameless. The vitality of the Church lies in the obedience of its members to the divine plan, and this vitality comes from the frequent communion of the Saints—meeting together often, and with contrite spirits, partaking of the sacrament of the Lord's supper.[17]

Priesthood Authority and Worthiness

- **D&C 20:76 The authority and worthiness of the officiator.** The sacred sacramental ordinance is to be administered by "the elder or priest" who shall "kneel with the church and call upon the Father in solemn prayer" (v. 76). Thus, a very important prerequisite to the performance of such covenant-bearing ordinances is that the person performing the ordinance must have proper priesthood authority and worthiness to do so. This is because the officiator symbolically represents the Lord.

Worthiness to Partake of the Sacrament

- **D&C 46:4 The unworthy are not to partake of the sacrament.** Another prerequisite is that the person receiving the ordinance must be worthy to do so. A person who is not already keeping the standards of the temple, for instance, cannot receive a temple recommend to go there and make temple covenants that will require him or her to keep those standards. Worthiness is required *before* making solemn covenants with the Lord.

  The Lord commands the Church "not to cast any one who belongeth to the church out of your sacrament meetings." Even the unworthy are welcome in our meeting houses. However, "if any have trespassed, let him not partake until he makes reconciliation."

President Joseph Fielding Smith wrote: "If any of the members are not in good standing; if they have in their hearts any feeling of hatred, envy, or sin of any kind, they should not partake of these emblems. If there are any differences or feelings existing between brethren, these differences should be adjusted before the guilty parties partake; otherwise they will eat and drink unworthily and bring upon them the condemnation spoken of by Paul (see 1 Corinthians 11:20–24; 3 Nephi 18:28–32; 20:8; Mormon 9:29). We should all see that our hearts and hands are clean and pure."[18]

We do not have to be perfect to partake of the sacrament, and I fear that sometimes we fail to take it when we most need to do so. Of course, we should never make such covenants if we have no intention of repenting of those wrong things we may have said or done during the week, or if we have been guilty of sins for which our priesthood leaders have restricted our access to the sacrament. But otherwise, the sacrament is a forward-looking ordinance—one in which we make covenants for the coming week. As such, it is an opportunity to promise to do better, not a statement that we have done well up to now.

Elder Melvin J. Ballard said: "If there is a feeling in our hearts that we are sorry for what we have done; if there is a feeling in our souls that we would like to be forgiven, then the method to obtain forgiveness is not through rebaptism; it is not to make confession to man, but it is to repent of our sins, to go to those against whom we have sinned or transgressed and obtain their forgiveness, and then repair to the sacrament table where, if we have sincerely repented and put ourselves in proper condition, we shall be forgiven, and spiritual healing will come to our souls. It will really enter into our being."[19]

Elder Dallin H. Oaks said: "In partaking of the sacrament, we can renew the effects of our baptism. . . . The renewal of our covenants by partaking of the sacrament should also be preceded by repentance, so we come to that sacred ordinance with a broken heart and a contrite spirit (see 2 Nephi 2:7; 3 Nephi 12:19; D&C 59:8). Then, as we renew our baptismal covenants and affirm that we will 'always remember him' (D&C 20:77), the Lord will renew the promised remission of our sins, under the conditions and at the time He chooses. . . . Out of the seemingly small act of consciously and reverently renewing our baptismal covenants comes a renewal of the blessings of baptism by water and by the Spirit, that we may always have His Spirit to be with us. In this way all of us will be guided, and in this way all of us can be cleansed."[20]

Elder Melvin J. Ballard said:

> I suggested that perhaps some of us are ashamed to come to the sacrament table because we feel unworthy and are afraid lest we eat and drink of these sacred emblems to our own condemnation. And so we want every Latter-day Saint to come to the sacrament table because it is the place for self-investigation, or self-inspection, where we may learn to rectify our course and to make right our own lives, bringing them into harmony with the teachings of the Church and with our brethren and sisters. It is the place where we become our own judges.
>
> There may be some instances where the elders of the Church could say, properly, to one who, in transgression, stretches forth his hands to partake of the emblems: You should not do this until you have made restitution; but ordinarily we will be our own judges. If we are properly instructed, we know that it is not our privilege to partake of the emblems of the flesh and blood of the Lord in sin, in transgression, or having injured and holding feelings against our brethren and sisters. . . . The one thing that would make for the safety of every man and woman would be to appear at the sacrament table every Sabbath day. We would not get very far away in one week—not so far away that, by the process of self-investigation, we could not rectify the wrongs we may have done.[21]

EVENTS AFTER THE SACRAMENT

- **John 13:23 John was next to Jesus, on His right.** John says that "one of [the] disciples" was "leaning on Jesus' bosom," and further identifies him as the disciple "whom Jesus loved." This disciple was none other than John himself. It may seem odd that John would not identify himself. But in the time of Jesus, writers simply did not identify themselves in the first person. It was considered bad form. Even in our own time, how many of us have been told by a teacher to not use the word "I" when writing a research paper? Somehow, it is supposed to be more scholarly not to do so. A similar rule existed when John wrote his gospel, and so he does not specifically identify himself.

LEONARDO DA VINCI, 1490–98

Nevertheless, he is called "John the Beloved" for a reason. He was the closest friend of Jesus among the Twelve Apostles and may also have been related through their mothers, who were probably sisters. On this occasion, John was located in the most honored position at the table—on the right hand of the Master.

Medieval paintings show all the disciples seated around a table. But such depictions are not correct. In Jesus' day, those at a banquet would adopt a reclining position, leaning upon their left elbows while eating with their right hands (see picture below). Thus, John would have been immediately in front of Jesus, with his back facing Jesus' bosom. This is what "leaning on Jesus' bosom" means.

Jesus Identifies His Betrayer

- **John 13:21–22 Jesus announces that one of the Twelve will betray Him.** Jesus was now "troubled in spirit," and testified ("Verily, verily I say unto you") to the Apostles that "one of you shall betray me" (v. 21). They were stunned, "look[ing upon] one . . . another, doubting of whom he spake" (v. 22). How could this be? They had been together in the Lord's company now for more than two years. They were, no doubt, very close friends, knit together by their devotion to the Master and having seen all of His mighty works. And now, one of them would betray Him? How could this be?

PROVIDENCE LITHOGRAPHIC CO., 1903, #42

- **Matthew 26:22 The shocked disciples ask Jesus, "Lord, is it I?"** They became "exceeding sorrowful, and began every one of them to say unto him, Lord, is it I?"

- **John 13:24–30 Jesus identifies Judas Iscariot as the betrayer.** Peter, their recognized leader, beckoned to John, urging him to "ask [Jesus] who it should be of whom he spake" (v. 24). And John, "lying on Jesus' breast," asked Him plainly, "Lord, who is it?" (v. 25). Jesus quietly answered John, "He it is, to whom I shall give a sop, when I have dipped it" (v. 26).

"In areas of the world where table utensils are not used at mealtime, it is common practice to place both broth and meat in a dish in the center of the table. Thin pieces of bread, often shaped to make a spoon, are used to extract both meat and broth from their repository. The bread thus dipped becomes a 'sop.' It is a mark of great honor for two friends to dip from the same sop-dish and an even greater mark of

CARL H. BLOCH, 1890

respect for one to dip for a friend and present the sop to him. Thus it was that Judas attempted to feign his love and loyalty for Jesus at the Passover meal by dipping his hand in the same dish with Him (see Matthew 26:23)."[22]

When Jesus had dipped the sop, "he gave it to Judas Iscariot, the son of Simon" (v. 26). "And after the sop Satan entered into him" (v. 27). Jesus said out loud to Judas, "That thou doest, do quickly," and "no man at the table knew for what intent he spake this unto him" (vv. 27–28). "For some of them thought, because Judas had the bag, that Jesus had said unto him, Buy those things that we have need of against the feast; or, that he should give something to the poor. He then having received the sop went immediately out: and it was night" (vv. 29–30).

Washing the Disciples' Feet

- **Luke 22:24–27 The Apostles again contend about "which of them should be accounted the greatest"** (see also Matthew 18:1; Luke 9:46). It was not a quiet philosophical discussion; it engendered strife (v. 24). They had debated this matter before, and Jesus had told them that in order to become great in the kingdom of heaven they would have to become like little children (see Matthew 18:1–4). But here they were again, debating their relative rewards for having served Him as His Apostles.

  Jesus explained, "The kings of the Gentiles exercise lordship over them; and they that exercise authority upon them are called benefactors. But ye shall not be so: but he that is greatest among you, let him be as the younger; and he that is chief, as he that doth serve" (vv. 25–26). True greatness, He said, comes through selfless service, and He has set the example by being "among you as he that serveth" (v. 27).

- **John 13:4–5 Jesus washes their feet to show them what true greatness means.** Jesus then "riseth from supper, and laid aside his garments; and took a towel, and girded himself" (v. 4). This was the garb of a slave—one who performed the most menial tasks in a household. With the towel girded about His waist, "he poureth water into a basin, and began to wash the disciples' feet, and to wipe them with the towel wherewith he was girded" (v. 5).

PROVIDENCE LITHOGRAPHIC CO., 1898, #41

- **John 13:6–8 Peter objects to the ordinance.** To touch someone's feet was the most humiliating task known in their culture. Even slaves were not required to do it. Yet, here was the Master humbly washing their filthy feet. Peter objected strenuously, "Lord, dost thou wash my feet?" (v. 6). Jesus counseled patience. "What I do thou knowest not now; but thou shalt know hereafter" (v. 7). But Peter was adamant, saying to the Lord, "Thou shalt never wash my feet" (v. 8).

- **John 13:8–11 "If I wash thee not, thou hast no part with me."** Jesus' answer to Peter is full of meaning for all of us. If we wish to be with Him, we must be perfect. And if we wish to be perfect, our sins must be washed away by Him. Therefore, if He washes us not, then we have no hope of ever being with Him or the Father hereafter. Realizing this, Peter then enthusiastically accepted the ordinance: "Lord, not my feet only, but also my hands and my head" (v. 9). Of course, the ordinance was symbolic and did not require the washing of any part of the body except the feet to make them "clean every whit" (v. 10). Jesus assured them that they would be made clean, "but not all"—a reference to Judas Iscariot who had already departed.

- **John 13:12–17 Jesus explains the meaning of the ordinance.** When He had finished washing their feet, Jesus put His outer garment back on and sat down, asking, "Know ye what I have done to you?" (v. 12). "Ye call me Master and Lord: and ye say well; for so I am. If I then, your Lord and Master, have washed your feet; ye also ought to wash one another's feet. For I have given you an example, that ye should do as I have done to you" (vv. 13–15). This was His way of showing them true leadership and greatness. He testified, "The servant is not greater than his lord; neither he that is sent greater than he that sent him" (v. 16), and if they wanted to be happy they must remember these principles (v. 17).

Elder Howard W. Hunter said: "As the hour of sacrifice approached, Jesus retreated with His twelve Apostles to the peace and privacy of an upper chamber. There the Master sought to fortify His special witnesses against the snares of the evil one by laying aside His outer garment, girding Himself with a towel, and washing the Apostles' feet. . . . To the very end of His mortal life Jesus was demonstrating the grandeur of His spirit and the magnitude of His strength. He was not, even at this late hour, selfishly engrossed with His own sorrows or contemplating the impending pain. He was anxiously attending to the present and future needs of His beloved followers. He knew their own safety, individually and as a church, lay only in their unconditional love one for another. His entire energies seem to have been directed toward their needs, thus teaching by example what He was teaching by precept. He gave them words of comfort and commandment and caution."[23]

— **D&C 88:140–141 Washing of the feet was restored in our day on December 27, 1832.** The Lord instructed Joseph Smith, "And again, the ordinance of washing feet is to be administered by the president, or presiding elder of the church. It is to be commenced with prayer; and after partaking of bread and wine, he is to gird himself according to the pattern given in the thirteenth chapter of John's testimony concerning me. Amen." This ordinance is performed from time to time among the First Presidency and Quorum of the Twelve Apostles in the most sacred places of our temples.

Notes

1. For an explanation of this and other precise dates that appear in this chapter, see John P. Pratt, "The Restoration of Priesthood Keys on Easter 1836, Part 1: Dating the First Easter," *Ensign*, June 1985, 59–68. See also *The Life and Teachings of Jesus and His Apostles* [1979], 136, 158.

2. *Jesus the Christ*, 3rd ed. [1916], 591.

3. *Doctrinal New Testament Commentary*, 3 vols. [1965–73], 1:703.

4. *Doctrinal New Testament Commentary*, 1:701–2.

5. *Doctrinal New Testament Commentary*, 1:702.

6. *Jesus the Christ*, 592.

7. For a detailed explanation of Passover symbolism, see John P. Pratt, "The Restoration of Priesthood Keys on Easter 1836, Part 2: Symbolism of Passover and of Elijah's Return," *Ensign*, July 1985, 55–64.

8. See *Jesus the Christ*, 618.

9. "The Feast of Unleavened Bread," http://endtimepilgrim.org/unleavened.htm

10. *Jesus the Christ*, 596–97.

11. In Conference Report, Oct. 1995, 88, 90; or *Ensign*, Nov. 1995, 67, 68.

12. See Conference Report, Oct. 1995, 90, 91; or *Ensign*, Nov. 1995, 68, 69.

13. *Matthew Cowley Speaks* [1954], 191.

14. "The Sacrament," address delivered May 8, 1956, in *1956 BYU Devotional Speeches of the Year* [1957], 5–6.

15. *History of the Church*, 1:106–8.

16. "Temple Worship," *The Utah Genealogical and Historical Magazine*, Apr. 1921, 60, 62.

17. *Matthew Cowley Speaks*, 191–92.

18. *Doctrines of Salvation*, comp. Bruce R. McConkie, 3 vols. [1954–56], 2:343.

19. "The Sacramental Covenant," *Improvement Era*, Oct. 1919, 1026–27.

20. In Conference Report, Oct. 1996, 81, 82; or *Ensign*, Nov. 1996, 61.

21. "The Sacramental Covenant," *Improvement Era*, Oct. 1919, 1027–28.

22. *Harper's Bible Dictionary* [1959], "Sop."

23. In Conference Report, Apr. 1974, 23, 24; or *Ensign*, May 1974, 18, 19.

CHAPTER 5

THE HOLY SPIRIT & JESUS' INTERCESSORY PRAYER

(JOHN 14–17)

THE FOURTH DAY

(Wednesday)[1]

Jesus was now ready to go out into the Garden of Gethsemane and do that for which He had come into the world—atone for the sins of all of God's children. He knew that this would be the last time in His mortal life that He could instruct His disciples. He also knew that they were full of anxiety concerning His leaving them. He therefore taught them about the Comforter who would be sent to help them once He departed. He also promised to continue to visit them Himself. And lastly, He offered a heartfelt prayer in their behalf.

THEBIBLEREVIVAL.COM, #47

- **John 14:1–3 "In my Father's house are many mansions."** Jesus began His instruction with words of comfort. "Let not your heart be troubled: ye believe in God, believe also in me" (v. 1). No doubt gesturing toward the heavens, He told them that "in my Father's house are many mansions: if it were not so, I would have told you. I go to prepare a place for you" (v. 2). "And if I go and prepare a place for you, I will come again, and receive you unto myself; that where I am, there ye may be also" (v. 3).

- **John 14:4–6 "I am the way, the truth, and the life."** Jesus had taught them concerning the plan of salvation and reminded them that "whither I go ye know, and the way ye know" (v. 4). But Thomas, wanting more certainty, said, "Lord, we know not whither thou goest; and how can we know the way?" (v. 5). To this desperate inquiry Jesus gave a succinct answer: "I am the way, the truth, and the life: no man cometh unto the Father, but by me" (v. 6).

  To say that He is "the way" means that He provides the path by which we can return to our Heavenly Father. To say that He is "the truth" means that *all* truth emanates from Him; it does not exist independent and apart from that Being who is the source of truth. To say that He is "the life" means that "in Him the light of life centers; except for Him and His power there would be no existence; should He withdraw the light of life, death would gain an immediate victory."[2] It also means that, through His Atonement and resurrection, He made immortality and eternal life possible for us.

  President David O. McKay said:

  > "How can we know the way?" asked Thomas, as he sat with his fellow Apostles and their Lord at the table after the supper on the memorable night of the betrayal; and Christ's divine answer was: "I am the way, the truth, and the life . . ." (John 14:5–6). And so He is! He is the source of our comfort, the inspiration of our life, the author of our salvation. If we want to know our relationship to God, we go to Jesus Christ. If we would know the truth of the immortality of the soul, we have it exemplified in the Savior's resurrection.
  >
  > If we desire to learn the ideal life to lead among our fellowmen, we can find a perfect example in the life of Jesus. Whatsoever our noble desires, our lofty aspirations, our ideals in any phase of life, we can look to Christ and find perfection. So, in seeking a standard for moral manhood, we need only to go to the Man of Nazareth and in Him find embodied all virtues that go to make the perfect man.[3]

THE FIRST COMFORTER (HOLY GHOST)

PROVIDENCE LITHOGRAPHIC CO., 1896, #41

- **John 14:15–17 Jesus promises to send the Comforter (Holy Ghost) to them.** The first requirement of this promise was, "If ye love me, keep my commandments" (v. 15). Then, if they would do this, Jesus said, "I will pray the Father, and he shall give you another Comforter, that he may abide with you for ever; Even the Spirit of truth; whom the world cannot receive, because it seeth him not, neither knoweth him: but ye know him; for he dwelleth with you, and shall be in you" (vv. 16–17).

- **John 14:18–20 Jesus promises to also visit them Himself.** "I will not leave you comfortless," He said, "I will come to you" (v. 18). In "yet a little while" Jesus would be leaving the earth and "the world seeth me no more" (v. 19). But the Apostles would see Him, and "because I live, ye shall live also" (v. 19). By this means they would learn and know that Jesus and the Father are united in purpose, "and ye in me, and I in you" (v. 20).

- **John 16:1–4 Jesus forewarned them so their faith would not fail under persecution** (v. 1). "They shall put you out of the synagogues," He warned, and "the time cometh, that whosoever killeth you will think that he doeth God service" (v. 2). They would do these things because they do not know the Father nor His Son (v. 3). "But these things have I told you, that when the time shall come, ye may remember that I told you of them" (v. 4). He had not told them of these things earlier in their ministries because He was still with them. But now that He was going away, they needed to know.

- **John 16:5–7 The Holy Ghost could not be with them so long as Jesus was there.** He was "go[ing His] way to him that sent me" (v. 5), and because of this "sorrow hath filled your heart" (v. 6). "Nevertheless I tell you the truth; It is expedient for you that I go away: for if I go not away, the Comforter will not come unto you; but if I depart, I will send him unto you" (v. 7).

  President Joseph Fielding Smith said: "The disciples of Jesus did not receive the gift of the Holy Ghost while He was with them. The reason for this, in part at least, was due to the fact that they had with them to guide and teach them the second member of the Godhead, even Jesus Himself. While He was with them there was no occasion for them to have the companionship of the Holy Ghost. Before the Savior left them, He promised to send them the Comforter, or Holy Ghost."[4]

  Elder Bruce R. McConkie said: "Since the divine law in all ages called for men to pray to the Father in the name of Christ, why had Jesus awaited this hour to institute the age-old system among His disciples? Perhaps it is a situation similar to that which is involved in receiving the gift of the Holy Ghost; as long as Jesus was with the disciples they did not enjoy the full manifestations of the Holy Ghost (see John 16:7). Perhaps as long as Jesus was personally with them many of their petitions were addressed directly to Him rather than to the Father. Such was the course followed by the Nephites when the resurrected and glorified Lord ministered among them. They prayed directly to Him and not to the Father [see 3 Nephi 19:17–18, 22]."[5]

The Roles of The Holy Ghost

The Holy Ghost is an actual being and a son of our Heavenly Father. Like Jesus, He achieved Godhood in the premortal world and became one of the three members of the Godhead that we worship. He has not yet received a body of flesh and bones, but will do so when the work of this world has been completed. He remains a spirit so that He can enter into our souls and communicate directly with our spirits in ways not possible with the physical senses (see D&C 130:22).

The Holy Ghost has many names, each of which is associated with one of the functions He performs. Following is a summary of His roles identified in the scriptures.

— **John 14:25–26** .... The Holy Ghost comforts. The Holy Ghost teaches. The Holy Ghost helps us remember.

Jesus had taught them while He was with them (v. 25). "But the Comforter, which is the Holy Ghost, whom the Father will send in my name, he shall teach you all things, and bring all things to your remembrance, whatsoever I have said unto you" (v. 26). With regard to teaching, the Lord revealed in our day that the *only* way we can teach another person is through the Holy Ghost, "and if ye receive not the Spirit ye shall not teach" (D&C 42:14).

— **John 16:7–11** .... The Holy Ghost witnesses against sin. The Holy Ghost witnesses of righteousness. The Holy Ghost judges our thoughts, words, and deeds.

Jesus promised that after He departed He would send the Comforter to them (v. 7). "And when he is come, he will reprove the world of sin, and of righteousness, and of judgment" (v. 8). He will witness against the sins of those that believe not in Christ (v. 9). He will witness of righteousness, being the only ever-present member of the Godhead in our lives (v. 10). And He will judge our behavior, being the one sure ever-present witness of our thoughts, words, and deeds (v. 11).

— **John 16:12–13** .... The Holy Ghost guides us to truth. The Holy Ghost testifies of Christ and the Father. The Holy Ghost provides revelation of things to come.

Jesus promised that "when he, the Spirit of truth, is come, he will guide you into all truth." Also, "he shall not speak of himself; but whatsoever he shall hear, that shall he speak" (which means He testifies of the Father and the Son and their teachings). And finally, "he will shew you things to come."

— **John 16:14** . . . . . The Holy Ghost glorifies Jesus and the Father. The Holy Ghost makes the gospel plain unto men.

Jesus taught that the Holy Ghost would "glorify" Him by receiving of His teachings and explaining them to those who are seeking truth.

— **Ephesians 1:13** . . . . . . The Holy Ghost seals us up unto eternal life.
Ephesians 4:30

"Sealed," in this case, does not mean "stuck together" like we would do with sealing tape. It means "certified"—the sort of thing that is done when a notary public "seals" a document that has been signed in his or her presence. If we have lived a life worthy of exaltation, that fact is "sealed [by] that holy Spirit of promise" (1:13). Thus, "the holy Spirit of God . . . seal[s us] unto the day of redemption" (4:30).

— **Moses 6:60**. . . . . .The Holy Ghost justifies us (testifies of our worthiness).

We obey God's command when we are baptized. After that, if we have done all that we can do, "by the Spirit [we] are justified." It is the blood of Christ that sanctifies us, but it is through the Holy Spirit that the effects of Christ's Atonement are made manifest in our individual lives. The Spirit literally "purges" us of sin when we come unto Christ and accept His Atonement in our lives.

— **Galatians 5:22–23**. . .The Holy Ghost bestows attributes of godliness.

Paul taught that "the fruit of the Spirit is love, joy, peace, longsuffering, gentleness, goodness, faith, meekness, [and] temperance." We are more godly in all our walk and conversation when we possess the Spirit in our lives.

— **Mosiah 4:3**. . . . . The Holy Ghost provides joy and peace in this world.

After hearing the words of King Benjamin, "the Spirit of the Lord came upon [his people], and they were filled with joy, having received a remission of their sins, and having peace of conscience, because of the exceeding faith which they had in Jesus Christ who should come, according to the words which king Benjamin had spoken unto them."

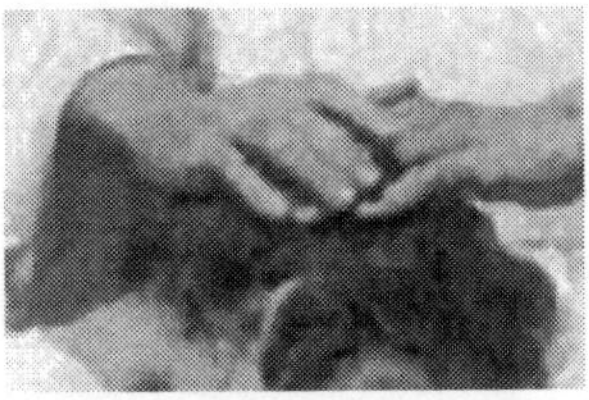

- **John 20:22 Jesus confers the Spirit upon them.** John says, "He breathed on them, and saith unto them, Receive ye the Holy Ghost." The Apostles had experienced the manifestations of the Holy Ghost during Jesus' mortal ministry, but did not receive the gift of the Holy Ghost until after His death and resurrec- tion. This was the bestowal of the gift of the Holy Ghost upon them.

  Elder Dallin H. Oaks said:

  > Manifestations of the Holy Ghost are given to lead sincere seekers to gospel truths that will persuade them to repentance and baptism. The gift of the Holy Ghost is more comprehensive. . . . [It] includes the right to constant companionship, that we may 'always have his Spirit to be with [us]' (D&C 20:77).
  >
  > A newly baptized member told me what she felt when she received that gift. This was a faithful Christian woman who had spent her life in service to others. She knew and loved the Lord, and she had felt the manifestations of His Spirit. When she received the added light of the restored gospel, she was baptized and the elders placed their hands upon her head and gave her the gift of the Holy Ghost. She recalled, "I felt the influence of the Holy Ghost settle upon me with greater intensity than I had ever felt before. He was like an old friend who had guided me in the past but now had come to stay."[6]

- **Acts 5:32 Only the righteous can enjoy the companionship of the Spirit.** After we have received the gift of the Holy Ghost, we must remain worthy of His constant companionship, or else the Spirit will depart from us. God has promised the Holy Ghost only "to them that obey him."

  — **D&C 6:14** The Lord told Oliver Cowdery that "thou hast inquired of me, and behold, as often as thou hast inquired thou hast received instruction of my Spirit." But had he not been worthy, "thou wouldst not have come to the place where thou art at this time."

— **D&C 20:77, 79** The sacramental prayers contain a solemn covenant between God the Eternal Father and each person who partakes of the sacramental emblems. We, for our part, promise to "take upon [us] the name of thy Son, and always remember him and keep his commandments which he has given them" (v. 77). And in return for this obedience, we are promised to always "have his Spirit to be with [us]" (vv. 77, 79).

— **D&C 76:116** The things of God "are only to be seen and understood by the power of the Holy Spirit, which God bestows on those who love him, and purify themselves before him."

— **D&C 121:45–46** If we "let [our] bowels . . . be full of charity towards all men, and to the household of faith, and let virtue garnish [our] thoughts unceasingly," then our confidence will "wax strong in the presence of God; and the doctrine of the priesthood shall distil upon [our souls] as the dews from heaven" (v. 45). "The Holy Ghost shall be [our] constant companion, and [our] scepter an unchanging scepter of righteousness and truth; and [our] dominion shall be an everlasting dominion, and without compulsory means it shall flow unto [us] forever and ever" (v. 46).

- **Galatians 5:22–23 How we can recognize the influence of the Holy Ghost.** As mentioned earlier, Paul said the Holy Spirit will confer upon us feelings of love, joy, peace, longsuffering, gentleness, goodness, faith, meekness, and temperance. When we feel these things we are receiving the Spirit of the Holy Ghost.

  — **D&C 6:15, 23** The Lord said to Oliver Cowdery, "Behold, thou knowest that thou hast inquired of me and I did enlighten thy mind; and now I tell thee these things that thou mayest know that thou hast been enlightened by the Spirit of truth. . . . Did I not speak peace to your mind concerning the matter? What greater witness can you have than from God?"

— **D&C 11:13** And the Lord said to Hyrum Smith, "I will impart unto you of my Spirit, which shall enlighten your mind, which shall fill your soul with joy."

President Boyd K. Packer said: "The Holy Ghost speaks with a voice that you *feel* more than you *hear*. It is described as a 'still small voice' (D&C 85:6). And while we speak of 'listening' to the whisperings of the Spirit, most often one describes a spiritual prompting by saying, 'I had a *feeling* . . .' Revelation comes as words we *feel* more than *hear*."[7]

The Prophet Joseph Smith said in a dream given to President Brigham Young: "[Teach the Saints that] the Spirit of the Lord . . . will whisper peace and joy to their souls; it will take malice, hatred, strife, and all evil from their hearts; and their whole desire will be to do good, bring forth righteousness, and build up the kingdom of God."[8]

THE SECOND COMFORTER (CHRIST)

THEBIBLEREVIVAL.COM, #30

- **John 14:18–23 "I will come to you."** Jesus promised His Apostles that He would not "leave you comfortless" but would "come to you" (v. 18). Though the world would not see Him again until His Second Coming, the Apostles would know that He lives, and "because I live, ye shall live also" (v. 19). But this promise is not restricted to Apostles. "He that hath my commandments, and keepeth them, he it is that loveth me: and he that loveth me shall be loved of my Father, and I will love him, and will manifest myself to him" (v. 21).

One of the Apostles did not fully understand, and asked, "Lord, how is it that thou wilt manifest thyself unto us, and not unto the world?" (v. 22). And He answered, "If a man love me, he will keep my words: and my Father will love him, and we will come unto him, and make our abode with him" (v. 23).

The Prophet Joseph Smith said: "Now what is this other Comforter? It is no more nor less than the Lord Jesus Christ Himself; and this is the sum and substance of the whole matter; that when any man obtains this last Comforter, he will have the personage of Jesus Christ to attend him, or appear unto him from time to time, and even He will manifest the Father unto him, and they will take up their abode with him, and the visions of the heavens will be opened unto him, and the Lord will teach him face to face, and he may have a perfect knowledge of the mysteries of the Kingdom of God; and this is the state and place the ancient Saints arrived at when they had such glorious visions—Isaiah, Ezekiel, John upon the Isle of Patmos, St. Paul in the three heavens, and all the Saints who held communion with the general assembly and Church of the Firstborn."[9]

PROVIDENCE LITHOGRAPHIC CO, 1903, #36

Elder Bruce R. McConkie said:

> These statements about the two Comforters climax and crown the teachings of the Son of God. We have no record of anything He ever said which can so completely withdraw the curtain of eternity and open to the faithful a vision of the glories of God. Based on love, born of obedience, Jesus promises the Saints that they can have, here and now in this life, the following:
>
> (1) The gift and constant companionship of the Holy Ghost; the comfort and peace which it is the function of that Holy Spirit to bestow; the revelation and the sanctifying power which alone will prepare men for the companionship of gods and angels hereafter;

(2) Personal visitations from the Second Comforter, the Lord Jesus Christ Himself, the resurrected and perfected being who dwells with His Father in the mansions on high; and

(3) God the Father . . . shall visit man in person, take up His abode with him, as it were, and reveal to him all the hidden mysteries of His kingdom.[10]

FINAL EVENTS BEFORE GETHSEMANE

Words of Consolation

- **John 15:15 Jesus calls His disciples His "friends."** Having shown Himself to be their servant as well as their Master, Jesus then punctuated His feelings for His disciples by saying, "Henceforth I call you not servants; for the servant knoweth not what his lord doeth: but I have called you friends; for all things that I have heard of my Father I have made known unto you." They had stood by Him through all of His ministry, and with the exception of Judas, they had remained faithful. We, too, are His friends if we do these things. We may, then, boldly proclaim that Jesus is our special Friend, as He said.

- **John 15:16 "Ye have not chosen me, but I have chosen you, and ordained you."** The Apostles were not self-appointed disciples, claiming the right to speak for the Lord simply because they desired to do so. This is the way of modern Christendom, whose ministers, lacking an official call from an Apostle, appoint themselves spokespersons for Christ. Jesus Himself corrected this notion at the last supper: "Ye have not chosen me," He reminded the Apostles, "but I have chosen you, and ordained you."

  And what was their mission? ". . . that ye should go and bring forth fruit, and that your fruit should remain." They were not simply acolytes—Jesus' "posse" as we would say today—but missionaries sent forth to gather scattered Israel into the kingdom. And then, having reaped that harvest, to ensure that their fruit remains faithful. And as they engaged in this work, He promised "that whatsoever ye shall ask of the Father in my name, he may give it you."

- **John 15:17 "Love one another."** Jesus again commanded "that ye love one another." He had said earlier in the evening, "A new command- ment I give unto you, That ye love one another; as I have loved you, that ye also love one another. By this shall all men know that ye are my disciples, if ye have love one to another" (John 13:34–35). Thus, if we would be considered disciples of Christ we must love each other. As we look across the landscape of Christianity in our day, we might easily determine who is and who is not a Christian. The determination is not made by whether one subscribes to the creeds of earthly councils that convened 300 years after the Savior lived and died. Whether or not one is a Christian is determined by the formula He Himself provided: whether we have love one to another.

THEBIBLEREVIVAL.COM, #27

- **John 15:18–21 The world will hate us because it hates Him.** We should not expect the world to love us, because "it hated [Christ] before it hated [us]" (v. 18). "If ye were of the world, the world would love his own: but because ye are not of the world, but I have chosen you out of the world, therefore the world hateth you" (v. 19). Jesus reminded His followers, "The servant is not greater than his lord. If they have persecuted me, they will also persecute you" (v. 20). "All these things will they do unto you for my name's sake, because they know not him that sent me" (v. 21).

- **John 16:33 We will have tribulation in the world, but will have peace in Him.** Jesus had told His disciples these things "that in me [they] might have peace." While they could not expect the world to love them, and "in the world [they would] have tribulation," they should still "be of good cheer" because He has "overcome the world." The victory over Satan is sure. We have need only to be patient and endure until the end.

- **John 15:13 "Greater love hath no man than this, that a man lay down his life for his friends."** Because Christ laid down His life and took it up again, we shall also be resurrected and live forever. Because Christ shed His blood, we can be washed clean of all our sins and shortcomings. He came and lived and died to save us. And there can be no greater evidence of His love than the Atonement He has wrought for all mankind. God be praised for this marvelous and eternal gift!

C. FARRAR, 1894

Jesus Foretells His Suffering and Death

- **John 16:16–20 Jesus tells the Apostles that He will soon die and be resurrected.** The sequence was this: "A little while, and ye shall not see me," followed by a period of time in "a little while, [when] ye shall see me." In the meantime, between His death and resurrection, He would "go to the Father" (v. 16). The Apostles were thoroughly confused and Jesus knew it (vv. 17–19). He told them that they would "weep and lament, but the world shall rejoice" at His death. Yet, while "ye shall be sorrowful, . . . your sorrow shall be turned into joy" (v. 20).

  We may all take consolation in this promise. We have all, at one time or another, laid down our friends or family members in vile graves. There, their bodies crumble into dust while their spirits live on. But on that wonderful, glorious day of the resurrection, our "sorrow shall be turned into joy." How will you feel on that day as you take into your arms once again your loved ones and friends—very much alive, never to die again? Jesus has promised this will happen, and we can look forward with absolute faith to that day.

The Prophet Joseph Smith reminisced about that day:

> Would you think it strange that I relate what I have seen in vision in relation [to] this interesting theme[?] Those who have died in Jesus Christ, may expect to enter into all that fruition of joy when they come forth, which they have pursued here.
>
> So plain was the vision I actually saw men before they had ascended from the tomb as though they were getting up slowly. They take each other by the hand. It was my father and my son, my mother and my daughter, my brother and my sister. When the voice calls, suppose I am laid by the side of my father. What would be the first joy of my heart? Where is my father, my mother, my sister? They are by my side. I embrace them and they me. . . .
>
> . . . All your losses will be made up to you in the resurrection provided you continue faithful. By the vision of the Almighty I have seen it. . . . God has revealed His Son from the heavens and the doctrine of the resurrection also. We have a knowledge that those we bury here God [will] bring them up again, clothed upon and quickened by the spirit of the Great God.[11]

The Great Intercessory Prayer

As one of His last, great acts before His death, Jesus offered a prayer in behalf of His Apostles and all of those who believe in Him. This prayer is often called the great intercessory prayer because as Jesus prayed, He interceded, or stood between us and Heavenly Father, to plead for our salvation.

A. BIDA, 1874

- **John 17:1–3 Christ prays to the Father and defines eternal life.** "These words spake Jesus, and lifted up his eyes to heaven, and said, Father, the hour is come; glorify thy Son, that thy Son also may glorify thee" (v. 1). Jesus knew why He had come to earth. He acknowledged that God the Father had "given him power over all flesh, that he should give eternal life to as many as thou hast given him" (v. 2). And how would He bestow this great gift? His answer is clear: "And this is life eternal, that they might know thee the only true God, and Jesus Christ, whom thou hast sent" (v. 3).

- **John 17:4–5 Christ had finished His work and glorified the Father.** In an act of "returning and reporting," Jesus said to the Father, "I have glorified thee on the earth: I have finished the work which thou gavest me to do. And now, O Father, glorify thou me with thine own self with the glory which I had with thee before the world was." Jesus was already a glorified, God-like being in the premortal world. We have known Him forever as the Creator of worlds and the designated Savior of all of God's children everywhere. He was now about to finish His work of salvation on this earth, and He desired the blessings of God to help Him do it.

- **John 17:6–10 Jesus prays for all of His believing disciples.** Jesus said to the Father, "I have manifested thy name unto the men which thou gavest me out of the world: thine they were, and thou gavest them me; and they have kept thy word" (v. 6). He acknowledged that His disciples now had their own testimonies of Him and of the Father and that the Father had sent Him (vv. 7–8). "I pray for them," Jesus said. "I pray not for the world, but for them which thou hast given me" (v. 9). He acknowledged that His disciples belonged to the Father as well as to Him, "and all mine are thine, and thine are mine; and I am glorified in them" (v. 10).

- **John 17:11–12 Jesus provided salvation to all of God's children.** Jesus knew that He would soon be "no more in the world," but these disciples would be in the world after He returned to the Father (v. 11). He prayed, "Holy Father, keep through thine own name those whom thou hast given me, that they may be one, as we are" (v. 11). While He was with them He supported and kept them, losing none except "the son of perdition" [Judas Iscariot] (v. 12). And the same would be true of all the children of God who believe in Jesus Christ in any dispensation. Christ saved them all except for those who become sons of perdition.

- **John 17:13–16 Jesus prays that they will be protected from worldliness.** Jesus prayed out loud for these things while He was still "in the world" so that "they might have my joy fulfilled in themselves" (v. 13). "I have given them thy word; and the world hath hated them, because they are not of the world, even as I am not of the world" (v. 14). Now He wished to pray for their protection—"not that thou shouldest take them out of the world, but that thou shouldest keep them from the evil" (v. 15).

  Elder M. Russell Ballard said:

  > In the Church, we often state the couplet: "Be in the world but not of the world." As we observe television shows that make profanity, violence, and infidelity commonplace and even glamorous, we often wish we could lock out the world in some way and isolate our families from it all. . . .
  >
  > Perhaps we should state the couplet previously mentioned as two separate admonitions. First, "*Be in the world.*" Be involved; be informed. Try to be understanding and tolerant and to appreciate diversity. Make meaningful contributions to society through service and involvement. Second, "*Be not of the world.*" Do not follow wrong paths or bend to accommodate or accept what is not right.
  >
  > We should strive to change the corrupt and immoral tendencies in television and in society by keeping things that offend and debase *out* of our homes. In spite of all of the wickedness in the world, and in spite of all the opposition to good that we find on every hand, we should *not* try to take ourselves or our children *out* of the world. Jesus said, "The kingdom of heaven is like unto leaven," or yeast (Matthew 13:33). We are to lift the world and help all to rise above the wickedness that surrounds us. The Savior prayed to the Father:
  >
  > "I pray not that thou shouldest take them out of the world, but that thou shouldest keep them from the evil" (John 17:15).[12]

- **John 17:17 Sanctification through the word of God.** Jesus asked the Father to "sanctify [those who believe in Him] through thy truth," which truth He defines as "thy word" (v. 17). Thus, He acknowledges that the scriptures and other words of God are the key to sanctification in the midst of a wicked world.

- **John 17:18–19 Sanctification through the Atonement of Christ.** "As thou hast sent me into the world, even so have I also sent them into the world" (v. 18). And despite the wickedness of that world, "for their sakes" Christ had sanctified Himself, living a spotless life in order to be worthy to effect the Atonement for all of us, "that they also might be sanctified through the truth" (v. 19).

- **John 17:20–23 Jesus prays that His disciples may be "one" as the Father and Jesus are "one."** He was not praying for the disciples in that room alone, "but for them also which shall believe on me through their word" (v. 20). That includes you and me. His wish was that "they all may be one; as thou, Father, art in me, and I in thee, that they also may be one in us" (v. 21). And to what purpose? Jesus mentioned several:

  (1) "That the world may believe that thou hast sent me" (v. 21).
  (2) "That they may be one, even as we are one: I in them, and thou in me" (vv. 22–23).
  (3) "That they may be made perfect in one" (v. 23).
  (4) "That the world may know that thou hast sent me, and hast loved them, as thou hast loved me" (v. 23).

  President Gordon B. Hinckley said: "They [the Father and the Son] are distinct beings, but they are one in purpose and effort. They are united as one in bringing to pass the grand, divine plan for the salvation and exaltation of the children of God. . . . It is that perfect unity between the Father, the Son, and the Holy Ghost that binds these three into the oneness of the divine Godhead."[13]

- **John 17:24 Jesus prays for their exaltation.** "Father, I will that they also, whom thou hast given me, be with me where I am; that they may behold my glory, which thou hast given me: for thou lovedst me before the foundation of the world."

- **John 17:25–26 Jesus prays that the love of God will be manifest through them.** "O righteous Father, the world hath not known thee: but I have known thee, and these have known that thou hast sent me. And I have declared unto them thy name, and will declare it: that the love wherewith thou hast loved me may be in them, and I in them."

Jesus Goes Out Into Gethsemane

- **John 14:30 "The prince of this world cometh, and hath nothing in me."** The great intercessory prayer ended and Jesus now prepared to take upon Himself the sins of the world. He told His disciples that "hereafter I will not talk much with you." The events of the next 24 hours would not permit it.

  Jesus acknowledged that "the prince of this world [Satan] cometh, and hath nothing in me." This was the great apex of the Father's entire plan of salvation. Satan had worked unceasingly to destroy the plan. He succeeded in getting Adam and Eve to fall. Now, all he needed to do was get Jesus to fail and we would all be in the devil's power forever. He really thought he could achieve it. But because Jesus had lived a perfect life and was about to atone for the sins of all men, Satan's efforts would, once and for all, be frustrated. He would "have nothing" because of Christ.

  President Harold B. Lee said: "So powerful was he in the Master's day that the Master referred to Satan as 'the prince of this world,' but He added, '. . . the prince of this world cometh, and hath nothing in me' (John 14:30). We must be able to say, as did the Master, that though the power is evil on every side, 'as for me and my house, we shall serve the God of this land.' The prince of this world is coming to tempt every one of us, and the only ones who will stand through these evil days are those who have founded their houses upon the rock, as the Master said; when the storms descended and the winds blew and the rains came and beat upon the house, it fell not because it was founded upon the rock. That is what the Lord is trying to say to us today."[14]

- **Matthew 26:30 They sang a hymn and then departed.** This verse bears witness to the importance of music in the Savior's life. The final thing He wanted to experience before descending below all things was the singing of a hymn. How often have we, also, been lifted and encouraged and strengthened by music? It is truly one of God's greatest gifts to His children. On this occasion, they sang a closing hymn and then went out into the Garden of Gethsemane on the Mount of Olives.

Notes

1. For an explanation of this precise date, see John P. Pratt, "The Restoration of Priesthood Keys on Easter 1836, Part 1: Dating the First Easter," *Ensign*, June 1985, 59–68. See also *The Life and Teachings of Jesus and His Apostles* [1979], 136, 164, 170.

2. *Mormon Doctrine*, 2nd ed. [1966], 832.

3. In Conference Report, Apr. 1968, 6–7; or *Improvement Era*, June 1968, 3.

4. *Answers to Gospel Questions*, comp. Joseph Fielding Smith Jr., 5 vols. [1957–66] 2:159.

5. *Doctrinal New Testament Commentary*, 3 vols. [1965–73], 1:758.

6. In Conference Report, Oct. 1996, 80; or *Ensign*, Nov. 1996, 60.

7. In Conference Report, Oct. 1994, 77; or *Ensign*, Nov. 1994, 60.

8. *Manuscript History of Brigham Young*, 1846–1847, comp. Elden J. Watson [1971], 529.

9. *History of the Church*, 3:381.

10. *Doctrinal New Testament Commentary*, 1:735.

11. *An American Prophet's Record: The Diaries and Journals of Joseph Smith*, ed. Scott H. Faulring [1989], 366–67.

12. In Conference Report, Apr. 1989, 100–1; or *Ensign*, May 1989, 80.

13. In Conference Report, Oct. 1986, 69; or *Ensign*, Nov. 1986, 51.

14. *Ensign*, Nov. 1971, 12.

CHAPTER 6

THE ATONEMENT IN GETHSEMANE

(MATTHEW 26:36–46; MARK 14:32–42; LUKE 22:39–46)

THE FOURTH DAY
(Wednesday)[1]

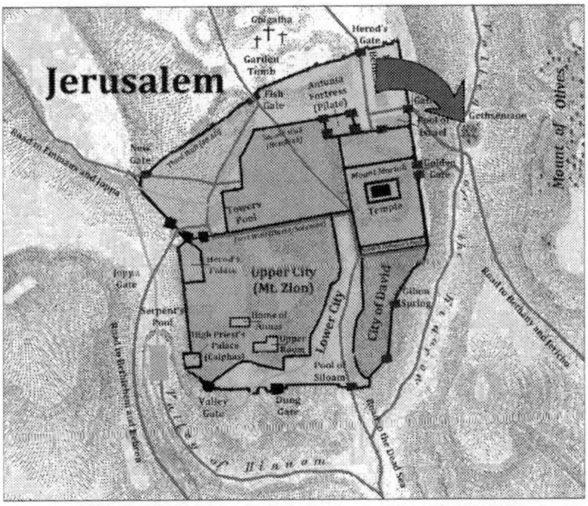

Following His last supper, discourse, and prayer, Jesus said: "Arise, let us go hence" (John 14:31). They sang a hymn together and then departed. Jesus led the eleven Apostles into a garden that lies on the western slope of the Mount of Olives, near its base (see arrows in photos at right).

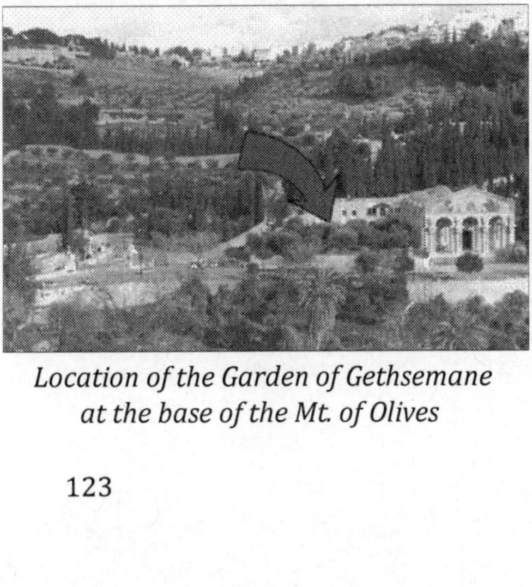

Location of the Garden of Gethsemane at the base of the Mt. of Olives

It is a small olive orchard, called *Gethsemane*. The designation means "oil press," so called because the olive grove contained a press to crush the olives from the orchard. "An old tradition identifies it with a garden still existing some 250 yards from the east wall of [Jerusalem]."[2]

- **John 18:1–2 Jesus went there often to pray and to teach His disciples.** At the base of the Kidron Valley is the brook named Cedron, and on the east side of the brook lay the garden. Jesus "went forth with his disciples" and they all entered into the garden (v. 1). The place was well known to them, "for Jesus ofttimes resorted thither with his disciples" (v. 2).

THE ATONEMENT OF CHRIST

The Importance of the Atonement

The Prophet Joseph Smith said: "The fundamental principles of our religion are the testimony of the Apostles and Prophets, concerning Jesus Christ, that He died, was buried, and rose again the third day, and ascended into heaven; and all other things which pertain to our religion are only appendages to it."[3]

President Ezra Taft Benson said: "In Gethsemane and on Calvary, He worked out the infinite and eternal Atonement. It was the greatest single act of love in recorded history. Thus He became our Redeemer—redeeming all of us from physical death, and redeeming those of us from spiritual death who will obey the laws and ordinances of the gospel."[4]

Elder Bruce R. McConkie said: "Nothing in the entire plan of salvation compares in any way in importance with that most transcendent of all events, the atoning sacrifice of our Lord."[5]

I have thrilled in recent years to read *The Infinite Atonement* by Elder Tad R. Callister,[6] which I consider to be the best book written on the subject in modern times. It contains all the depth of Talmage's *Jesus the Christ*, but in more understandable language. Concerning the significance of Christ's Atonement, Elder Callister wrote:[7]

The final week of the Savior's mortal ministry had arrived. For four thousand years prophets had preached and prophesied of the events that would culminate in this particular week. All events in history, memorable as they had been or would yet be, paled in comparison to this moment. This was the focal point of all history.

He who had created worlds without number was about to enter a quiet, secluded garden, a humble plot of ground in His vast cosmic universe. There was no fanfare, no pressing throng to witness the most profound event His creations would ever know. This was a moment so sacred, so sublime, that no human eye could fully pierce, no human mind could fully comprehend its transcending importance. Only three other mortals—Peter, James, and John—would be near, and even their witness would be tempered by the twilight and shrouded by sleep.

HEINRICH HOFMANN

The appointed hour was at hand. The Son of God stood alone in all His majestic power against all the artillery of the Evil One. Here was divine love in its consummate expression battling diabolic evil in its cruelest proportions. This was the place and the time for the Atonement of Jesus Christ.

If a survey were taken of history's most significant events, common answers might include the harnessing of fire, the discovery of America, the splitting of the atom, landing on the moon, or the invention of the computer. Each is a wondrous event, but absent the backdrop of the Atonement each is of but transitory importance—no more than a shooting star illuminating the sky for a brief moment, and then vanishing into the night. The Atonement gives purpose and potency to every event in history.

President Gordon B. Hinckley spoke of its relationship to other events in world history: "When all is said and done, when all of history is examined, when the deepest depths of the human mind have been explored, there is nothing so wonderful, so majestic, so tremendous as this act of grace."[8] This was not just another great event in the chronicles of history. It was, as Hugh Nibley observed, "the one supreme reality of our life upon this earth!"[9]

The prophet Alma shared this belief. He had stepped down as chief judge so he might fully devote his time to the ministry. With prophetic vision he looked down the stream of time and saw "many things to come" (Alma 7:7), and then concluded, "... There is one thing which is of more importance than they all—for behold, the time is not far distant that the Redeemer liveth and cometh among his people" (Alma 7:7).

Elder Bruce R. McConkie added his testimony to that of Alma: "The most transcendent event in His entire eternal existence, the most glorious single happening from creation's dawn to eternity's endless continuance, the crowning work of His infinite goodness—such took place in a garden called Gethsemane."[10]

Initial Instructions to the Apostles

- **Luke 22:39 Jesus went often to Gethsemane to pray.** Luke tells us that, on this occasion, Jesus "went, as he was wont, to the mount of Olives." Thus we see that He liked to go there and this was not His first visit to this beautiful and quiet grove.

- **Matthew 26:36–38 Jesus asks Peter, James, and John to be witnesses of the Atonement.** He instructed eight of the apostles to "sit ye here, while I go and pray yonder" (v. 36), then took Peter, James, and John into the interior of the garden (v. 37). He plunged into depression, becoming "sorrowful and very heavy," and remarked to His three companions that He was "exceeding sorrowful, even unto death" (vv. 37–38). He asked them to "tarry ye here, and watch with me" (v. 38). According to footnote *b*, to "watch" means to "stay awake." Thus, He wanted them to be witnesses of the Atonement.

COURTESY DAVID HALL, ISRAEL PHOTOS II, 2006

- **Luke 22:40 "Pray that ye enter not into temptation."** Luke's version of this event tells us that Jesus not only told them to stay awake but also to "pray that ye enter not into temptation." He had already told them that Satan was coming to confront Him (see John 14:30), and the presence of that prince of darkness might have implications for their own safety and spirituality. But perhaps also, He wanted them to observe the price He would pay for sin that they might be less prone in the future to "enter . . . into temptation."

Phase One of the Atonement

Many do not realize that Jesus' Atonement occurred in three phases, not all at once. His suffering was interrupted briefly twice as He went back to check on Peter, James, and John, who were supposed to be "watching" and witness-ing this eternally significant event.

HEINRICH HOFMANN

- **Luke 22:41–42 Jesus goes a "stone's cast" farther and prays.** Leaving Peter, James, and John within sight, He withdrew "about a stone's cast" from them (100 feet) "and kneeled down, and prayed" (v. 41).

- **Matthew 26:39 Sensing the severity, He says: "If it be possible, let this cup pass."** The prophets teach that Jesus took upon Himself not only the demands of justice for all our sins, but also the pain of our disappointments, our sorrows, our infirmities, and every other evil consequence that has ever befallen every child of God (see Isaiah 53:4; Mosiah 3:7; Alma 7:12). To call it an unfathomable burden would be a gross understatement. We cannot comprehend such suffering. And as it pressed down upon Him, He said to the Father, ". . . If it be possible, let this cup pass from me: nevertheless not as I will, but as thou wilt." He was determined to fulfill His duty, no matter how difficult it might be.

— **D&C 19:18–19 The severity of His suffering.** "Which suffering caused myself, even God, the greatest of all, to tremble because of pain, and to bleed at every pore, and to suffer both body and spirit—and would that I might not drink the bitter cup, and shrink—Nevertheless, glory be to the Father, and I partook and finished my preparations unto the children of men."

— **D&C 19:17, 15 The terrible price of sin.** The severity of Christ's suffering teaches us concerning the terrible price that must be paid for sin. We can escape such suffering through repentance, but if we do not repent, then we "must suffer even as [He]" (v. 17). And those sufferings will be "sore—how sore you know not, how exquisite you know not, yea, how hard to bear you know not" (v. 15).

Elder B. H. Roberts said: ". . . Let the severity of the Christ's Atonement for man's sin bear witness; for it required all that the Christ gave in suffering and agony of spirit and body, to lay the grounds for man's forgiveness and reconciliation with God. The severity of the Atonement should impress men with the fact that we live in a world of stern realities; that human actions draw with them tremendous consequences that may not be easily set aside if the actions in which they have their origin are wrong. . . . Suffering is the consequence or the penalty of violating divine, moral law; and the penalty must be paid, either by the one sinning or by another who shall suffer vicariously for him."[11]

— **D&C 19:16–17, 20 We can avoid suffering for our sins if we repent.** "For behold, I, God, have suffered these things for all, that they might not suffer if they would repent; But if they would not repent they must suffer even as I" (vv. 16–17). "Wherefore, I command you again to repent, lest I humble you with my almighty power; and that you confess your sins, lest you suffer these punishments of which I have spoken" (v. 20).

President John Taylor said:

> Jesus had to take away sin by the sacrifice of Himself . . . And as He in His own person bore the sins of all, and atoned for them by the sacrifice of Himself, so there came upon Him the weight and agony of ages and generations, the indescribable agony consequent upon this great sacrificial Atonement wherein He bore the sins of the world, and suffered in His own person the consequences of an eternal law of God broken by man. Hence His profound grief, His indescribable anguish, His overpowering torture, all experienced in the submission to the eternal fiat of Jehovah and the requirements of an inexorable law.
>
> The suffering of the Son of God was not simply the suffering of personal death; for in assuming the position that He did in making an Atonement for the sins of the world He bore the weight, the responsibility, and the burden of the sins of all men, which, to us, is incomprehensible. . . .
>
> Groaning beneath this concentrated load, this intense, incomprehensible pressure, this terrible exaction of Divine Justice, from which feeble humanity shrank, and through the agony thus experienced sweating great drops of blood, He was led to exclaim, 'Father, if it be possible, let this cup pass from me.' He had wrestled with the superincumbent load in the wilderness, He had struggled against the powers of darkness that had been let loose upon Him there; placed below all things, His mind surcharged with agony and pain, lonely and apparently helpless and forsaken, in His agony the blood oozed from His pores.[12]

— **D&C 122:7–8 Jesus descended below us all.** To the Prophet Joseph Smith, our Lord said, that "if thou shouldst be cast into the pit, or into the hands of murderers, and the sentence of death passed upon thee; if thou be cast into the deep; if the billowing surge conspire against thee; if fierce winds become thine enemy; if the heavens gather blackness, and all the elements combine to hedge up the way; and above all, if the very jaws of hell shall gape open the mouth wide after thee," it would still not surpass His suffering in Gethsemane (v. 7). In that one eventful night, "the Son of Man . . . descended below them all" (v. 8).

— **Alma 7:11–13 Jesus suffered "pains and afflictions and temptations of every kind."** This included all the "pains and the sicknesses of his people" (v. 11). It also included "their infirmities, that his bowels may be filled with mercy, according to the flesh, that he may know according to the flesh how to succor his people according to their infirmities" (v. 12). And of course it also included suffering for "the sins of his people, that he might blot out their transgressions according to the power of his deliverance" (v. 13).

We can turn to Christ in our suffering, sorrow, and repentance, knowing that He can understand completely because *He* felt those pains *for us*, even before we felt them, as part of the Atonement. How this is possible we do not know. But anyone who has felt His tender mercies in times of trouble knows that it is true. Elder Jeffrey R. Holland said: "*To succor* means 'to run to.' I testify that in my fears and in my infirmities the Savior has surely run to me. I will never be able to thank Him enough for such personal kindness and such loving care."[13]

Elder Neal A. Maxwell spoke several times about this topic:

> As part of His infinite Atonement, Jesus knows "according to the flesh" all that through which we pass (see Alma 7:11–12). He has borne the sins, griefs, sorrows, and . . . pains of every man, woman, and child (see 2 Nephi 9:21).[14]
>
> The agonies of the Atonement were infinite and first-hand! Since not all human sorrow and pain is connected to sin, the full intensiveness of the Atonement involved [Jesus] bearing our pains, infirmities, and sicknesses, as well as our sins.[15]
>
> . . . Jesus knows and understands when we are stressed and perplexed . . . The complete consecration which effected the Atonement ensured Jesus' perfect empathy; He felt our very pains and afflictions before we did and knows how to succor us.[16]
>
> Can we, even in the depths of disease, tell Him anything at all about suffering? In ways we cannot comprehend, our sicknesses and infirmities were borne by Him even before they were borne by us. The very weight of our combined sins caused Him to descend below all. We have never been, nor will we be, in depths such as He has known. Thus His Atonement made perfect His empathy and His mercy and His capacity to

succor us, for which we can be everlastingly grateful as He tutors us in our trials.[17]

- **Mark 14:36 Jesus addresses the Father as "Abba" ("daddy").** Mark's version of this event (probably obtained from Peter, with whom Mark served) says that Jesus' appeal was, "Abba, Father, all things are possible unto thee; take away this cup from me: nevertheless not what I will, but what thou wilt." The name "Abba" was a term of endearment in those days, the equivalent of which today would be to refer to our father as "daddy" or "papa."

C. H. BLOCH

- **Luke 22:43 An angel (perhaps Adam) appears unto Jesus and strengthens Him.** The Father's answer to His prayer was to send "an angel unto him from heaven" to strengthen Him (v. 43).

  Elder Tad R. Callister asked:[18]

  > Do we presume that He, a God, was so weakened by this ordeal that He now needed strengthening? What divine messenger offered such aid? Was it Adam? Noah? Abraham? Certainly at such a critical moment in the destiny of man, this angel must have been a being of towering stature.
  >
  > Elder Bruce R. McConkie suggests it was "mighty Michael [Adam]."[19] While we do not know with certainty the identity of this heaven-sent comforter, there are at least four reasons why it may indeed have been Adam.[20]
  >
  > First, Adam, who was a joint creator of this earth and father of mortal man, would have had a supreme interest in man's ultimate destiny. Certainly he had a vested interest to see that this earth and all its dominions were not created in vain. Second, it seems appropriate that he who triggered in part the

need for the Atonement should now be the agent for mankind to assist Him who pled for its redemption. Third, as taught by Joseph Smith, Adam has a presiding role in the hierarchy of divine beings, since all "angels are under the direction of Michael or Adam,"[21] and thus it seems no messenger would be more suited to strengthen and bless than he who was the presiding archangel. Fourth, Adam enjoyed a unique relationship with the Savior. Not only did he join with Him in the creation process, but likewise as he led the heavenly forces in battle (see Revelation 12:7). Now, once again, Adam might momentarily stand by Him as the Savior participated in the most crucial battle of all. Adam could not take the Savior's place (for the Savior must bear this alone), but what he could do, he no doubt wanted to do. Perhaps he was there to console Him, to comfort Him, to support Him, maybe even to bless Him.

The scriptures are silent as to the nature of the exchange between Christ and His angelic visitor. No doubt this was one of those moments so sacred it was not to be recorded in the annals of man. Evidently certain thoughts of the spirit are so lofty, so poignant, that they cannot be reduced to the oral language or written word of man. They simply defy mortal expression. Surely this was one of those moments.

Whatever the details of that divine encounter, surely the angelic guest must have extended to Christ the fullest blessing heaven could offer. Certainly this was a moment of transcendent pathos. Perhaps each wept and transmitted an intensity of love known only by the gods and angels. Perhaps the angel offered words of comfort and reassurance. Or perhaps the strength of his silent presence was sufficient. Whatever the divine exchange may have been, the Savior found sufficient strength, in the midst of unfathomable pain, to press on. Truman Madsen reminds us that the angel came "strengthening—not delivering."[22]

- **Luke 22:44 Jesus' suffering intensifies, causing blood to extrude from His pores.** His suffering is now described as "agony," and it caused Him to "pray . . . more earnestly" as He began to "sweat . . . great drops of blood" that fell down to the ground.

W. Jeffrey Marsh said: "Spiritual anguish and physical pain pressed down upon Him so greatly that blood oozed from every pore in His body (JST Luke 22:44; Mosiah 3:7; D&C 19:18). The medical term for such a condition is hematidrosis. Under extreme distress and pressure the capillaries burst and produce a bloody sweat. Christ's was the most severe instance of hematidrosis ever experienced."[23]

- **Mosiah 3:7 Jesus' agony was more than any man could have borne.** Can we imagine the burden of suffering the pain of every sin, in addition to every "pain of body, hunger, thirst, and fatigue" that has ever been felt by any child of God in every age and throughout the universe? King Benjamin said that such pain was "more than man can suffer, except it be unto death."

  Elder James E. Talmage said:

  > Christ's agony in the garden is unfathomable by the finite mind, both as to intensity and cause. . . . He struggled and groaned under a burden such as no other being who has lived on earth might even conceive as possible. It was not physical pain, nor mental anguish alone, that caused Him to suffer such torture as to produce an extrusion of blood from every pore; but a spiritual agony of soul such as only God was capable of experiencing. No other man, however great his powers of physical or mental endurance, could have suffered so; for his human organism would have succumbed . . . In that hour of anguish Christ met and overcame all the horrors that Satan, "the prince of this world," could inflict. . . . In some manner, actual and terribly real though to man incomprehensible, the Savior took upon Himself the burden of the sins of mankind from Adam to the end of the world.[24]

  President Joseph Fielding Smith said:

  > This is what He did: He carried, in some way that I cannot understand and you cannot understand, the burden of the combined weight of the sins of the world. It is hard enough for me to carry my own transgressions, and it is hard enough for you to carry yours. . . . I have seen men in the gall of bitterness, in the torments and the anguish of their souls, because of their sins. I have seen them cry out in anguish because of their transgressions— just one individual's sins. Can you comprehend the suffering of Jesus Christ when He carried, not

merely by physical manifestation but in some spiritual and mental condition or manner, the combined weight of sin? . . . A great many people have an idea that when He was on the cross, and nails were driven into His hands and feet, that was His great suffering. His great suffering was before He ever was placed upon the cross. It was in the Garden of Gethsemane that the blood oozed from the pores of His body . . .

Now I cannot comprehend that pain. I have suffered pain, you have suffered pain, and sometimes it has been quite severe; but I cannot comprehend pain, which is *mental anguish more than physical*, that would cause the blood, like sweat, to come out upon the body. It was something terrible, something terrific.[25]

Elder Bruce R. McConkie said:

Where and under what circumstances was the atoning sacrifice of the Son of God made? Was it on the Cross of Calvary or in the Garden of Gethsemane? It is to the Cross of Christ that most Christians look when centering their attention upon the infinite and eternal Atonement. And certainly the sacrifice of our Lord was completed when He was lifted up by men; also, that part of His life and suffering is more dramatic and, perhaps, more soul stirring. But in reality the pain and suffering, the triumph and grandeur, of the Atonement took place primarily in Gethsemane.

It was there Jesus took upon Himself the sins of the world on conditions of repentance. It was there He suffered beyond human power to endure. It was there He sweat great drops of blood from every pore. It was there His anguish was so great He fain would have let the bitter cup pass. It was there He made the final choice to follow the will of the Father. It was there that an angel from heaven came to strengthen Him in His greatest trial.

Many have been crucified and the torment and pain [are] extreme. But only one, and He the Man who had God as His Father, has bowed beneath the burden of grief and sorrow that lay upon Him in that awful night, that night in which He descended below all things as He prepared Himself to rise above them all.[26]

- **Matthew 26:40–41 Peter, James, and John grow weary and fall asleep.** Jesus' suffering persisted into the night, and it had already been a long day. Thus, in the midst of His suffering, when He took a brief respite and went back to where they were supposed to be watching, He "findeth them asleep, and saith unto Peter, What, could ye not watch with me one hour?" (v. 40). This mild rebuke was for their own sakes, not for His. He wanted them to observe the price of sin that they might be less prone in the future to "enter . . . into temptation" (v. 41).

C. FARRAR, 1894

- **JST Mark 14:43 It was the Apostles who said: "The Spirit truly is ready, but the flesh is weak."** The King James account says that Jesus remarked at this time that "the spirit . . . is willing, but the flesh is weak" (Matthew 26:41). But the Joseph Smith Translation makes it clear that it was the Apostles who said this, not Jesus. It was their excuse for dosing while the Savior was suffering.

Phase Two of the Atonement

- **Matthew 26:42 Jesus' suffering returns.** Returning to His lonely agony, Jesus felt the weight of suffering and sorrow "again the second time." But His prayer now acknowledges that the suffering cannot be removed from Him: "O my Father, if this cup may not pass away from me, except I drink it, thy will be done."

- **Mark 14:40 Jesus again returns to His three disciples and finds them "asleep again."** Whereas before they had said that "the flesh is weak," this time they did not know what excuse to give to Him. It must have been embarrassing, but "their eyes were heavy" after a long and eventful day.

Phase Three of the Atonement

- **Matthew 26:44 Jesus returns to His suffering a third time.** Matthew records that He left the three disciples as before and "went away again, and prayed the third time, saying the same words." The Atonement was so vast and all-inclusive that it required the entire night and three separate sessions of suffering to accomplish.

- **Matthew 26:45 Returning again to the three, He says, "Sleep on now, and take your rest."** They would need rest, because "the hour [was] at hand, [when] the Son of man [would be] betrayed into the hands of sinners." This new day would be a long and emotional one, culminating in the crucifixion and death of their Master.

THE INFINITE SCOPE OF THE ATONEMENT

Our Savior's Atonement was "infinite" in many ways. In *The Infinite Atonement*, Elder Tad R. Callister explains that it was infinite because of the divine nature of Jesus, but also because it was infinite in its power, in the eternities of time that it covers, in the scope of its coverage, in the depth of its redeeming power, in the immensity of suffering endured by Jesus, and in the love of the Father and the Son that was manifest in its performance.[27] I will mention only three of his ideas here, but would suggest that my readers obtain and read his entire book if they wish a full and profound understanding of the Atonement of Jesus Christ.

Christ Atoned for All Men, Animals, and Plants[28]

Adam and Eve were not the only living things that were affected by the Fall. The animals and plants that lived in the garden were also subject to the changes in the earth's status as it passed from a terrestrial state to a telestial one. Thus, they and we need to be redeemed from this fallen earth. Elder Callister wrote:

Are the mortals who walk this earth the only beneficiaries of the Atonement? What about other worlds and other forms of life? Who saves them from temporal, and where necessary, spiritual death?

The Atonement covers more than mankind. President Joseph Fielding Smith spoke directly to this point: "It is a very inconsistent notion which is held by some, that the resurrection will only come to human souls, that the animals and plants have no spirits and therefore are not redeemed by the sacrifice of the Son of God, and hence they are not entitled to the resurrection."[29]

Joseph Smith taught: "I suppose John saw beings there [in heaven], that had been saved from ten thousand times ten thousand earths like this, strange beasts of which we have no conception all might be seen in heaven. John learned that God glorified Himself by saving all that His hands had made whether beasts, fowl, fishes or man."[30] The Lord promised that "all old things shall pass away, and all things shall become new, . . . both men and beasts, the fowls of the air, and the fishes of the sea" (D&C 29:24). But how does the Atonement apply to these other forms of life? Are they resurrected and granted immortal bodies for eternity? Do they also need to overcome spiritual death?

Elder McConkie addresses this issue by asking the following question as though it were a statement of response: "Is it the doctrine of the gospel . . . that this temporal death passed upon all forms of life, upon man and animal and fish and fowl and plant life; *that Christ came to ransom man and all forms of life from the effects of the temporal death* brought into the world through the Fall, *and in the case of man from a spiritual death also; and that this ransom includes a resurrection for man and for all forms of life?"*[31]

Jacob seems to confirm that redemption from spiritual death is limited to man, for he taught that Christ "suffereth the pains of all men, yea, the pains of every living creature, both men, women, and children, *who belong to the family of Adam*" (2 Nephi 9:21; emphasis added).

Christ Atoned for the Earth Itself[32]

The earth itself has passed through similar stages to those experienced by the children of God. Like Adam and Eve, it fell from terrestrial glory and became telestial. Like Adam, it had to be baptized—in the earth's case by the Flood. And like all who are baptized, it will also be baptized with fire at the end of the earth. Eventually, it will become celestialized and dwell near the throne of God. But first, the earth, like we, must be saved from impurities and death. Elder Callister continued:

What of the earth itself? Does it have a need for redemption? It does. Like plants and animals it needs to be redeemed from physical death.

President Brigham Young express-ed such sentiments: "Christ is the author of this Gospel, of this earth, of men and women, of all the posterity of Adam and Eve, and of every living creature that lives upon the face of the earth, that flies in the heavens, that swims in the waters, or dwells in the field. Christ is the author of salvation to all this creation; to all things pertaining to this terrestrial globe we occupy. . . . He has redeemed the earth; He has redeemed mankind and every living thing that moves upon it."[33]

Elder McConkie discusses certain heresies concerning the Fall, one being that Adam was the final product of the evolutionary process. In response he comments, "When those who espouse this view talk of a fall and an atonement, they falsely assume such applies only to man rather than to the earth and all forms of life, as the scriptures attest."[34]

Elder Talmage shared similar feelings: "We learn from Scripture that Adam's transgression brought about a fallen condition, not of mankind alone, but likewise of the earth itself. In this and in numerous other epochal events, . . . nature is seen to be in intimate relation with man."[35]

How then, has the Savior redeemed the earth? Will it die? The scriptures clearly so state. Isaiah spoke of the time when "the earth shall wax old like a garment, and they that dwell therein shall die in like manner" (Isaiah 51:6; see also 2 Nephi 8:6). Latter-day revelation confirms this truth, for in speaking of this terrestrial sphere the Lord observed, "It shall be sanctified; yea, notwithstanding it shall die, it shall be quickened again, and shall abide the power by which it is quickened, and the righteous shall inherit it" (D&C 88:26).

President Joseph Fielding Smith likewise spoke of the death of the earth and its subsequent quickening or resurrection made possible only by the Atonement: *"The earth, as a living body, will have to die and be resurrected, for it, too, has been redeemed by the blood of Jesus Christ."*[36]

Christ Atoned for the Entire Universe

PHOTO COURTESY OF NASA

We know, of course, that Christ suffered for all mankind. President John Taylor said: "And this provision [the Atonement] applies not only to the living, but also to the dead, so that all men who have existed in all ages, who do exist now, or who will exist while the earth shall stand, may be placed upon the same footing, and that all men may have the privilege, living or dead, of accepting the conditions of the great plan of redemption provided by the Father, through the Son, before the world was; and that the justice and mercy of God may be applied to every being, living or dead, that ever has existed, that does now exist, or that ever will exist."[37]

But what about God's children who live on other planets? Do they have their own Savior or did Christ's Atonement cover them as well? Elder Callister addressed this also:[38]

> Does the Savior's Atonement extend beyond this world? Elder McConkie taught: ". . . Our Lord's jurisdiction and power extend far beyond the limits of this one small earth on which we dwell. He is, under the Father, the Creator of worlds without number (see Moses 1:33). And through the power of His Atonement the inhabitants of these worlds, the revelation says, 'are begotten sons and daughters unto God' (D&C 76:24), *which means that the Atonement of Christ, being literally and truly infinite, applies to an infinite number of earths.*"[39]
>
> What a mind-expanding concept! [Enoch] postulated that even if we could number millions of earths, "it would not be a beginning to the number of thy [God's] creations; and thy curtains are stretched out still" (Moses 7:30).
>
> Elder Marion G. Romney, who authored an article on Christ as the creator of worlds without number, wrote: "Jesus Christ, in the sense of being its Creator *and Redeemer, is the Lord of the whole universe.* Except for His mortal ministry accomplished on this earth, His service and relationship to other worlds and their inhabitants are the same as His service and relationship to this earth and its inhabitants."[40] Elder Romney discussed the Savior's role in the premortal existence as the chosen Redeemer and added, "In short, Jesus Christ, through whom God created the universe, was chosen [as the Redeemer in the pre-earthly councils] to put into operation throughout the universe Elohim's great plan 'to bring to pass the immortality and eternal life of man.'"[41] He concluded with his witness of the Savior's universality as the Atoning One: "All who have a true concept of Jesus Christ and who have received a witness by the Spirit of His divinity are ever stirred by the records of His life. They see in all that He said and did confirmation of His universal Lordship, both as Creator and Redeemer. . . ."[42]
>
> The headnote to Doctrine and Covenants 76 summarizes verses 18–24 in this manner: *"Inhabitants of many worlds* are begotten sons and daughters unto God through the Atonement of Jesus Christ" (emphasis added).
>
> [President] Lorenzo Snow alluded to this doctrine when speaking of the Father's trust in His Son. He observed: "Thousands of years

before He [the Savior] came upon earth, the Father had watched His course and knew that He could depend upon Him when the salvation of *worlds* should be at stake; and He was not disappointed."[43]

In other words, the Savior is a multi-planet redeemer. This seems consistent with the fact He is also a multi-planet creator, as taught through Moses, "Worlds without number have I created; . . . and by the Son I created them, which is mine Only Begotten" (Moses 1:33). Paul taught the same: "God . . . hath in these last days spoken unto us by his Son, . . . by whom also he made the *worlds*" (Hebrews 1:1–2; emphasis added). Since the Son "made the worlds," a fair interpretation of Doctrine and Covenants 76:42—"that through him *all might be saved* whom the Father had put into his power and *made by him*" (emphasis added)—would suggest that the Savior saved all people from all worlds "made by him." The next verse seems to further substantiate this point: "Who [the Savior] glorifies the Father, and saves all the works of his hands" (D&C 76:43). Elder Russell M. Nelson confirmed these thoughts [when he said:] ". . . The mercy of the Atonement extends not only to an infinite number of people, but also to an infinite number of worlds created by Him."[44]

Hugh Nibley quotes the Gospel of Truth, which says, "All the other worlds look to the same God as to a common sun," and then adds his own observation, "The crucifixion is effective in worlds other than this one."[45] Brother Nibley cites other ancient writers who had insights into the Savior's universal lordship. Speaking of other worlds, the Twelfth Ode of Solomon records: "'They know Him who made them because they are in concord. They have a common ruler, *a common lord*, so they are in concord with each other, and they communicate with Him and through Him with each other, for the mouth of the Most High has spoken to them."[46] Another writing of the ancient Church (1 Clement) records: "God is the Father of all the worlds. . . . As the Father of greatness is in the glorious world, so His Son rules among those cosmoses as first chief lord of all the powers."[47] Finally, Robert J. Matthews put it about as simply as it can be stated: "The question often arises, Is Jesus the Savior of other worlds? The answer is yes."[48]

It Had to Be an Infinite Atonement

- **2 Nephi 9:7 It had to be an "infinite atonement" in order to save us.** Nephi's brother Jacob explained that "save it should be an infinite atonement this corruption could not put on incorruption." Unless we are purged from all earthly corruption we cannot live in the presence of our perfectly Holy Father. Yet, because of our mortal weaknesses we all sin and fall short of that kind of holiness. "Wherefore, [at] the first judgment . . . man must needs have remained [in sin] to an endless duration. And if so, this flesh must have laid down to rot and to crumble to its mother earth, to rise no more." What to do? The answer was and is the Atonement and resurrection of Jesus Christ.

- **Alma 34:10–12 Nothing short of an infinite Atonement would suffice.** The sacrifice of which Amulek speaks is "not a sacrifice of man, neither of beast, neither of any manner of fowl; for it shall not be a human sacrifice; but it must be an infinite and eternal sacrifice" (v. 10). Justice does not permit "any [mortal] man [to] sacrifice his own blood [to] atone for the sins of another" (v. 11). This is because we all sin and are unworthy to provide vicarious salvation to others. "Nothing . . . short of an infinite atonement . . . will suffice for the sins of the world" (v. 12). Thus, there was no other (and never will be) who could provide an infinite Atonement except Him who was sinless, Jesus the Christ.

  President Joseph Fielding Smith said:

  > The Fall brought death. That is not a desirable condition. We do not want to be banished from the presence of God. We do not want to be subject forever to mortal conditions. We do not want to die and have our bodies turn to dust, and the spirits that possess these bodies by right, turned over to the realm of Satan and become subject to him.
  >
  > But that was the condition; and if Christ had not come as the atoning sacrifice, in demand of the law of justice, to *repair* or to *atone* or to *redeem* us from the condition that Adam found himself in, and that we find ourselves in; then mortal death would have come; the body would have gone back to the dust from where it came; the spirit would have gone into the realms of Satan's domain, and have been subject to him forever.[49]

- **Alma 34:13–14 His was the great and last sacrifice.** This means "the last sacrifice for sin," because sacrifices at the temple continued for about 37 years following Christ's Atonement, and they will be practiced again at the Millennial temple as an ordinance of the priesthood. But after Jesus' sacrifice in Gethsemane and on Golgotha, "it [was] expedient there should be . . . a stop to the shedding of blood [for sin]" because such sacrifices under the law of Moses had now been fulfilled (v. 13). Indeed, "the whole meaning of the law [and its sacrifices for sin]" pointed to the "great and last sacrifice [of] the Son of God, [which sacrifice was] infinite and eternal."

- **3 Nephi 11:11 He drank from the bitter cup which the Father gave to Him.** To the Nephites, Christ said, "I have drunk out of that bitter cup which the Father hath given me, and have glorified the Father in taking upon me the sins of the world." In this, Jesus fulfilled "the will of the Father in all things from the beginning."

- **3 Nephi 27:14–15 The Father sent Him specifically to do what He did for us.** "My Father sent me that I might be lifted up upon the cross; and after that I had been lifted up upon the cross, that I might draw all men unto me, that as I have been lifted up by men even so should men be lifted up by the Father, to stand before me, to be judged of their works, whether they be good or whether they be evil—And for this cause have I been lifted up; therefore, according to the power of the Father I will draw all men unto me, that they may be judged according to their works."

- **John 10:17–18 He was commanded by the Father to die and then resurrect Himself.** The Father asked Him to "lay down my life, that I might take it again. No man taketh it from me, but I lay it down of myself. I have power to lay it down, and I have power to take it again. This commandment have I received of my Father."

  Elder Robert D. Hales said: "What we must remember about the Savior is that He and He alone had the power to lay down His life and take it up again. He had the ability to die from His mortal mother, Mary, and the ability to overcome death from

His immortal Father. Our Savior, Jesus Christ, went willingly and deliberately to His death, having told His followers that this would happen. Why? one might ask. The answer: to give immortality to all mankind and the promise of eternal life to those who believed in Him (see John 3:15), to give His own life for a ransom for others (see Matthew 20:28), to overcome Satan's power, and to make it possible for sins to be forgiven. Without Jesus' Atonement, there would be an impassable barrier between God and mortal men and women. When we comprehend the Atonement, we remember Him with awe and gratitude."[50]

A Vision of the Atonement

The Apostle Orson F. Whitney received a vision of the Savior in Gethsemane, which he later shared with the members of the Church. His vision provides a firsthand witness of what happened there, perhaps very much like the scene that was seen by Peter, James, and John, who accompanied the Master into the Garden. We will close this chapter by reading his account and imagining that we were also gazing upon those scenes. And in fact, we may have been from our heavenly home where we all were when the Atonement occurred.

> I seemed to be in the Garden of Gethsemane, a witness of the Savior's agony. I saw Him as plainly as ever I have seen anyone. Standing behind a tree in the foreground, I beheld Jesus, with Peter, James, and John as they came through a little wicket gate at my right.
>
> Leaving the three Apostles there, after telling them to kneel and pray, the Son of God passed over to the other side, where He also knelt and prayed. It was the same prayer with which all Bible readers are familiar: "O my Father, if it be possible, let this cup pass from me: nevertheless not as I will, but as thou wilt."
>
> As He prayed, the tears streamed down His face, which was toward me. I was so moved at the sight that I also wept, out of pure sympathy. My whole heart went out to Him; I loved Him with all my soul, and longed to be with Him as I longed for nothing else.
>
> Presently He arose and walked to where those Apostles were kneeling—fast asleep! He shook them gently, awoke them, and in a tone of tender reproach, untinctured by the least show of anger or

impatience, asked them plaintively if they could not watch with Him one hour.

There He was, with the awful weight of the world's sins upon His shoulders, with the pangs of every man, woman, and child shooting through His sensitive soul—and they could not watch with him one poor hour!

Returning to His place, He offered up the same prayer as before; then went back and again found them sleeping. Again He awoke them, readmonished them, and once more returned and prayed. Three times this occurred, until I was perfectly familiar with His appearance—face, form, and movements. He was of noble stature and majestic mien—not at all the weak, effeminate being that some painters have portrayed; but the very God that He was and is, as meek and humble as a little child. [51]

Notes

1. For an explanation of this precise date, see John P. Pratt, "The Restoration of Priesthood Keys on Easter 1836, Part 1: Dating the First Easter," *Ensign*, June 1985, 59–68. See also *The Life and Teachings of Jesus and His Apostles* [1979], 136, 170.
2. Bible Dictionary, "Gethsemane," 680.
3. *History of the Church*, 3:30.
4. *The Teachings of Ezra Taft Benson* [1988], 14.
5. *Mormon Doctrine*, 2nd ed. [1966], 60.
6. *The Infinite Atonement* [2000].
7. *The Infinite Atonement* [2000], 2–3.
8. *Teachings of Gordon B. Hinckley* [1997], 28.
9. *Of All Things!*, compiled and edited by Gary P. Gillum [1981], 12.
10. *The Promised Messiah: The First Coming of Christ* [1978], 2.
11. *The Seventy's Course in Theology*, 5 vols. [1907–12], Fourth Year, 128.

12. *The Mediation and Atonement* [1882], 149–50.

13. In Conference Report, Oct. 1997, 89; or *Ensign*, Nov. 1997, 66.

14. In Conference Report, Apr. 1987, 89; or *Ensign*, May 1987, 72.

15. *Not My Will, But Thine* [1988], 51.

16. In Conference Report, Oct. 1995, 29; or *Ensign*, Nov. 1995, 24.

17. *Even As I Am* [1982], 116–17.

18. *The Infinite Atonement*, 123–24.

19. In Conference Report, Apr. 1985, 10; or *Ensign,* May 1985, 9.

20. While this conclusion seems logical, it is not a scriptural certainty. Elder Maxwell wrote of this heavenly messenger: *"An angel, whose identity we do not know, came to strengthen Him"* ("Enduring Well," *Ensign*, Apr. 1997, 10; emphasis added).

21. *History of the Church*, 4:208.

22. "The Olive Press," *Ensign*, Dec. 1982, 61.

23. *His Final Hours* [2000], 47–48.

24. *Jesus the Christ*, 3rd ed. [1916], 613.

25. *Doctrines of Salvation*, comp. Bruce R. McConkie, 3 vols. [1954–56], 1:129–30.

26. *Doctrinal New Testament Commentary*, 3 vols. [1965–73], 1:774–75.

27. See *The Infinite Atonement*, 58–60.

28. *The Infinite Atonement*, 83–84.

29. *Answers to Gospel Questions*, comp. Joseph Fielding Smith Jr., 5 vols. [1957–66], 5:7.

30. *The Words of Joseph Smith*, compiled and edited by Andrew F. Ehat and Lyndon W. Cook [1980], 185.

31. "The Seven Deadly Heresies," BYU fireside address, June 1, 1980, in *1980 Devotional Speeches of the Year* [1981], 76; emphasis added.

32. *The Infinite Atonement*, 84–85.

33. In *Journal of Discourses*, 3:80–81.

34. *A New Witness for the Articles of Faith* [1985], 99.

35. *The Essential James E. Talmage*, edited by James P. Harris [1997], 211.

36. *Doctrines of Salvation*, 1:74. On another occasion, Joseph Fielding Smith wrote: ". . . Through His death, through His ministry, the shedding of His blood, He has brought to pass redemption from death to *all men, to all creatures*—not alone to man, but to *every living thing*, and *even to this earth itself*, upon which we stand, for we are informed through the revelations that it too shall receive the resurrection" (*Doctrines of Salvation*, 1:138).

37. *The Mediation and Atonement*, 181.

38. *The Infinite Atonement*, 87–89.

39. *Mormon Doctrine*, 65; emphasis added.

40. "Jesus Christ, Lord of the Universe," *Improvement Era*, Nov. 1968, 46; emphasis added.

41. "Jesus Christ, Lord of the Universe," *Improvement Era*, Nov. 1968, 48.

42. "Jesus Christ, Lord of the Universe," *Improvement Era*, Nov. 1968, 48.

43. *The Teachings of Lorenzo Snow*, comp. Clyde J. Williams [1998], 93; emphasis added.

44. In Conference Report, Oct. 1996, 46; or *Ensign*, Nov. 1996, 35.

45. *Old Testament and Related Studies* [1986], 142.

46. *Old Testament and Related Studies*, 142; emphasis added.

47. *Old Testament and Related Studies*, 143.

48. *A Bible! A Bible!* [1990], 210.

49. *Doctrines of Salvation*, 1:122.

50. In Conference Report, Oct. 1997, 34; or *Ensign*, Nov. 1997, 26.

51. *Through Memory's Halls* [1930], 82–83; see also *Ensign*, Aug. 1975, 20–21.

Chapter 7

Jesus' Crucifixion and Death

(Matthew 26–27; Mark 14–15; Luke 22–23; John 18–19)

THE FIFTH DAY
(Thursday)

SEVERAL ILLEGAL TRIALS

The leaders of the Jews had long sought to arrest Jesus. They followed Him during His entire ministry, seeking one word or action by which they might find legal fault in Him and demand His arrest and death. After Jesus publicly raised Lazarus from the dead, they became even more determined.

A. BIDA, 1874

- **John 11:47–53 "What do we? for this man doeth many miracles."** They reasoned, "If we let him thus alone, all men will believe on him: and the Romans shall come and take away both our place and nation" (v. 48). The high priest Caiaphas said "it is expedient for us, that one man should die for the people, and that the whole nation perish not" (v. 50). So, "then from that day forth they took counsel together for to put him to death" (v. 53). Elder Bruce R. McConkie said: ". . . It should be remembered that, according to the prophetic word, it was 'because of priestcrafts and iniquities' that our Lord was 'crucified' (2

Nephi 10:5)."[1] He also said: "Persecution is one of the chief weapons in the hands of false priests; they use it to preserve their false religions. . . . False ministers fear the truth because by it their crafts are in danger. They practice priestcrafts to get gain and the praise of the world, neither of which will be theirs if true religion sweeps them into a deserved oblivion."[2]

Jesus Is Arrested

We get different details from each of the Gospels with regard to Jesus' arrest. We must piece them together in order to get an entire picture of what took place.

- **Matthew 26:45–46 "The hour is at hand."** When Jesus found Peter, James, and John sleeping for the third time during His Atonement, He said, "Sleep on now, and take your rest," knowing they would need it because "the hour is at hand, and the Son of man is betrayed into the hands of sinners" (v. 45). Then, sometime later, He woke them with the command, "Rise, let us be going: behold, he is at hand that doth betray me" (v. 46).

GUSTAVE DORÉ, 1896

- **Matthew 26:47–50 Judas betrays Jesus with a kiss.** It was still dark when "Judas, one of the twelve, came, and with him a great multitude with swords and staves, from the chief priests and elders of the people" (v. 47). He had told his partners in crime that "whom- soever I shall kiss, that same is he: hold him fast" (v. 48). So now, in keeping with the conspiratorial sign, "he came to Jesus, and said, Hail, master; and kissed him" (v. 49). Jesus greet- ed him with kindness, saying, "Friend, wherefore art thou come?" (v. 50). But after the kiss, Luke records that Jesus asked Judas, "Betrayest thou the Son of man with a kiss? (Luke 22:48). Then, they who had come with Judas "laid hands on Jesus, and took him" (v. 50).

— **John 18:2–3 Judas knew Jesus would be in the Garden of Gethsemane.** John records, "Judas . . . knew the place: for Jesus ofttimes resorted thither with his disciples" (v. 2). So Judas led "a band of men and officers from the chief priests and Pharisees" to the spot "with lanterns and torches and weapons" (v. 3).

— **John 18:4–7 Jesus did not run nor hide but boldly identified Himself.** He "went forth, and said unto them, Whom seek ye?" (v. 4). When "they answered him, Jesus of Nazareth[,] . . . Jesus saith unto them, I am he" (v. 5). Stunned by His presence and also fearful, "they went backward, and fell to the ground" (v. 6), whereupon Jesus asked again, "Whom seek ye? And they said, Jesus of Nazareth" (v. 7).

— **John 18:8, 12 Jesus shows concern for His disciples in this moment of danger.** He said to the armed guard, "I have told you that I am he: if therefore ye seek me, let these go their way" (v. 8). And then "the band and the captain and officers of the Jews took Jesus, and bound him" (v. 12).

PROVIDENCE LITHOGRAPHIC CO, 1898, #42

- **Matthew 26:51–54 Jesus heals the high priest's servant's ear.** Matthew tells us that "one of them which were with Jesus stretched out his hand, and drew his sword, and struck a servant of the high priest's, and smote off his ear" (v. 51). John reveals that this was Peter, and the servant's name, whose right ear was severed, was Malchus (see John 18:10). Jesus said to Peter, "Put up again thy sword into his place: for all they that take the sword shall perish with the sword. Thinkest thou that I cannot now pray to my Father, and he shall presently give me more than twelve legions of angels? But how then shall the scriptures be fulfilled, that thus it must be?" (vv. 52–54).

- **Matthew 26:55 Jesus chides His captors for their secrecy in coming in the night.** What they were doing was illegal, and they knew it. They feared the multitudes if they tried to take him publicly. Knowing this, Jesus asked them, "Are ye come out as against a thief with swords and staves for to take me? I sat daily with you teaching in the temple, and ye laid no hold on me" (v. 55).

- **Matthew 26:56 All of Jesus' disciples flee.** They had boasted that they would defend Him even unto death (see Matthew 26:35; Mark 14:31). But in this moment of grave danger, "all the disciples forsook him, and fled."

The Trial Before the High Priest

The leaders of the Jews were determined to destroy Jesus, and engaged in every conceivable stratagem to accomplish it. They cared not a whit that their actions violated their own laws. Jesus had to be stopped, and they would stop at nothing to put an end to His ministry. Every circumstance of His Jewish trial was illegal. Not only did His enemies hold it at night, but they also obtained false witnesses.[3] Jesus knew this but chose to remain silent throughout the ordeal, just as Isaiah had said He would (see Isaiah 53:7).

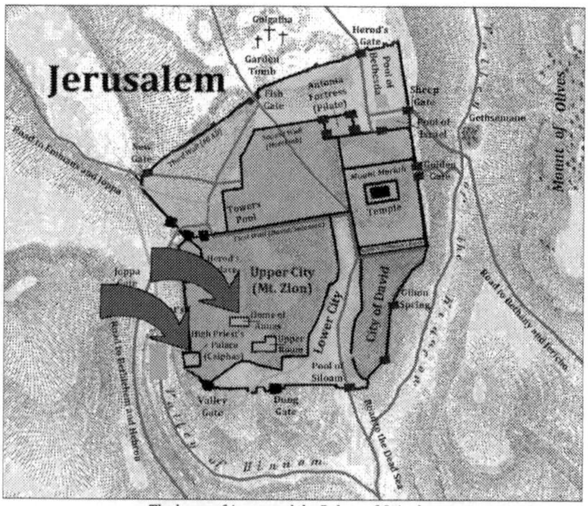

The home of Annas and the Palace of Caiaphas

- **John 18:12–13 Only John mentions that Jesus was taken before Annas**, a former high priest and father-in-law of Caiaphas, the sitting high priest. He records that after "the captain and officers of the Jews took Jesus, and bound him," they "led him away to Annas first; for he was father in law to Caiaphas, which was the high priest that same year."

- **John 18:19–21 Jesus is interrogated before Caiaphas.** The high priest inquired concerning "his disciples, and of his doctrine" (v. 19). Jesus answered, "I spake openly to the world; I ever taught in the synagogue, and in the temple, whither the Jews always resort; and in secret have I said nothing" (v. 20). The high priest knew full well what Jesus had taught and who had followed Him. This pompous interview was all show. "Why askest thou me?" Jesus retorted, "ask them which heard me, what I have said unto them: behold, they know what I said" (v. 21).

PROVIDENCE LITHOGRAPHIC CO., 1910, #42

- **John 18:22–23 One of the high priest's servants slaps Jesus.** Incensed at Jesus' response to the high priest, "one of the officers which stood by struck Jesus with the palm of his hand, saying, Answerest thou the high priest so?" (v. 22). And Jesus answered, "If I have spoken evil, bear witness of the evil: but if well, why smitest thou me?" (v. 23).

The Trial Before the Sanhedrin

The private interview at the home of the high priest Annas was useless as a tool to entrap Jesus because nothing He said to them was worthy of arrest, let alone death. Thus, they took Him to the full Sanhedrin at the palace of the high priest Caiaphas (see Matthew 26:57; see also map on this page).

Jesus appeared before the Sanhedrin

— **Matthew 26:57–58 Peter follows Him there.** Peter appeared nearby again, going into the high priest's palace "where the scribes and elders were assemled," and "sat with the servants, to see the end."

— **John 18:15 John also follows.** John tells us that "Simon Peter followed Jesus, and so did another disciple: that disciple was known unto the high priest, and went in with Jesus into the palace of the high priest." We assume that this unnamed disciple was John himself.

- **Matthew 26:59–63 False witnesses testify against Jesus.** The purpose of this council was not to seek justice, but to condemn. "The chief priests, and elders, and all the council, sought false witness against Jesus, to put him to death" (v. 59). But they could find no reliable witness among the many who came (v. 60). Then, at last, two liars perjured themselves before the council. One testified, "This fellow said, I am able to destroy the temple of God, and to build it in three days" (v. 61). They pretended not to understand that Jesus was referring to the resurrection of His own body, though their actions after His death would demonstrate that they clearly did understand (see Matthew 27:62–66). For now, it was convenient to accept the ruse. "The high priest arose, and said unto him, Answerest thou nothing? what is it which these witness against thee?" (v. 62). Even so, this was not enough to condemn Jesus to death, and Jesus held His peace, answering them not at all (v. 63).

- **Matthew 26:63 The high priest asks Jesus if He is the Christ, the Son of the Living God.** Next, "the high priest . . . said unto him, I adjure thee by the living God, that thou tell us whether thou be the Christ, the Son of God." Jesus had plainly said so in public on several occasions, but they wanted Him to say it before the council. That would be blasphemy under their law, and sufficient to condemn Him to death, though under Roman law they had no power to execute Him.

- **Mark 14:62 Jesus answers, "I am."** Matthew says Jesus answered with an idiomatic expression of those times, "Thou hast said," meaning essentially "You said it" (Matthew 26:64). But Mark quotes Jesus' answer as, "I am" (Mark 14:62). Then, to emphasize His answer Jesus said further, "Hereafter shall ye see the Son of man sitting on the right hand of power, and coming in the clouds of heaven" (Matthew 26:64).

- **Matthew 26:65–66 The council convicts Jesus of blasphemy.** At this answer, "the high priest rent his clothes, saying, He hath spoken blasphemy; what further need have we of witnesses? behold, now ye have heard his blasphemy" (v. 65). This is what they were hoping to accomplish with their illegal nighttime tribunal. "What think ye?" the high priest asked his council colleagues, and "they answered and said, He is guilty of death" (v. 66).

- **Matthew 26:67–68 Council members abuse Jesus with slapping and spitting.** As Isaiah had predicted (see Isaiah 50:6), they "spit in his face, and buffeted him; and . . . smote him with the palms of their hands" while mocking Him with taunts of, "Prophesy unto us, thou Christ, Who is he that smote thee?"

Peter Denies That He Knows Jesus

- **Matthew 26:69–74 Confront-ed by people outside the palace of Caiaphas, Peter denies three times that he even knows Jesus.** While all these events were transpiring, "Peter sat without in the palace: and a damsel came unto him, saying, Thou also wast with Jesus of Galilee. But he denied before them all, saying, I know not what thou sayest" (v. 70). That was the first denial. Then, "when he was gone out into the porch, another maid saw him, and said unto them that were there, This fellow was also with Jesus of Nazareth. And again he denied with an oath, I do not know the man" (vv. 71–72). That was the second denial, and it was compounded by his making an oath to the contrary. Then finally, "after a while came unto him they that stood by, and said to Peter, Surely thou also art one of them; for thy speech bewrayeth thee. Then began he to curse and to swear, saying, I know not the man" (vv. 73–74).

- **Matthew 26:74–75 "And immediately the cock crew"** (v. 74). Only then did Peter remember the words of Jesus, who had said to him at the last supper, "Before the cock crow, thou shalt deny me thrice" (Matthew 26:34). And Peter "went out, and wept bitterly" (v. 75).

President Gordon B. Hinckley said:

> . . . My heart goes out to Peter. So many of us are so much like him.

We pledge our loyalty; we affirm our determination to be of good courage; we declare, sometimes even publicly, that come what may we will do the right thing, that we will stand for the right cause, that we will be true to ourselves and to others.

Then the pressures begin to build. Sometimes these are social pressures. Sometimes they are personal appetites. Sometimes they are false ambitions. There is a weakening of the will. There is a softening of discipline. There is capitulation. And then there is remorse, followed by self-accusation and bitter tears of regret. . . .

. . . If there be those throughout the Church who by word or act have denied the faith, I pray that you may draw comfort and resolution from the example of Peter, who, though he had walked daily with Jesus, in an hour of extremity momentarily denied the Lord and also the testimony which he carried in his own heart. But he rose above this and became a mighty defender and a powerful advocate. So, too, there is a way for any person to turn about and add his or her strength and faith to the strength and faith of others in building the kingdom of God.[4]

The Trial Before Pilate

- **Matthew 27:1–2 Jewish leaders conspire to have Jesus killed.** Jesus had been charged by the Sanhedrin with blasphemy, worthy of death under Jewish law, but not under Roman law. Only the Romans could put Him to death, and so they had to seek occasion to condemn Him before Pilate or Herod.

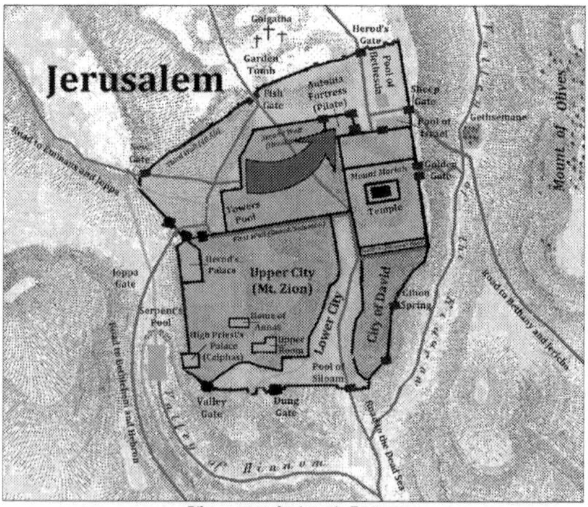

Pilate was at the Antonia Fortress

So, "when the morning was come, all the chief priests and elders of the people took counsel against Jesus to put him to death" (v. 1), and took Him first "to Pontius Pilate the governor" (v. 2), who was at the Antonia Fortress.

- **Matthew 27:3–Judas declares, "I have betrayed the innocent blood" and commits suicide.** Apparently, Judas had sought to get rich by having Jesus arrested, but did not realize that they would kill Him. Thus, "when [Judas] saw that [Jesus] was condemned, repented himself, and brought again the thirty pieces of silver to the chief priests and elders, Saying, I have sinned in that I have betrayed the innocent blood. And they said, What is that to us? see thou to that" (vv. 3–4).

E. ARMITAGE, THE BIBLE & ITS STORY, 1908

He could not undo the damage and Jesus was certainly headed toward His death. In all of history there had been no more "innocent blood" than the blood of Jesus Christ, and to shed innocent blood makes one a son of perdition. Judas was now inevitably headed toward that fate.

Judas "cast down the pieces of silver in the temple, and departed, and went and hanged himself" (v. 5). The Joseph Smith Translation of the Bible adds detail concerning Judas' death. It says that Judas "hanged himself on a tree.

J. S. V. CAROLSFELD, 1852-60

And straightway he fell down, and his bowels gushed out, and he died" (JST Matthew 27:6).

The chief priests "took the silver pieces, and said, It is not lawful for to put them into the treasury, because it is the price of blood. And they took counsel, and bought with them the potter's field, to bury strangers in" (vv. 6–7). At the time Matthew wrote his account, that field was still called "the field of blood" (v. 8). Matthew says all of this was done in fulfillment of the prophecy of Jeremiah ("Jeremy"), though we do not have this prophecy today in the book of Jeremiah. But we do have the prophecy of Zechariah which said the same thing (see Zechariah 11:12–13).

- **Luke 23:1–2 Seeking Jesus' death, Jewish leaders accuse Him of being an enemy to Caesar.** The entire "multitude" of the council then "arose, and led him unto Pilate" (v. 1). There, "they began to accuse him, saying, We found this fellow perverting the nation, and forbidding to give tribute to Cæsar, saying that he himself is Christ a King" (v. 2).

- **Luke 23:3–7 Learning that Jesus is a Galilean, Pilate turns Him over to Herod Antipas**, the tetrarch or ruler of Galilee. Pilate asked Jesus if He was "the King of the Jews[,]" and Jesus answered again with the idiomatic expression, "Thou sayest it" (v. 3). That was not enough to concern Pilate, and he said "to the chief priests and to the people, I find no fault in this man" (v. 4). They argued fiercely that Jesus "stirreth up the people, teaching throughout all Jewry, beginning from Galilee to this place" (v. 5). Then Pilate, realizing he had an out from this ridiculous situation, "as soon as he knew that [Jesus] belonged unto Herod's jurisdiction, he sent him to Herod, who himself also was at Jerusalem at that time" (vv. 6–7).

The Trial Before Herod

- **Luke 23:8–9 Christ remains silent before Herod.** Herod was excited to meet Jesus, because although he had heard of Him for a very long time, he had never before met Him, and "he hoped to have seen some miracle done by him" (v. 8).

He asked Jesus many questions, but Jesus "answered him nothing" (v. 9). This fulfilled the prophecy of Isaiah which said He would be "oppressed, and. . .afflicted, yet he [would] open . . . not his mouth; he [will be] brought as a lamb to the slaughter, and as a sheep before her shearers is dumb, so he [will] open . . . not his mouth" (Isaiah 53:7).

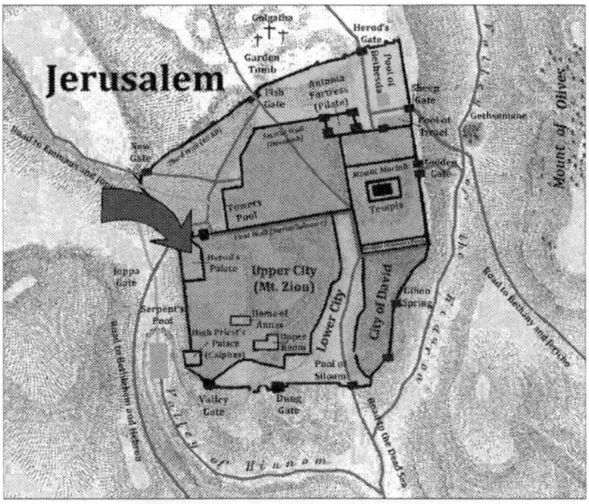

Location of Herod's Palace

- **Luke 23:10–12 Christ is mocked and returned to Pilate.** Frustrated by Herod's inability to condemn Jesus, "the chief priests and scribes stood and vehemently accused him" (v. 10).

  Meanwhile, "Herod with his men of war set him at nought, and mocked him, and arrayed him in a gorgeous robe, and sent him again to Pilate" (v. 11). And although Herod and Pilate "were at enmity between themselves" at the time, in the matter of Jesus they "were made friends together" (v. 12).

Another Trial Before Pilate

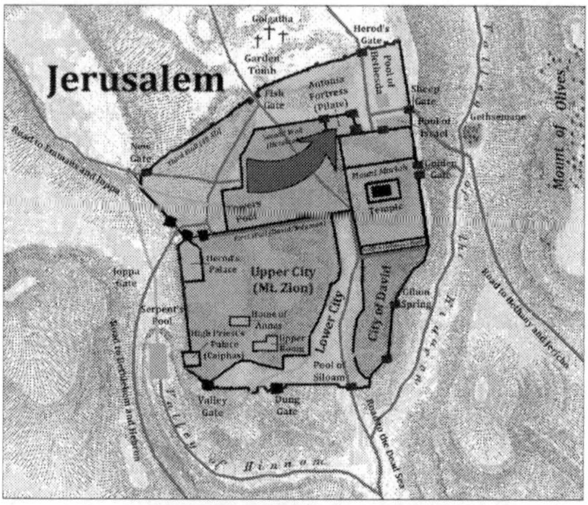

Jesus was returned again to Pilate

- **John 18:36–37 Pilate again asks Jesus if He is a king.** Jesus answered, "My kingdom is not of this world: if my kingdom were of this world, then would my servants fight, that I should not be delivered to the Jews: but now is my kingdom not from hence" (v. 36).

  Pressing the point, Pilate asked again, "Art thou a king then?" and Jesus answered, "Thou sayest that I am a king. To this end was I born, and for this cause came I into the world, that I should bear witness unto the truth. Every one that is of the truth heareth my voice" (v. 37). He was not a political threat to anyone, but a man sent from God to proclaim the truth.

PROVIDENCE LITHOGRAPHIC CO., 1904, #37

- **Luke 23:13–16 Pilate concludes that Jesus is innocent.** Having heard enough, Pilate "called together the chief priests and the rulers and the people" and said to them, "Ye have brought this man unto me, as one that perverteth the people: and, behold, I, having examined him before you, have found no fault in this man touching those things whereof ye accuse him:

No, nor yet Herod: for I sent you to him; and, lo, nothing worthy of death is done unto him. I will therefore chastise him, and release him."

- **Matthew 27:15–19 Pilate seeks to set Jesus free.** Each year at the Passover Feast, the Judean governor would "release unto the people a prisoner"—whomever they wanted to be set free (v. 15; see also Luke 23:17). That particular year there was "a notable prisoner, called Barabbas," and, of course, Jesus (v. 16).

The crowd chose to release Barabbas

"Therefore when they were gathered together, Pilate said unto them, Whom will ye that I rellease unto you? Barabbas, or Jesus which is called Christ?" (v. 17).

He hoped they would choose Jesus because Pilate's wife had sent a message to him, saying, "Have thou nothing to do with that just man: for I have suffered many things this day in a dream because of him" (v. 19).

- **Matthew 27:20–23 The crowd demands that Jesus be crucified.** Though Barabbas was a well-known criminal, "the chief priests and elders persuaded the multitude that they should ask Barabbas, and destroy Jesus" (v. 20). So, when Pilate asked, "Whether of the twain will ye that I release unto you? They said, Barabbas" (v. 21). And when he asked of them,

"What shall I do then with Jesus which is called Christ? They all say unto him, Let him be crucified" (v. 22). Pilate was astounded, protesting, "Why, what evil hath he done?" but they "cried out the more, saying, Let him be crucified" (v. 23).

GUSTAVE DORÉ, 1896

- **John 19:12–15 The Jews hypocritically declare their loyalty to Rome.** In reality, the Jews hated the Romans. The Pharisees, in particular, despised anyone who collected their taxes, and the people longed for a deliverer to set them free from Roman oppression. Yet, when Pilate sought to release Jesus, "the Jews cried out, saying, If thou let this man go, thou art not Cæsar's friend: whosoever maketh himself a king speaketh against Cæsar" (v. 12).

  Such boldfaced hypocrisy! Pilate sat himself down in his judgment seat and cried out to them, "Behold your King!" (vv. 13–14). "But they cried out, Away with him, away with him, crucify him." And when Pilate asked a final time, "Shall I crucify your King? The chief priests answered, We have no king but Cæsar" (v. 15).

- **Matthew 27:24–26 Pilate washes his hands of responsibility for Jesus' death and gives in to the crowd's wishes.** Lacking courage when he saw that he could not prevail over the demands of the mob before him, Pilate "took water, and washed his hands before the multitude, saying, I am innocent of the blood of this just person: see ye to it" (v. 24). And "then answered all the people, and said, His blood be on us, and on our children" (v. 25). Pilate then "released . . . Barabbas unto them" (v. 26).

SCOURGING AND HUMILIATION

Jesus Is Scourged

- **Matthew 27:26 Jesus is scourged.** Matthew observed simply, "And when he had scourged Jesus, he delivered him to be crucified." Elder James E. Talmage explained: "Scourging was a frightful preliminary to death on the cross. The instrument of punishment was a whip of many thongs, loaded with metal and edged with jagged pieces of bone. . . . The condemned [sometimes] died under the lash and so escaped the horrors of living crucifixion."[5]

A. GIOACCHINO, 1640s

This cruel torture was predicted by Isaiah, who said that the Savior would give His "back to the smiters" (Isaiah 50:6). And although He had bled all night in the Garden of Gethsemane, He would have bled even more profusely as the thongs of the whip ripped out great chunks of flesh with every one of the 39 lashes He received.

Jesus Is Humiliated

- **Matthew 27:27–31 Jesus is stripped, humiliated, and mocked.** Bruised, broken, and torn, Jesus was then taken by Pilate's soldiers "into the common hall," where "the whole band of soldiers" gathered to mock Him (v. 27). "They stripped him [presumably naked], and put on him a scarlet robe. And when they had platted a crown of thorns, they put it upon his head, and a reed in his right hand: and they bowed the knee before him, and mocked him, saying, Hail, King of the Jews!" (vv. 28–29). Then, "they spit upon him, and took the reed, and smote him on the head" (v. 30). Then after they had finished mocking Him, "they took the robe off from him, and put his own raiment on him, and led him away to crucify him" (v. 31).

GUSTAVE DORÉ, 1896

Elder James E. Talmage explained:

In accordance with the brutal customs of the time, Jesus, weak and bleeding from the fearful scourging He had undergone, was given over to the half-savage soldiers for their amusement. He was no ordinary victim, so the whole band came together in the Pretorium, or great hall of the palace, to take part in the diabolical sport. They stripped Jesus of His outer raiment, and placed upon Him a purple robe.

Then with a sense of fiendish realism they platted a crown of thorns, and placed it about the Sufferer's brows; a reed was put into His right hand as a royal scepter; and, as they bowed in a mockery of homage, they saluted Him with: "Hail, King of the Jews!"

G. RENI

Snatching away the reed or rod, they brutally smote Him with it upon the head, driving the cruel thorns into His quivering flesh; they slapped Him with their hands, and spat upon Him in vile and vicious abandonment.[6]

Jesus Carries His Cross to Calvary

RAPHAEL, 1516-17

- **Luke 23:26 The soldiers compel Simon the Cyrenian to bear Jesus' cross.** By now, He would have been too weak to carry the heavy beam that would become His cross. So, "they laid hold upon one Simon, a Cyrenian, coming out of the country, and on him they laid the cross, that he might bear it after Jesus."

- **Luke 23:27–31 Jesus prophesies the coming destruction of Jerusalem.** A "great company" of people followed Jesus to Calvary, including "women, which also bewailed and lamented him" (v. 27). "But Jesus turning unto them said, Daughters of Jerusalem, weep not for me, but weep for yourselves, and for your children" (v. 28).

  The days were coming, Jesus prophesied, when people would say, "Blessed are the barren, and the wombs that never bare, and the paps which never gave suck" (v. 29). Such people would be too burdened to flee the destruction that would come upon them. "Then shall they begin to say to the mountains, Fall on us; and to the hills, Cover us" (v. 30), but there would be no escape from the Romans, who destroyed Jerusalem in A.D. 70. "For if they [the Romans] do these things in a green tree [when times are good], what shall be done in the dry [when things are not so good]?" (v. 31).

THE CRUCIFIXION

Jesus Is Nailed to His Cross

- **Matthew 27:33 Jesus is crucified at Golgotha on the Hill of Calvary.** *Golgotha* means "a place of a skull," and was an appropriate name for the place where many enemies of Rome

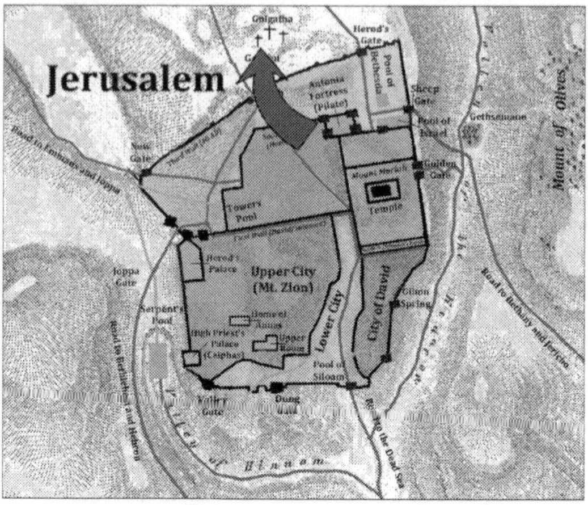

were crucified near Jerusalem. It was located on the Hill of Calvary, north of the city. And there, after all they had already done to Him, they crucified our Lord.

Crucifixion was an execution used by the Romans to humiliate and torture criminals and enemies. A man was generally stripped of his clothing and then nailed to the cross he had been compelled to drag to the site of the execution.

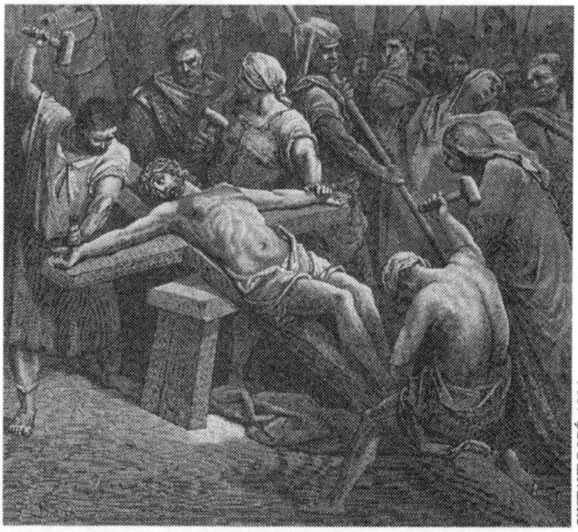
GUSTAVE DORÉ, 1896

One large spike was driven into the palm of each hand, thereby affixing his arms to the cross-beam in an outstretched fashion. Then, lest the weight of his body should cause the nail to tear through the flesh of the hand, another spike was driven through each wrist as well.

The feet of the victim were affixed with one spike driven through both of them into a small angled platform beneath the sufferer. This would keep the man from flailing his legs around in agony and would also increase the pain of his suffering. To relieve the pain in his hands and wrists, the sufferer could push his body up with his feet, but that would only cause the nail in his feet to tear deeper as well. Thus, he might periodically push up to relieve his hands and wrists, and then hang from his wrists to relieve his feet. Either way, there was no relief.

The contorted position of the body would produce excruciating pain in the back, abdomen, and thighs, which would cramp continuously under the burden of the dead weight pressing down upon them. The body would quickly dehydrate from the sweat that would break out from every pore, leaving the man thirsty as well as in pain.

Since the crucifixion was generally done near the highway into the city, passers-by would often pause to pity or to mock the naked sufferer, who, in Roman culture, was considered a disgrace to society. There would be no way to help him, and only his family to stand by him as he very slowly succumbed to dehydration, loss of blood, and pain. It could sometimes take days for the relief of death to come.

Harry Emerson Fosdick wrote:

> Let a man stand before some great picture of the crucifixion like that of Rubens' in Antwerp; let him imagine that he had himself seen such a thing done to a human being and knew that it was going to be done to him, and he can a little understand the conditions under which the latter part of Jesus' ministry was passed.

RUBENS, 1619–20

> As Rubens pictures it, one thief is gasping for breath; the other, struck upon the leg by a Roman soldier to see if he is dead, is crying out in . . . agony, and writhing, tears one foot loose from the nail that pierced it. The Master's mother and John are weeping with averted eyes, unable to endure the sight, and Mary Magdalene, in passionate grief, is trying with vain hands to ward away the soldier who from horseback drives the spear into the Savior's side. The body of the Master hangs limp and dead.

> Jesus had probably seen crucifixions, and knew that He was going to be crucified. Our words *fortitude*, *courage*, and *patient resolution* need an expanded meaning before they are qualified to cover the case.[7]

Elder S. Dilworth Young said: "I read that He was hung on a cross. I look at my own hands and feet and try to imagine the pain of such torture—to hang there in the heat of the day, the weight of His body on those tearing nails, every muscle and nerve drawn tight in agony. No stopping, no escape until He, having said: 'It is finished' (John 19:30), gave up the ghost. I realize that this was endured for me and for you; I bow my head; it is hard to hold back the tears. Even now, [about 2,000] years later, it is as poignant as though it occurred yesterday."[8]

Elder Gordon B. Hinckley said:

> . . . No member of this Church must ever forget the terrible price paid by our Redeemer who gave His life that all men might live—the agony of Gethsemane, the bitter mockery of His trial, the vicious crown of thorns tearing at His flesh, the blood cry of the mob before Pilate, the lonely burden of His heavy walk along the way to Calvary, the terrifying pain as great nails pierced His hands and feet, the fevered torture of His body as He hung that tragic day, the Son of God crying out, "Father, forgive them; for they know not what they do" (Luke 23:34).
>
> This was the cross, the instrument of His torture, the terrible device designed to destroy the Man of Peace, the evil recompense for His miraculous work of healing the sick, of causing the blind to see, of raising the dead. This was the cross on which He hung and died on Golgotha's lonely summit.
>
> We cannot forget that. We must never forget it, for here our Savior, our Redeemer, the Son of God, gave Himself a vicarious sacrifice for each of us.[9]

The Last Recorded Statements of Christ

- **Luke 23:34 <u>Statement #1</u>: "Father, forgive them [the soldiers]; for they know not what they do."** This, while the soldiers greedily "parted his raiment, and cast lots" over who would receive the bounty of His last earthly possessions.

Jesus' view from the cross

"Father, forgive them; for they know not what they do," Jesus said, referring to those Roman soldiers who carried out the orders of their superiors. Jesus' utterance of this prayer unto the Father is a demonstration of His magnanimity, His forgiving nature, and of His personal compliance with the command to forgive one's enemies. Yet, appreciating the fact that Jesus had the largeness of soul to pray in behalf of His crucifiers, we should not see His utterance as a means of absolving their personal sins.

Elder Bruce R. McConkie said:

> This first "word" from the cross is equally as important for what it does not say as for what it does. It is not an utterance whereby anyone's sins are forgiven, but it is a petition asking for forgiveness in a particular and limited sense of the word. Jesus was the Son of God; as such He had power to forgive sins, a power which He had freely exercised in proper cases (see Matthew 9:2–8).
>
> But no such power is exercised here. He does not say, "Thy sins be forgiven thee," as had been His wont on other occasions. Nor does He ask the Father to forgive the sins of those involved, in the sense of cleansing them from sin so as to qualify them for church membership or celestial inheritance. The law whereby such forgiveness is gained requires repentance and baptism. But He says, rather, "Father, lay not this sin to their charge, for they are acting under orders, and those upon whom the full and real guilt rests are their rulers and the Jewish conspirators who caused me to be condemned. It is Caiaphas and Pilate who know I am innocent; these soldiers are just carrying out their orders."

Jesus did not, it should be noted, pray for Judas who betrayed Him; for Caiaphas and the chief priests who conspired against Him; for the false witnesses who perjured their souls before the Sanhedrin and in the judgment halls of Rome; for Pilate and Herod, either of whom could have freed Him; nor for Lucifer whose power and persuasive ability underlay the whole wicked procedure. All these are left in the hands of Eternal Justice to be dealt with according to their works. Mercy cannot rob justice; the guilty do not go free simply because the righteous bring no railing accusation against them.

Here on the cross Jesus is simply complying with His own command to forgive your enemies and to bless those who curse you.[10]

- **Luke 23:39–43 <u>Statement #2</u>: "Today shalt thou [the thief] be with me in paradise."** One thief had selfishly challenged Jesus (as Satan had done), saying, "If thou be Christ, save thyself and us" (v. 39). But the other thief rebuked the first one, saying, "Dost not thou fear God, seeing thou art in the same condemnation? And we indeed justly; for we receive the due reward of our deeds: but this man hath done nothing amiss" (vv. 40–41). Then, turning to Jesus, he asked, "Lord, remember me when thou comest into thy kingdom" (v. 42). "And Jesus said unto him, Verily I say unto thee, To day shalt thou be with me in paradise" (v. 43).

  The Prophet Joseph Smith said that Jesus told the thief, "This day thou shalt be with me in the world of spirits."[11] "Jesus did not lend any credence to a death-bed repentance of the malefactor. What Jesus did do was give recognition to the seeds of faith and repentance that were evidenced by a penitent man. As always, the Lord's efforts were directed toward offering as much hope as possible to one who would turn from darkness unto the everlasting light."[12]

- **John 19:25–27 <u>Statement #3</u>: To Mary: "Behold thy son!" and to John: "Behold thy mother!"** Other than John, the disciples had all abandoned Jesus in fear. But His mother Mary "stood by the cross of Jesus" along with "his mother's sister [Salome], Mary the wife of Cleophas, and Mary Magdalene"

(v. 25). Looking down upon his mother in total compassion, Jesus said to her, referring to John, "Woman, behold thy son!" (v. 26). And then, to John the Beloved, referring to Mary, "Behold thy mother! And from that hour that disciple took her unto his own home" (v. 27).

Elder Thomas S. Monson said: "There remained yet a few faithful followers. From His tortured position on the cruel cross, He sees His mother and the disciple whom He loved standing by. He speaks: '. . . woman, behold thy son! Then saith he to the disciple, Behold thy mother! . . .' (John 19:26–27). From that awful night when time stood still, when the earth did quake and great mountains were brought down—yes, through the annals of history, over the centuries of years and beyond the span of time, there echoes His simple yet divine words, 'Behold thy mother!'"[13]

— **Matt. 27:55–56 James and John were Jesus' cousins.** The women who stood at Jesus' cross had "followed Jesus from Galilee, ministering unto him" (v. 55). They included "Mary Magdalene, and Mary the mother of James and Joses," and Salome, who was "the mother of Zebedee's children" (v. 56). It is from this reference, combined with John's statement above, that we get the idea that the Apostles John the Beloved

and James were Jesus' cousins, because they were sons of Salome—sister of Mary, the mother of Jesus Christ.

- **Matthew 27:46 <u>Statement #4</u>: To God the Father: "My God, my God, why hast thou forsaken me?"** At about "the ninth hour" [3:00 P.M.], "Jesus cried with a loud voice, saying, *Eli, Eli, lama sabachthani*? that is to say, My God, my God, why hast thou forsaken me?" (emphasis added). Apparently, at this time, just prior to His death, God the Father withdrew His comforting Spirit from Jesus, leaving Him absolutely alone to finish His mission.

President J. Reuben Clark Jr. said: ". . . His being cast off by the world and by His own did not fill His cup of rejection. At the crucifixion, while the passers-by and the soldiers mocked, scoffed and reviled Him, He hung on the cross alone, save for a thief on either side, forsaken not only by the throngs of the idle curious, but forsaken by the scores He had healed, by the multitudes He had fed, by the greedy crowds that would have made Him king; He hung, forsaken by His disciples, even by His Apostles who had boasted they would be devoted and loyal, even to death itself; forsaken by all except His mother, her sister, and Mary Magdalene, and John the Beloved, and some women who stood afar off. So crucified and hanging in His infinite, forsaken loneliness, His spirit about to go, His mighty grief burst forth in that cry of mortal near-despair, 'My God, my God, why hast thou forsaken me?'"[14]

Elder Jeffrey R. Holland said: "Because He must ultimately tread this winepress of redemption unaided, can He endure the darkest moment of them all, the shock of the greatest pain? This comes not with thorns and with nails, but with the terror of feeling utterly alone: '. . . My God, my God, why hast thou forsaken me?' (Mark 15:34). Can He bear all of our sins *and* our fear and loneliness too? He did and He does and He will."[15]

Elder James E. Talmage said: "It seems, that in addition to the fearful suffering incident to crucifixion, the agony of Gethsemane had recurred, intensified beyond human power to endure. In that bitterest hour the dying Christ was alone, alone in most terrible reality. That the supreme sacrifice of the Son might be consummated in all its fulness, the Father seems to have withdrawn the support of His immediate Presence, leaving to the Savior of men the glory of complete victory over the forces of sin and death."[16]

- **John 19:28–29 <u>Statement #5</u>: "I thirst."** At that point, "knowing that all things were now accomplished," Jesus said, "I thirst" (v. 28). John says He uttered this request to fulfill prophecy (see Psalm 69:21). And beneath Him on the ground lay "a vessel full of vinegar: and they filled a spunge with vinegar, and put it upon hyssop, and put it to his mouth" (v. 29). This was apparently a better way to satiate thirst than water would have been, plus it would have served as somewhat of an anaesthetic for the pain.

  Elder James E. Talmage said: "The period of faintness, the conception of utter forsakenness soon passed, and the natural cravings of the body reasserted themselves. The maddening thirst, which constituted one of the worst of the crucifixion agonies, wrung from the Savior's lips His one recorded utterance expressive of physical suffering. 'I thirst' He said. . . . John affirms that Christ uttered the exclamation, 'I thirst,' only when He knew 'that all things were now accomplished'; and the Apostle saw in the incident a fulfilment of prophecy [see Psalm 69:21]."[17]

- **John 19:30 <u>Statement #6</u>: "It is finished."** After Jesus had received the vinegar, He exclaimed in triumph, "It is finished" (v. 30), knowing that His atoning sacrifice had been accepted by the Father (see John 19:28). JST Matthew 27:54 records Jesus as saying: "Father, it is finished, thy will is done." Jesus had obediently come to earth, taught our Father's children, established His Church, and made His atoning sacrifice. This is the mission for which He had volunteered in the premortal world (see Abraham 3:27), and because of it, all of God's children could now have hope of redemption from sin and a return to their Father's presence. He had taken no shortcuts, avoided no responsibility, made no compromise with sin. He saw it through to the bitter end, and then "bowed his head, and gave up the ghost."

- **Luke 23:46 Statement #7: "Father, into thy hands I commend my spirit."** Luke records that, as Jesus bowed His head and died, He made one last statement of prayer to His father, saying, "Father, into thy hands I commend my spirit: and having said thus, he gave up the ghost."

  Elder James E. Talmage said: "Jesus the Christ was dead. His life had not been taken from Him except as He had willed to permit. Sweet and welcome as would have been the relief of death in any of the earlier stages of His suffering from Gethsemane to the cross, He lived until all things were accomplished as had been appointed. In the latter days the voice of the Lord Jesus has been heard affirming the actuality of His suffering and death, and the eternal purpose thereby accomplished. Hear and heed His words: 'For, behold, the Lord your Redeemer suffered death in the flesh; wherefore he suffered the pain of all men, that all men might repent and come unto him' (D&C 18:11)."[18]

- **Jesus died at "the ninth hour," in the late afternoon, about 3:00 P.M.** This would have been just before sundown, which would have ushered in the Sabbath. The sixth hour was about noon, and the ninth hour about three o'clock in the afternoon.

The Earth Reacts to the Death of Christ

- **Matthew 27:50–51, 54 Earthquakes rock Jerusalem.** When Jesus "yielded up the ghost," we are told that "the veil of the temple was rent in twain from the top to the bottom; and the earth did quake, and the rocks rent" (vv. 50–51). The earth convulsed in both anger and pain at the death of its Creator. And when "the centurion, and they that were with him, watching Jesus, saw the earthquake, and those things that were done, they feared greatly, saying, Truly this was the Son of God" (v. 54).

- **3 Nephi 8 Intense destruction rocks the Western Hemisphere.**

  — **3 Nephi 8:2–4 About 33 years after the sign of Jesus' birth, the people "began to look with great earnestness" for the fulfillment of Samuel's words concerning Jesus' death.** It was now A.D. 33, and the Nephites knew that this was the time when Samuel the Lamanite predicted great destructions would come to the Nephites. They were now firmly entrenched in wickedness, ripe for destruction, with their central government destroyed, and mostly unwilling to listen to the warnings of their prophets.

  Yet, they had not forgotten about the predictions, and "the people began to look with great earnestness for the sign which had been given by the prophet Samuel"—which was "that there should be darkness for the space of three days over the face of the land" (v. 3). Just as had happened when the signs of Christ's birth had appeared, the people engaged in "great doubtings and disputations . . . , notwithstanding so many signs had been given" (v. 4).

  — **3 Nephi 8:5–18 The predicted destruction occurs.** We are told that the destruction began "in the thirty and fourth year, in the first month, on the fourth day of the month"(in other words, 33 years had passed since Christ's birth and the 34th year had just begun) (v. 5). The destruction began at the death of the Savior, which coincides with early April on our modern calendars. One by one, the predicted destructions came.

Samuel's Prophecies	The Predictions and Their Fulfillment
Helaman 14:21, 23	Great storms & earthquakes 3 Nephi 8:5–7, 16–18
Helaman 14:24	Highways & cities destroyed 3 Nephi 8:8–10, 14
Helaman 14:20, 27	Darkness for three days 3 Nephi 8:20–21

— **3 Nephi 8:5–7, 16 Great storms and tempests.**

It started with "a great storm, such an one as never had been known in all the land" (v. 5), accompanied by "a great and terrible tempest" (v. 6), probably hurricane-force winds blowing in from the sea. There was "terrible thunder . . . that . . . did shake the whole earth as if it was about to divide asunder" (v. 6), caused by "exceedingly sharp lightnings, such as never had been known in all the land" (v. 7). Some people "were carried away in the whirlwind," which suggests terrible tornadoes, "and whither they went no man knoweth, save they know that they were carried away" (v. 16).

Such storms are rare but not unheard of on the West Coast of the Americas. We usually hear of them coming in from the Atlantic Ocean and striking the East Coast or the Gulf of Mexico. When they do, they can be unbeliev-ably devastating, as we all learned with Hurricane Katrina in New Orleans. Hurri-canes are almost always accompanied by severe rainstorms, thunderstorms, and tornadoes in the affected areas.

"John L. Sorenson quotes the report of a 1793 eruption in the Tuxtla Mountains which has some interesting parallels: 'Don

Joseph Mozino reports that it all started with a buildup of towering clouds over the mountains and great grand thunderclaps, but underground, that sounded like all the artillery in Veracruz going off.' The account estimates the number of these thunderclaps at 400, says that they could be heard hundreds of miles away, and concludes, 'No doubt the thunder was of two kinds. One resulted from exceptionally violent storms caused by the heat and dust and the other from the fracturing of the strata underground.'"[19]

"Even though much of Mesoamerica receives heavy seasonal rains, the situation would be further complicated by [a] volcano . . . The heat [a massive volcano] injects . . . into the atmosphere would trigger torrential rains as a side effect as [the volcano's] heated material contact[s] the stratosphere's colder wet air."[20]

— **3 Nephi 8:12–13, 17–18 Great earthquakes and volcanoes.** As these storms raged, "the whole earth became deformed, because of the tempests, and the thunderings, and the lightnings, and the quaking of the earth" (v. 17). As a result of these earthquakes and volcanoes, "the whole face of the land was changed" (v. 12). "The rocks were rent in twain [and] they were broken up upon the face of the whole earth, insomuch that they were found in broken fragments, and in seams and in cracks, upon all the face of the land" (v. 18). ". . . Highways were broken up, and the level roads were spoiled, and many smooth places became rough" (v. 13).

If there were such massive upheavals that "the whole earth became deformed" (v. 17), we would expect to see evidence of it at the time of Christ's death somewhere in the Americas. And we do.

__Earthquakes__: ". . . If there is any weakness in the underlying rock strata, earthquakes would be triggered by volcanic action. Near the coast, this seismic activity would create tidal waves of huge heights and immense power. A common Mesoamerican pattern is for an erupting volcano to trigger an earthquake. In some cases, an earthquake can also cause a [volcanic eruption]. The noise, needless to say, would be deafening: lightning, thunder, great cracks where rock strata are giving way, and the noises of the eruption itself."[21]

"Mesoamerica . . . is known for its seismic activity. One text on the archaeology of Mesoamerica is called *The Sons of the Shaking Earth*, taking its title from a common characteristic of the whole area. . . . From the Valley of Mexico on the north to El Salvador on the south, we have a pattern of major volcanic eruptions. [At the time of Christ's death,] [t]he north [experienced] lava flows over thirty feet thick [and] the south saw ash layers of up to sixty-five feet deep."[22]

"Ixtlilxochitl, Mexico's sixteenth century historian, working from records which preceded the coming of the Spaniards, describes and dates to the time of the crucifixion events as they occurred in southern Mexico. The darkness and the quaking and the rending of rocks at the very time of the crucifixion are described [in the *Works of Ixtlilxochitl*]:

"'It was 166 years since they had adjusted their years and times with the equinox, and 270 since the ancient ones had been destroyed, when the sun and the moon eclipsed, and the earth trembled, and the rocks broke, and many other things and signs took place, although there was no calamity whatever toward men. This happened in the year of ce Calli, which, adjusting this count with ours, comes to be at the same time when Christ our Lord suffered, and they say it happened during the first days of the year.'"[23]

Volcanoes: "Interestingly, [there is] evidence of at least four different volcanic eruptions. . . . Volcanic activity can be dated as early as the time of Christ. Not far away near the border of Guatemala is the site of Chalchuapa, a large . . . site that was occupied [both before and after the time of Christ]. A layer of volcanic ash between the archaeological strata has been dated by radiocarbon processes to A.D. 30, a date that provides a correlation with the crucifixion of Christ. . . .

"Copilco [experienced] a lava flow thirty feet thick, covering architecture, burials, and pottery vessels. This layer of lava dates from the time of Christ. . . . About thirty miles northeast [of Copilco] is the huge site of Teotihuacan. Between two architecture levels [there] appears a layer of volcanic ash probably blown in from that eruption. By radiocarbon dating, that eruption dates to A.D. 30."[24]

— **3 Nephi 8:8–10, 14–15 Cities and countrysides are destroyed.** Many important Nephite cities were destroyed by various means.

- Zarahemla took fire (v. 8).
- Moroni sank into the depths of the sea, drowning its inhabitants (v. 9).
- Moronihah was buried by landslides, such that "in the place of the city there became a great mountain" (v. 10).
- Many other great and notable cities were sunk, burned, and shaken by earthquakes until their buildings collapsed, killing their inhabitants and leaving them desolate (v. 14).
- Cities that were not utterly destroyed had significant damage and deaths (v. 15).
- There was "great and terrible destruction in the land southward" (v. 11).
- There was even greater and more terrible destruction in the land northward (v. 12).

Landslides and Mud Flows: How could entire cities be covered in three hours, and others washed out to sea? The answer may lie in mud flows. ". . . A 1964 volcanic eruption in Nicaragua created such huge quantities of ash that the area experienced ninety mud flows in a single year. Because mud flows are deep deposits of ash, they are highly unstable. The impact of any significant amount of rain makes the ash flow down slopes, seeking a lower resting bed. Speeds of these mud flows can vary from twenty to thirty miles an hour and one flow was clocked at fifty-nine miles an hour. According to the records, the distances a single mud flow has moved can range from five miles (the average is between five and ten miles) up to the record-holder: ninety-nine miles."[25]

Cities Buried by Water: "In highland Guatemala to the west of Guatemala City lies a large inland lake, Lake Atitlan [possibly the Waters of Mormon]. During a period of low water in the 1930s, ruins were detected in the water. . . . [Ceramics recovered from this underwater site] dated from about the time of Christ . . . It is reasonable to hypothesize that this city in the lake was . . . occupied near the time of Christ, and was covered subsequently by the lake waters. There are, interestingly, several volcanoes in the mountains surrounding the lake."[26]

All of the events described here occurred upon the occasion of the Savior's death on the cross at Jerusalem. The earth broke forth into spasms of fury, as its Creator was so brutally slain. We are told that all these destructive forces lasted for "about the space of three hours" (v. 19). Three hours! Most earthquakes with which we are familiar last a few seconds or minutes. Can we imagine what kind of damage could occur in three hours, while, at the same time, hurricanes, tornadoes, violent thunderstorms, and landslides are occurring everywhere? It must have been unbelievably frightening and destructive.

The Burial of Christ

- **John 19:31 The next day (Saturday) was a "high day"—the Sabbath day during the week of the Passover and the first day of the Feast of Unleavened Bread.** Jewish days began at sunset and continued until the following sunset. Jesus' Friday had begun the previous sunset at the last supper, continued through the night with His Atonement, and ended just before the next sunset that ushered in the Jewish Sabbath day (Saturday). Though it was a blessed day for all humankind, on which we were set free from the grasp of sin, it had been a horrific day for Jesus and His disciples. His body now hung limp and dead upon the cross, and those who loved Him had little time for a proper burial. It had to be accomplished before sunset because the "high day" Sabbath celebration was upon them. Since sunset would have been about 6:00 P.M., they had less than three hours to accomplish it.

- **John 19:31–37 The soldiers pierce Jesus' dead body with a spear.** Since, under the law, "bodies should not remain upon the cross on the sabbath day, (for that sabbath day was an high day,)" they "besought Pilate that their legs might be broken, and that they might be taken away" (v. 31). Breaking their legs was a way to ascertain if they were dead, and if not, to induce death.

RUBENS, 1616–17

The soldiers "brake the legs of the first [thief], and of the other which was crucified with him" (v. 32). "But when they came to Jesus, and saw that he was dead already, they brake not his legs: But one of the soldiers with a spear pierced his side, and forthwith came there out blood and water" (vv. 33–34).

Had Jesus been alive, His pumping heart would have sent forth streams of blood spurting from His side. But with no blood pressure to cause such a fountain, His body simply seeped whatever blood and water remained inside His torso. This was proof positive that Jesus was dead.

Even these acts, performed after His death, fulfilled the prophecies that said, "A bone of him shall not be broken" (see Exodus 12:46; Numbers 9:12), and another which said, "They shall look upon [Him] whom they have pierced" (Zechariah 12:10) (vv. 36–37).

- **Matthew 27:57–60 Joseph of Arimathaea's tomb.** After Jesus was crucified, His body was wrapped in clean linen cloths and placed in a tomb belonging to Joseph of Arimathaea. This was done quickly because the Sabbath was about to begin. The Bible describes him as a "rich man" who "went to Pilate, and begged the body of Jesus" and was granted the privilege of receiving the lifeless body of the Lord (vv. 57–58).

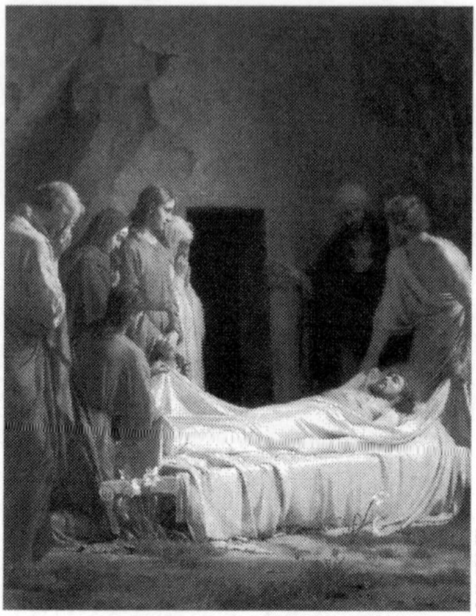

C. H. BLOCH

Matthew tells us that "he wrapped it in a clean linen cloth, and laid it in his own new tomb, which he had hewn out in the rock: and he rolled a great stone to the door of the sepulchre, and departed" (vv. 59–60).

— **Luke 23:50–53 Joseph did not "consent . . . to the counsel and deed" of the Sanhedrin** (v. 51). He was "a good man, and a just . . . who also himself waited for the kingdom of God" (vv. 50–51). Luke adds that his tomb was so new that no other man had ever been laid there (v. 53).

— **John 19:38–40 He was "a disciple of Jesus, but secretly for fear of the Jews"** (v. 38). He was assisted in the task of removing Jesus' body by "Nicodemus, which at the first came to Jesus by night" (v. 39), another member of the Sanhedrin who was a secret admirer of Jesus.

— **John 19:38–42 The tomb was near the place of crucifixion.** Joseph and Nicodemus "brought a mixture of myrrh and aloes, about an hundred pound weight" and "took . . . the body of Jesus, and wound it in linen clothes with the spices, as the manner of the Jews is to bury" (v. 40). Then they laid Jesus' body in Joseph's tomb, which was "in [near] the place where [Jesus] was crucified . . . in . . . a new sepulchre, wherein was never man yet laid" (v. 41). They selected this place because of the fast-approaching Sabbath day and because "the sepulchre was nigh at hand" (v. 42).

THE SIXTH & SEVENTH DAYS

(Friday & Saturday)

CHRIST'S MISSION TO THE SPIRIT WORLD

Three Days in the Tomb

Elder James E. Talmage said: "Our Lord definitely predicted His resurrection from the dead on the third day (Matthew 16:21; 17:23; 20:19; Mark 9:31; 10:34; Luke 9:22; 13:32; 18:33) . . . This specification of the third day must not be understood as meaning after three full days. The Jews began their counting of the daily hours with sunset; therefore the hour before sunset and the hour following belonged to different days. Jesus died and was interred during Friday afternoon. His body lay in the tomb, dead, during part of Friday (first day), throughout Saturday, or as we divide the days, from sunset Friday to sunset Saturday (second day), and part of Sunday (third day). We know not at what hour between Saturday sunset and Sunday dawn He rose."[27]

Prophetic Descriptions of this Mission

- **John 5:25–29 Jesus predicts His mission to the spirit world.** To the unbelieving Jews He said very early in His ministry, "Verily, verily, I say unto you, The hour is coming, and now is, when the dead shall hear the voice of the Son of God: and they that hear shall live" (v. 25). He was and is the Lord of Life, "for as the Father hath life in himself; so hath he given to the Son to have life in himself; and hath given him authority to execute judgment also, because he is the Son of man" (vv. 26–27). This means that He not only decides when a man shall die, but also when and how a man will be judged—including those in the spirit world. "Marvel not at this," He said, "for the hour is coming, in the which all that are in the graves shall hear his voice, and shall come forth; they that have done good, unto the resurrection of life; and they that have done evil, unto the resurrection of damnation" (vv. 28–29).

- **1 Peter 3:18–20; 4:6 Peter describes Christ's mission to the spirit world.** Peter points out that it was Christ who "suffered for sins, the just for the unjust, that he might bring us to God" (v. 18). Who else, then, can decide when and how a man will be judged? And although Christ was "put to death in the flesh," He was "quickened by the Spirit" and "went and preached unto the spirits in prison" (vv. 18–19). Who were these spirits? Peter says they were those who were "disobedient, when once the longsuffering of God waited in the days of Noah, while the ark was a preparing, wherein few, that is, eight souls were saved by water" (v. 20). And why did Christ take the gospel to them now? "For . . . this cause was the gospel preached also to them that are dead, that they might be judged according to men in the flesh, but live according to God in the spirit" (4:6).

- **Alma 40:11–14 There are two separate places in the spirit world.** Alma was taught by an angel concerning "the state of the soul between death and the resurrection"—that "the spirits of all men, as soon as they are departed from this mortal body, . . . whether they be good or evil, are taken home to that God who gave them life" (v. 11). Does this mean that they go immediately home to the place where God the Father lives? No. Alma explained that the "righteous are received into a state of happiness, which is called paradise, a state of rest, a state of peace, where they shall rest from all their troubles and from all care, and sorrow" (v. 12). But "the spirits of the wicked, yea, who are evil—for behold, they have no part nor portion of the Spirit of the Lord; for behold, they chose evil works rather than good; therefore the spirit of the devil did enter into them, and take possession of their house—[are] cast out into outer darkness; there shall be weeping, and wailing, and gnashing of teeth, and this because of their own iniquity, being led captive by the will of the devil" (v. 13). This is what we call the "spirit prison" where the wicked dwell "in darkness, and a state of awful, fearful looking for the fiery indignation of the wrath of God upon them; thus they remain in this state, as well as the righteous in paradise, until the time of their resurrection" (v. 14).

It is not too difficult to see where the Christian world got its idea of souls being consigned to either "heaven" or "hell" upon their deaths. Over the millennia, the doctrine of the spirit world has devolved into this belief, with no possible repentance for the wicked. But the Bible simply does not support such creeds. Both the Savior and Peter spoke plainly of redemption for the dead in the spirit world.

- **D&C 138:11–17 The hosts of the dead were awaiting the arrival of Christ.** President Joseph F. Smith received a vision on October 3, 1918, concerning what happened when Christ visited the spirits in prison. As he sat pondering these things, he said that "the eyes of my understanding were opened, and the Spirit of the Lord rested upon me, and I saw the hosts of the dead, both small and great. And there were gathered together in one place an innumerable company of the spirits of the just, who had been faithful in the testimony of Jesus while they lived in mortality" (vv. 11–12). These were the righteous in Old Testament times—those who looked forward steadfastly to the coming of Christ. They had "departed the mortal life, firm in the hope of a glorious resurrection, through the grace of God the Father and his Only Begotten Son, Jesus Christ" (v. 14).

  Knowing that Jesus had now atoned for their sins and was coming to visit them, "they were filled with joy and gladness, and were rejoicing together because the day of their deliverance was at hand" and "were assembled awaiting the advent of the Son of God into the spirit world, to declare their redemption from the bands of death" (vv. 15–16). Indeed, once Christ rose from the dead, they too would rise from the dead and receive again their bodies (see Matthew 27:52–53). "Their sleeping dust was to be restored unto its perfect frame, bone to his bone, and the sinews and the flesh upon them, the spirit and the body to be united never again to be divided, that they might receive a fulness of joy" (v. 17).

- **D&C 138:18–22 The Lord went not in person among the wicked.** President Smith said that "while this vast multitude waited and conversed, rejoicing in the hour of their deliverance from the chains of death, the Son of God appeared, declaring liberty to the captives who had been faithful; And there he preached to them the everlasting gospel, the doctrine of the resurrection and the redemption of mankind from the fall, and from individual sins on conditions of repentance" (vv. 18–19).

This occurred in the place that Alma called paradise (see Alma 40:12).

"But unto the wicked [Jesus] did not go, and among the ungodly and the unrepentant who had defiled themselves while in the flesh, his voice was not raised; Neither did the rebellious who rejected the testimonies and the warnings of the ancient prophets behold his presence, nor look upon his face. Where these were, darkness reigned" (vv. 20–22). This is spirit prison.

- **D&C 138:22–26 Jesus and His message are universally received and accepted by the righteous.** "Among the righteous there was peace" and "the saints rejoiced in their redemption, and bowed the knee and acknowledged the Son of God as their Redeemer and Deliverer from death and the chains of hell. Their countenances shone, and the radiance from the presence of the Lord rested upon them, and they sang praises unto his holy name" (vv. 22–24). We might compare this reception to the limited one He received while on earth, where, despite "his mighty works, and miracles, and proclamation of the truth, in great power and authority, there were but few who hearkened to his voice, and rejoiced in his presence, and received salvation at his hands" (vv. 25–26).

- **D&C 138:27–32 The gospel is preached to the unfaithful dead by the faithful.** "His ministry among those who were dead was limited to the brief time intervening between the crucifixion and his resurrection" (v. 27). Thus, He did not have time to visit the wicked in spirit prison. President Smith observed that "the Lord went not in person among the wicked and the disobedient who had rejected the truth, to teach them" (v. 29). Instead, "from among the righteous, he organized his forces and appointed messengers, clothed with power and authority, and commissioned them to go forth and carry the light of the gospel to them that were in darkness, even to all the spirits of men; and thus was the gospel preached to the dead" (v. 30). By this means, "the gospel [is] preached to those who . . . died in their sins, without a knowledge of the truth, or in transgression, having rejected the prophets" (v. 32).

- **Matthew 27:52–53 Many faithful Saints are resurrected shortly after Christ rises from the tomb.** Matthew testified that "the graves were opened; and many bodies of the saints which slept arose, And came out of the graves after his resurrection, and went into the holy city, and appeared unto many."

Notes

1. *The Mortal Messiah: From Bethlehem to Calvary,* 4 vols. [1979–81], 1:252.
2. *The Mortal Messiah: From Bethlehem to Calvary,* 2:393.
3. For a detailed discussion of the trial's illegalities, see *Jesus the Christ,* 3rd ed. [1916], 644–48, note 4.
4. "And Peter Went Out and Wept Bitterly," *Ensign,* Mar. 1995, 2, 4, 6.
5. *Jesus the Christ,* 638.
6. *Jesus the Christ,* 638–39.
7. *The Manhood of the Master* [1913], 69–70; emphasis added.
8. In Conference Report, Apr. 1973, 167; or *Ensign,* July 1973, 114.
9. In Conference Report, Apr. 1975, 137; or *Ensign,* May 1975, 93.
10. *Doctrinal New Testament Commentary,* 3 vols. [1965–73], 1:818–19.
11. *History of the Church,* 5:424–25.
12. *The Life and Teachings of Jesus and His Apostles* [1979], 186.
13. In Conference Report, Oct. 1973, 30; or *Ensign,* Jan. 1974, 31–32.
14. *Behold the Lamb of God* [1962], 301.
15. In Conference Report, Oct. 1989, 32; or *Ensign,* Nov. 1989, 26.
16. *Jesus the Christ,* 661.
17. *Jesus the Christ,* 661.

18. *Jesus the Christ*, 662.

19. In Bruce W. Warren and Thomas Stuart Ferguson, *The Messiah in Ancient America* [1987], 45.

20. *The Messiah in Ancient America*, 42–43.

21. *The Messiah in Ancient America*, 43.

22. *The Messiah in Ancient America*, 40, 44.

23. In *The Messiah in Ancient America*, 35.

24. *The Messiah in Ancient America*, 43, 44.

25. *The Messiah in Ancient America*, 42.

26. *The Messiah in Ancient America*, 44.

27. *Jesus the Christ*, 697, note 1.

Section Two

Resurrection, 40-Day Ministry, & Ascension

(April 3–May 12, A.D. 33)[1]

The events described in this section include:

THE RESURRECTION OF CHRIST
THE 40-DAY POST-RESURRECTION MINISTRY
CHRIST'S ASCENSION INTO HEAVEN

The chapters in this section are:

8. The Resurrection of Jesus Christ
9. Christ's 40-Day Ministry and Ascension

These events also include the accounts of literally hundreds of people who saw the resurrected Christ after His death upon the cross.

They also include Jesus' teachings to His disciples during the 40 days between His resurrection and His ascension into heaven. It was during this period that He taught them concerning the preaching of the gospel to the dead and ordinances that may be performed on earth in their behalf. He also charged them to take the gospel to every nation, kindred, tongue, and people. And He promised John that he would not die, but instead would be translated and continue his ministry until the Second Coming of Christ.

Finally, it relates the Savior's final words and ascension into heaven from the Mount of Olives, with a promise that He would one day return "in like manner" to that same place (Acts 1:11).

Following is a chronological list of events that took place during this period and the scriptures from the four Gospels that tell the story.[2]

RESURRECTION & 40-DAY MINISTRY

	Matt.	Mark	Luke	John
THE FIRST DAY OF THE WEEK				
The Tomb Is Opened	28:2–4			
Mary Magdalene & Other Women Visit the Tomb	28:1, 5–7	16:1–8	24:1–8	20:1
Mary Tells Peter and John			24:9–11	20:2
Peter, Mary, and John Visit the Tomb			24:12	20:3–10
The Savior Appears to Mary		16:9		20:11–i7
Mary Tells the Apostles		16:10–11		20:18
Christ Appears to the Other Women	28:9–10			
Guards Tell Priests of Resurrection	28:11–15			
2 Disciples see Christ on Emmaus Rd		16:12–13	24:13–32	
Christ Appears unto Peter			24:34	
Christ Appears to Apostles Except Thomas		16:14	24:33–49	20:19–23
AFTER THE FIRST DAY OF THE WEEK				
Jerusalem				
Christ Appears to the Eleven Apostles				20:24–29
Sea of Galilee				
Christ Appears to the Disciples				21:1–14
"Feed My Sheep"				21:15–19
John Is to Be Translated				21:20–23
Jerusalem				
Christ Appears to a Great Multitude	(1 Corinthians 15:6)			
Christ Appears to James	(1 Corinthians 15:7)			
Galilee				
Christ Appears to the Disciples	28:16–20	16:15–18	(See Acts 1:1–8)	
Bethany, Judea				
The Ascension of Jesus Christ		16:19	24:50–51	
The Disciples Return to Jerusalem		16:20	24:52–53	
John's Concluding Words				20:30–31 21:24–25

Notes:

1. For an explanation of these and other precise dates that appear in this section, see John P. Pratt, "The Restoration of Priesthood Keys on Easter 1836, Part 1: Dating the First Easter," *Ensign*, June 1985, 59–68. See also Bruce R. McConkie, *The Mortal Messiah: From Bethlehem to Calvary*, 4 vols. [1979–81], 1:168–69; 4:283, 286 (note 4), 404. See also James E. Talmage, *Jesus the Christ*, 3rd ed. [1916], 718, note 2.

2. Adapted from *The Life and Teachings of Jesus and His Apostles* [1979], 190, 198.

CHAPTER 8

THE RESURRECTION OF JESUS CHRIST

(MATTHEW 28; LUKE 24; JOHN 20–21)

RESURRECTION MORNING

(Sunday, April 3, A.D. 33)[1]

"Very Early in the Morning"

- **Matthew 28:1 Mary Magdalene and other women return to the tomb** with spices and ointments to anoint and embalm the body of Jesus.
  - **Luke 24:1 It was "upon the first day of the week, very early in the morning."** The Sabbath would have ended at 6:00 P.M. on Saturday evening, but the scriptures are clear that the women came to the tomb "as it began to dawn" toward daylight (Matthew 28:1). The precise time of the resurrection is not known. We only know that these women arrived at daylight and found the tomb empty.
  - **Mark 15:47; 16:1 Mark identifies the women.** In addition to Mary Magdalene, he mentions "Mary the mother of Joses [and] . . . of James," and also "Salome"—the wife of Zebedee and mother of the Apostles John the Beloved and James.

— **Mark 16:1; Luke 24:1 They brought "sweet spices"** which "they had prepared" in order that they might "come and anoint him."

- **The Location of the Tomb.** There is disagreement among Christians as to the location of the tomb of Jesus. Many (including many Church members) believe that it is the Garden Tomb, located outside the city walls near Golgotha, in what is believed to be the family garden of Joseph of Arimathaea. The traditional site (favored by Orthodox churches) is inside the city walls and is covered by the Church of the Holy Sepulchre, which was built by the emperor Constantine and his mother Helena.

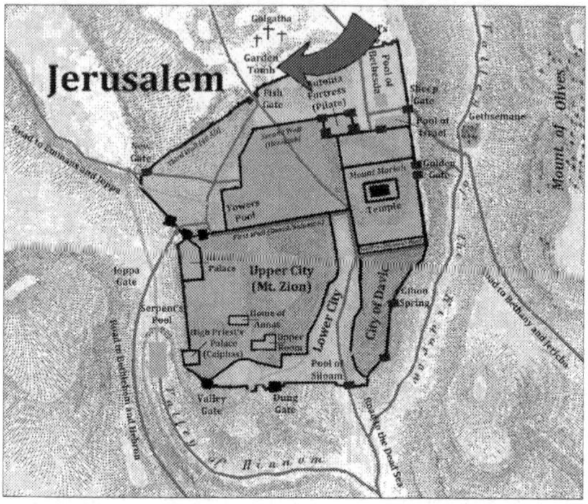

PHOTO COURTESY TTAYLOR@MIDWEST.NET

The Garden Tomb

- **Matthew 28:2–4 The stone is rolled back.** Matthew tells us that "there was a great earthquake: for the angel of the Lord descended from heaven, and came and rolled back the stone from the door, and sat upon it. His countenance was like lightning, and his raiment white as snow" (vv. 2–3). The Joseph Smith Translation of the Bible says that there were two angels (see JST Matthew 28:2), which is consistent with what Luke says in Luke 24:4. Where Matthew obtained this information is not clear, but he may have gotten it from the soldiers who were posted there, guarding the tomb, because he says that "for fear of [the angels] the keepers did shake, and became as dead men" (v. 4).

W. BOUGUEREAU, THE BIBLE AND ITS STORY, 1908

- **Luke 24:2–4 They find the tomb empty.** When "they found the stone rolled away from the sepulchre . . . they entered in, and found not the body of the Lord Jesus" (vv. 2–3). They were "much perplexed" (worried), but were comforted by "two men" who "stood by them in shining garments" (v. 4).

- **Matthew 28:5–6 "He is not here: for he is risen."** The angels standing by the tomb "said unto the women, Fear not ye: for I know that ye seek Jesus, which was crucified" (v. 5). Then they spoke the words that thrill every believer in Christ to this day: "He is not here: for he is risen, as he said. Come, see the place where the Lord lay" (v. 6).

  — **Luke 24:5–8 They remember Jesus' words concerning the resurrection.** Luke says that "they were afraid, and bowed down their faces to the earth" when they saw the angels (v. 5). These heavenly messengers asked them, "Why seek ye the living among the dead? He is not here, but is risen: remember how he spake unto you when he was yet in Galilee, Saying, The Son of man must be delivered into the hands of sinful men, and be crucified, and the third day rise again" (vv. 5–7). And then, "they remembered his words" (v. 8).

WITNESSES OF THE RESURRECTED CHRIST

The resurrection of Christ is at the heart of the Christian faith. Either He rose from the dead or He did not. If so, then He is divine—the Son of God with power over life and death—as He repeatedly taught that He was. If He did not rise, then He was a fraud, for He never claimed to be simply another prophet or a wise teacher. The intellectual sophists of our time (some of whom even claim to be Christians) have sought to "spiritualize" the resurrection, saying that it did not physically occur, but only spiritually. If this is so, then the New Testament is full of false witnesses.

Early Witnesses of the Resurrection

There were thousands of witnesses of the resurrected Christ:

- The guards at the tomb who saw the angel roll back the stone (Matthew 28:2–4).
- Mary Magdalene, who was the first to see the resurrected Christ (John 20:11–18).
- The other women who saw Christ on their way to tell the disciples (Matthew 28:9–10).
- Peter, who went to the tomb and shortly thereafter saw the risen Lord (Luke 24:12, 34).
- Luke and Cleopas whom the the Lord visited on the road to Emmaus (Luke 24:13–32).
- The Apostles without Thomas, whom the Lord visited that evening (John 20:19–25).
- The Apostles including Thomas, whom He visited 8 days later (John 20:24–29).
- All eleven Apostles, whom the Lord met on a mountain in Galilee (Matthew 28:16–18).

- Seven Apostles while fishing on the shores of the Sea of Galilee (John 21:1–19).
- More than 500 disciples at once on one occasion (1 Corinthians 15:3–6).
- James, the brother of the Lord, at Jerusalem (1 Corinthians 15:7).
- Saul of Tarsus (who later became the Apostle Paul), to whom He appeared on the road to Damascus (Acts 9:1–6).
- The Apostle John, to whom He appeared on the Isle of Patmos (Revelation 1:10–19).
- Many faithful Saints were resurrected shortly after Christ rose from the dead and were seen by many of Jesus' disciples (Matt. 27:52–53).
- About 2,500 Nephites to whom He appeared in the Western Hemisphere, and who individually handled His body (3 Nephi 11:14–15).

We will review these witnesses in this chapter, recounting their experiences with the living, resurrected Christ. The message of that glorious resurrection morning echoes through the words of all these witnesses.

President Gordon B. Hinckley said: "Those who hated Jesus thought they had put an end to Him forever when the cruel spikes pierced His quivering flesh and the cross was raised on Calvary. But this was the Son of God, with whose power they did not reckon. . . . No force beneath the heavens could now hold back the power of the Son of God. It was as if His Almighty Father could stand no more. The earth trembled. The guards fled. The stone was moved. The Lord of heaven and earth arose from the bier, shook off the burial clothes, and stepped forth to become the first fruits of them that slept. The empty tomb bore testimony of this greatest of all miracles. With the appearance of the risen Lord first to Mary and then to many others, even to upwards of five hundred, came the undeniable testimony of His everlasting power over life and death."[2]

The Guards at the Tomb

HEINRICH HOFMANN

- **Matthew 28:1–4 The guards at the tomb see an angel roll back the stone.** This happened sometime early Sunday morning "as it began to dawn," either before or at the same time that "Mary Magdalene and the other Mary [came] to see the sepulchre" (v. 1). "There was a great earthquake" as an "angel of the Lord descended from heaven, and came and rolled back the stone from the door, and sat upon it" (v. 2). "His countenance was like lightning, and his raiment white as snow: And for fear of him the keepers did shake, and became as dead men" (vv. 3–4).

- **Matthew 28:7–8 The women run quickly to tell the disciples that Christ has risen.** Meanwhile, the angel instructed the women at the tomb to "go quickly, and tell his disciples that he is risen from the dead; and, behold, he goeth before you into Galilee; there shall ye see him" (v. 7). The women "departed quickly from the sepulchre with fear and great joy; and did run to bring his disciples word" (v. 8; see also Luke 24:9).

E. BURNAND, THE BIBLE AND ITS STORY, 1908

- **John 20:1–10 Two of the disciples go to the tomb and find it empty.** When Mary Magdalene returned to tell the Apostles, she spoke first to "Simon Peter, and to the other disciple, whom Jesus loved [John himself]" (vv. 1–2). Mary said, "They have taken away the Lord out of the sepulchre, and we know not where they have laid him" (v. 2).

Peter and John hastened to the tomb, running together but with John arriving first (vv. 3–4). John, "stooping down, and looking in, saw the linen clothes lying; yet went he not in" (v. 5). When Peter arrived, he "went into the sepulchre, and seeth the linen clothes lie, And the napkin, that was about his head, not lying with the linen clothes, but wrapped together in a place by itself" (vv. 6–7). John followed him into the tomb, and when he saw the burial clothes lying there, he "believed" (v. 8). But believed what? Probably only that someone had stolen the body, because "they knew not the scripture, that he must rise again from the dead" (v. 9). They returned, confused, to their homes (v. 10).

The Witness of Mary Magdalene

Mary Magdalene was the first to see the resurrected Christ. Why Mary? This has produced much speculation—even some heresy—concerning her status with regard to the Lord. Some claim she was His wife, for which there is absolutely no scriptural support, although if He were not married He would have been subject to great criticism from His enemies. Others point out that Mary Magdalene was one of the faithful women who followed Him during His ministry (see Luke 23:27, 49, 55). She had been healed by Jesus of seven devils (see Mark 16:9; Luke 8:1–3). She was at Calvary when He died on the cross (see Mark 15:40). She cared deeply about her Lord, and was devastated by His cruel death. She was among the small group of women who came to the tomb on resurrection morning to lovingly anoint the body of Jesus with spices (see Mark 16:1). And she heard the words of the angels concerning His resurrection.

- **John 20:11–13 Mary remained behind, weeping.** When all others had departed the tomb, Mary Magdalene remained "at the sepulchre weeping: and as she wept, she stooped down, and looked into the sepulchre" (v. 11). There within the tomb she saw "two angels in white sitting, the one at the head, and the other at the feet, where the body of Jesus had lain" (v. 12). And when they asked her, "Woman, why weepest thou?" she answered, "Because they have taken away my Lord, and I know not where they have laid him" (v. 13).

THEBIBLEREVIVAL.COM, #27

- **John 20:14–16 Mary sees the resurrected Christ.** Turning away from the tomb, Mary then saw "Jesus standing, and knew not that it was Jesus" (v. 14). When He also asked her, "Woman, why weepest thou? whom seekest thou? She, supposing him to be the gardener, saith unto him, Sir, if thou have borne him hence, tell me where thou hast laid him, and I will take him away" (v. 15). The witness of the angels notwithstanding, Mary did not yet fully comprehend that Christ had risen from the dead. With great compassion, Jesus then said to her, "Mary," whereupon "she turned herself, and saith unto him, Rabboni; which is to say, Master" (v. 16).

- **John 20:17 "Touch me not."** We can imagine that Mary would have rushed into the Savior's arms when she realized who He was. But John records that Jesus said to her, "Touch me not; for I am not yet ascended to my Father" (v. 17). He was resurrected but had not yet returned and reported to the Father, which He must immediately do. The past three days had been spent in the spirit world organizing the work there.

  There may have been some compelling reason why Mary should not touch Jesus at this time, but it is more likely that the translation is in error. The word that is translated "touch" might more accurately be rendered "hold" or "restrain." Thus, while we can imagine that Mary was holding Him tight in her arms, He could not tarry with her. He had to return to His Father for further instructions, prepare for His 40-day post-resurrection ministry among the Jews, and visit the Nephites in the Western Hemisphere.

- **John 20:17–18 Mary bears witness to the Apostles.** Jesus told her to "go to my brethren, and say unto them, I ascend unto my Father, and your Father; and to my God, and your God" (v. 17). She did so, telling them that "she had seen the Lord, and that he had spoken these things unto her" (v. 18).

- **Mark 16:10–11 They do not believe her.** Obedient to the Lord's command, Mary "went and told [the Apostles], as they mourned and wept" (v. 10). But "when they had heard that he was alive, and had been seen of her, [they] believed not" (v. 11). How could this be? Had Peter and John not been at the tomb themselves? They were two of the First Presidency, and surely if the Lord had risen He would have come first to them. They had seen no such thing at the tomb, and they did not believe Mary.

The Witness of the Other Women

PROVIDENCE LITHOGRAPFIC CO., 1903, #42

- **Matthew 28:9–10 Jesus appears to the other women on their way to the disciples.** They had departed the tomb earlier, and now, in obedience to the instructions of the angels, they "went to tell his disciples" (v. 9). As they did so, "behold, Jesus met them, saying, All hail. And they came and held him by the feet, and worshipped him" (v. 9). These women included Joanna (wife of Chuza); Mary (wife of Cleophas and mother of James and Joses); and Salome (wife of Zebedee and mother of the Apostles John the Beloved and James). Jesus said to them, "Be not afraid: go tell my brethren that they go into Galilee, and there shall they see me" (v. 10).

Elder Neal A. Maxwell said: "Does it not tell us much about the intrinsic intelligence of women to read of the crucifixion scene at Calvary, 'And many women were there beholding afar off' (Matthew 27:55). Their presence was a prayer; their lingering was like a litany. And who came first to the empty tomb of the risen Christ? Two women. Who was the first mortal to see the resurrected Savior? Mary of Magdala. Special spiritual sensitivity keeps the women of God hoping long after many others have ceased."[3]

Elder Bruce R. McConkie said: "How much there is incident to the death, burial, and resurrection of our Lord which ennobles and exalts faithful women. They wept at the cross, sought to care for His wounded and lifeless body, and came to His tomb to weep and worship for their friend and Master. And so it is not strange that we find a woman, Mary of Magdala, chosen and singled out from all the disciples, even including the Apostles, to be the first mortal to see and bow in the presence of a resurrected being. Mary, who had been healed of much and who loved much, saw the risen Christ! . . . Jesus appeared first to Mary Magdalene and then to other women."[4]

- **Luke 24:10–11 The Apostles do not believe the women's witnesses.** Luke says that "Mary Magdalene, and Joanna, and Mary the mother of James, and other women that were with them . . . told these things unto the apostles," but "their words seemed to them as idle tales, and they believed them not."

  I wonder, brethren, if we are guilty of the same thing when we do not take seriously the contributions of our faithful women. What is it about the male ego that responds this way? Our ward and stake councils are not whole if they do not include the advice and the testimony of our sisters. These good men had heard the Savior say on multiple occasions that He would die and rise again. Yet, they did not remember those words until the Savior Himself reminded them after His resurrection. He also chided them for their faithlessness when they rejected the multiple witnesses of the women and of the disciples who saw the Lord on the road to Emmaus (see Mark 16:14).

The Witness of Simon Peter

- **Luke 24:12, 33–34 After his visit to the tomb, Peter sees the risen Lord.** Luke says that he "departed, wondering in himself at that which was come to pass" (v. 12). Then later, when the two disciples who were on the way to Emmaus returned to "the eleven gathered together, and them that were with them," the Apostles said to them, "The Lord is risen indeed, and hath appeared to Simon" (vv. 33–34).

THEBIBLEREVIVAL.COM, #26

It was no longer a "women's tale," but a certainty of which Peter was now a personal witness. He received that witness sometime between his visit to the empty tomb and the arrival from Emmaus of the other disciples.

We should not fail to notice that the first of the apostles to see the risen Lord was Peter, who Jesus had selected to lead the Church after His departure.

The Witness of Luke and Cleopas

THEBIBLEREVIVAL.COM, #25

- **Luke 24:13–24 Christ appears to Luke and Cleopas on their way to Emmaus.** Cleopas and his companion (Luke) were traveling on the road toward Emmaus (v. 13). They "talked together of all these things which had happened" and "while they communed together and reasoned, Jesus himself drew near, and went with them," but "their eyes were holden that they should not know him" (vv. 14–16). Jesus asked them what they were discussing and why they were so sad (v. 17). Cleopas answered, "Art thou only a stranger in Jerusalem, and hast not known the things which are come to pass there in these days?" (v. 18). And when Jesus asked "What things?" they said, "Concerning Jesus of Nazareth, which was a prophet mighty in deed and word before God and all the people: And how the chief priests and our rulers delivered him to be condemned to death, and have crucified him" (vv. 19–20).

They were sad because they "trusted that it had been he which should have redeemed Israel," but now He was gone and "to day is the third day since these things were done" (v. 21). They spoke of "certain women also of our company made us astonished, which were early at the sepulchre; And when they found not his body, they came, saying, that they had also seen a vision of angels, which said that he was alive" (vv. 22–23). But when "certain of them which were with us went to the sepulchre," they "found it . . . as the women had said: but him [Jesus] they saw not" (v. 24).

- **Luke 24:25–27 Christ teaches them as they walk.** He remonstrated, "O fools, and slow of heart to believe all that the prophets have spoken: Ought not Christ to have suffered these things, and to enter into his glory? And beginning at Moses and all the prophets, he expounded unto them in all the scriptures the things concerning himself."

- **Luke 24:28–31 "Abide with us . . . for it is toward evening."** They arrived at their destination and Jesus "made as though he would have gone further," when they "constrained him, saying, Abide with us: for it is toward evening, and the day is far spent" (vv. 28–29). He agreed "to tarry with them" and "sat at meat with them," and "took bread, and blessed it, and brake, and gave to them" (vv. 29–30).

C. H. BLOCH

- **Luke 24:31–32 Having felt the Spirit, they now recognize that the man is Jesus.** "Their eyes were opened, and they knew him; and he vanished out of their sight" (v. 31). "And they said one to another, Did not our heart burn within us, while he talked with us by the way, and while he opened to us the scriptures?" (v. 32). This was the sure sign of the Spirit, bearing witness to their souls that Jesus is the Christ. They felt it as they discussed and pondered the scriptures concerning Him, just as we do when we sincerely seek Him.

- **Mark 16:13–14 The Apostles do not believe them.** They hastened back to where the Apostles were gathered and told them of their experience, but just as they had not believed the witness of Mary, "neither believed they them" (v. 13). For this, the Lord later "upbraided them [for] their unbelief and hardness of heart, because they believed not them which had seen him after he was risen" (v. 14).

- **Luke 24:33–35 The witness of Peter changes their minds.** Luke says that when the two Emmaus witnesses returned to Jerusalem, the Apostles said, "The Lord is risen indeed, and hath appeared to Simon" (vv. 33–34). So apparently, after so many witnesses, now including their leader Peter, their hearts softened and they believed the report: Christ is risen. He had conquered death. And He would visit them soon.

"A Spirit Hath Not Flesh and Bones, as Ye See Me Have"

- **Luke 24:36 Jesus appears to the Apostles.** They had gathered together to speak of recent events, and "as they thus spake, Jesus himself stood in the midst of them, and saith unto them, Peace be unto you."

- **Luke 24:37–43 Resurrected beings have "flesh and bone" and can eat.** At first, they were "terrified and affrighted, and supposed that they had seen a spirit" (v. 37). But Jesus calmed their fears and showed them the *physical* nature of His resurrected body. "Behold my hands and my feet, that it is I myself: handle me, and see; for a spirit hath not flesh and bones, as ye see me have" (vv. 38–39).

Having never seen a resur ected person before, they "believed not for joy, and wondered" how this could be. So, to demonstrate, He said unto them, "Have ye here any meat? And they gave him a piece of a broiled fish, and of an honeycomb. And he took it, and did eat before them" (vv. 40–43).

"Handle me and see

His resurrection was not merely spiritual. He rose physically from the dead and took great pains on this occasion to make" that fact perfectly clear. How, then, can believing Christians, who claim to believe the Bible, say otherwise? The scriptures are very clear on this matter.

- **Luke 24:44–48 Jesus teaches them and calls them "witnesses of these things."** He reminded them of "the words which I spake unto you, while I was yet with you, that all things must be fulfilled, which were written in the law of Moses, and in the prophets, and in the psalms, concerning me" (v. 44). Then He expounded upon the scriptures so that they might understand them (v. 45). "And [Jesus] said unto them, Thus it is written, and thus it behoved Christ to suffer, and to rise from the dead the third day: And that repentance and remission of sins should be preached in his name among all nations, beginning at Jerusalem. And ye are witnesses of these things" (vv. 46–48).

- **John 20:24–25 Thomas was not there and did not believe them.** For whatever reason, he "was not with them when Jesus came" (v. 24). So, when the other disciples said to him, "We have seen the Lord," he did not believe them. He declared, "Except I shall see in his hands the print of the nails, and put my finger into the print of the nails, and thrust my hand into his side, I will not believe" (v. 25).

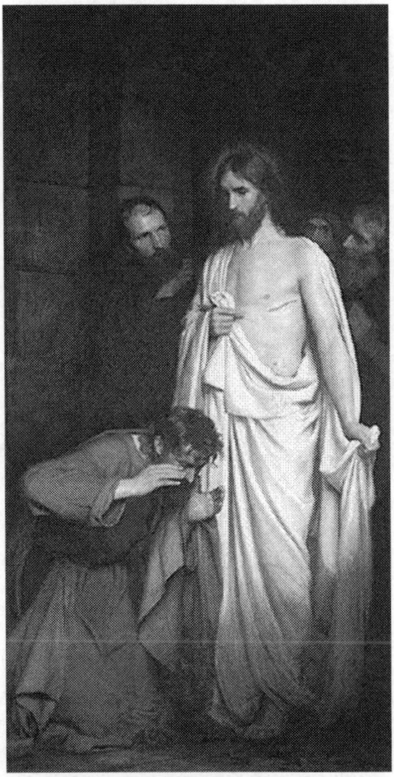
C. H. BLOCH

- **John 20:26–29 Jesus appears 8 days later to all of the Apostles, including Thomas.** This time Thomas was with them, and "then came Jesus, the doors being shut, and stood in the midst, and said, Peace be unto you" (v. 26). Turning toward Thomas, the Lord commanded, "Reach hither thy finger, and behold my hands; and reach hither thy hand, and thrust it into my side: and be not faithless, but believing" (v. 27). Thomas apparently did so, and then exclaimed, "My Lord and my God" (v. 28).

  Thomas, of course, has become a metaphor for faithlessness— "doubting Thomas"—and is frequently cited in discussions of those who demand signs in order to believe. But Jesus did not severely condemn him. He said, "Thomas, because thou hast seen me, thou hast believed: blessed are they that have not seen, and yet have believed" (v. 29).

  Elder Gordon B. Hinckley said: "Have you not heard others speak as Thomas spoke? 'Give us,' they say, 'the empirical evidence. Prove before our very eyes, and our ears, and our hands, else we will not believe.' This is the language of the time in which we live. Thomas the Doubter has become the example of men in all ages who refuse to accept other than that which they can physically prove and explain—as if they could prove love, or faith, or even such physical phenomena as electricity. . .

To all within the sound of my voice who may have doubts, I repeat the words given Thomas as he felt the wounded hands of the Lord: 'Be not faithless, but believing.'"[5]

Thomas continued faithful the rest of his life. Although the apocryphal sources do not strictly agree on the exact destination of Thomas, they all concur that he went to the East. Eusebius says Parthia (India) was allotted to Thomas. *The Acts of Thomas*, a work originally composed in Syriac at an unknown date, claims to chronicle Thomas's activities as the Apostle to India. According to legend, Thomas died when he was run through with a lance, on the coast of Coromandel, in the East Indies.[6]

The Apostles in Galilee

- **Matthew 28:16–18 All eleven Apostles meet Him on a mountain in Galilee.** This was the fulfillment of the promise of the newly-resurrected Lord given to them through the women: "Be not afraid: go tell my brethren that they go into Galilee, and there shall they see me" (Matthew 28:10).

Obedient to this instruction, "the eleven disciples went away into Galilee, into a mountain where Jesus had appointed them. And when they saw him, they worshipped him," but surprisingly Matthew records that "some doubted" (vv. 16–17). We know nothing more about this comment. But while teaching them there, the Lord explained that, now that He had risen from the dead, "All power is given unto me in heaven and in earth" (v. 18).

Seven Apostles at the Sea of Galilee

GUSTAVE DORÉ, 1896

- **John 21:1–15 The Lord appears again on the shores of the Sea of Galilee.** We will discuss what happened there in more detail in the following chapter on Christ's 40-day ministry. For purposes of this summary, suffice it to say that "Jesus shewed himself again to [seven of] the disciples at the sea of Tiberias" (v. 1).

  Those in attendance were Peter, Thomas, Nathanael, James and John (the sons of Zebedee), and two other of His disciples (v. 2). They had evidently returned to their fishing activities (v. 3), which they had abandoned three years earlier when they chose to follow Jesus.

  As He had done when He first met them, the Lord inquired whether they had had any success (which they hadn't), and then provided a miracle catch for them, which "they were not able to draw it for the multitude of fishes" (vv. 5–6). These two "miracles of the fishes" stand like bookends on the ministry of Jesus Christ. By this means He called His chief disciples and by the same means He announced His presence again on this occasion.

  They rushed to shore and there Jesus taught them. We will discuss the details of those teachings in the following chapter. But it is interesting that, although they had by now seen Him at least twice before (three times for some of them), they didn't recognize Him at first. Peter declared, "It is the Lord," jumping into the water and swimming to the shore (v. 7). The others came by boat, and when they arrived they found "a fire of coals there, and fish laid thereon, and bread" (v. 9)—apparently prepared by the Lord. None of the disciples dared ask Him,

"Who art thou? knowing that it was the Lord" (v. 12). Then they all dined together, presumably including the resurrected Lord (v. 15).

More than 500 Disciples at Once

- **1 Corinthians 15:3–6 More than 500 disciples saw Him** on one occasion. The Apostle Paul testified that He had heard the witnesses of "Cephas [Peter], then of the twelve," and finally of more than "five hundred brethren" who had seen Him "at once" (vv. 5–6), presumably during His 40-day post-resurrection ministry in Galilee. Paul noted that "the greater part" of these 500-plus witnesses "remain unto this present, but some are fallen asleep" (v. 6).

James, the Brother of the Lord

EARLY IMAGE OF JAMES, THE BROTHER OF THE LORD

- **1 Corinthians 15:7 James presided over the Church at Jerusalem.** Paul reports in this scripture that the resurrected Lord was "seen of James." This James was a son of Mary and a half-brother to our Lord. He apparently accepted the gospel after the resurrection of Christ, because John reports that prior to Jesus' last journey to Jerusalem and His crucifixion, "neither did his brethren believe" that He was the Christ (John 7:5). Perhaps this vision was part of that conversion.

He is the author of the book of James in our modern Bible. When Peter was delivered from prison he gave instruction that word should be taken to "James, and to the brethren" in Jerusalem (Acts 12:17). This would indicate that James had oversight over the church at Jerusalem (see Acts 15:13), and he is therefore widely referred to as "the Bishop of Jerusalem." Later, after the death of some Apostles, James may have been ordained an Apostle, and may even have replaced John's brother James in the First Presidency after the earlier James was martyred at Jerusalem.

According to Paul's own words, there were only two Apostles at Jerusalem when he was taken there to report on his missionary work—Peter and James the brother of the Lord (see Galatians 1:18–19). In fact, James conducted that Jerusalem Council. And Paul called Peter, John, and James the brother of the Lord the "pillars" of the Church (Galatians 2:9). Tradition says that James the brother of the Lord was eventually martyred in Jerusalem.[7]

The Apostle Paul

REMBRANT

- **Acts 9:1–6 The Apostle Paul saw Him in vision on the road to Damascus.** It was an open vision in broad daylight, given when Paul was on the way to persecute some of the Master's most faithful disciples. When the Being who appeared to Paul asked him why he was persecuting Him, and Paul responded, "Who art thou, Lord?" He identified Himself plainly as "Jesus whom thou persecutest" (vv. 4–5). This life-changing vision was sufficient to sustain Paul through every travail and in every circumstance for the remainder of his life. He knew personally the Lord whom he served.

The Apostle John

RUBENS, 1613

- **Revelation 1:10–19 The Apostle John saw Him in vision on the Isle of Patmos.** He reports being "in the Spirit on the Lord's day," when he "heard behind me a great voice, as of a trumpet, Saying, I am Alpha and Omega, the first and the last: and, What thou seest, write in a book" (vv.

10–11), which became the book of the Revelations of John. He saw "seven golden candlesticks; And in the midst of the seven candlesticks one like unto the Son of man, clothed with a garment down to the foot, and girt about the paps with a golden girdle. His head and his hairs were white like wool, as white as snow; and his eyes were as a flame of fire; And his feet like unto fine brass, as if they burned in a furnace; and his voice as the sound of many waters" (vv. 12–15). This description is very much like those described by Ezekiel and Daniel in Old Testament times. "And when I saw him, I fell at his feet as dead. And he laid his right hand upon me, saying unto me, Fear not; I am the first and the last: I am he that liveth, and was dead; and, behold, I am alive for evermore, Amen; and have the keys of hell and of death" (vv. 17–18). This was, without doubt, the Lord Jesus Christ who stood before John.

Many Who Saw Other Resurrected Beings

- **Matthew 27:52–53 Many faithful Saints were resurrected shortly after Christ arose.** Matthew testified that "the graves were opened; and many bodies of the saints which slept arose, And came out of the graves after his resurrection, and went into the holy city, and appeared unto many."

Elder Bruce R. McConkie explained that "Christ was the firstfruits of the resurrection (1 Corinthians 15:23), and because of His resurrec-tion, 'by the power of God,' all men shall come forth from the grave (Mormon 9:13). . . . To those who lived before the resurrection of Christ, the day of His coming forth from the dead was known as the first resurrection. Abinadi and Alma, for instance, so considered it (Mosiah 15:21–25; Alma 40). To those who have lived since that day, the first resurrection is yet future and will take place at the time of the Second Coming (D&C 88:96–102). We have no knowledge that the resurrection is going on now or that any persons have been resurrected since the day in which Christ came forth excepting Peter, James, and Moroni, all of whom had special labors to perform in this day which necessitated tangible resurrected bodies."[8]

The Nephites in the Western Hemisphere

- **3 Nephi 11:14–15 Jesus appeared also to the Nephites.** To a world that now openly doubts the reality of the resurrection of Christ, the Lord has provided another witness of His divinity—the Book of Mormon. According to this book of scripture, derived from the Lord's prophets in the Western Hemisphere, Jesus Christ appeared to His faithful followers shortly after His resurrection. Descending from the skies, He stood before them and invited them to come forward, one at a time, and handle Him. Thus, as with Thomas, about 2,500 men, women, and children received their own special witness that Jesus is the Christ and that He lives (see 3 Nephi 17:25). On the occasion of His visit to the Nephites, He said:

©JOSEPH BRICKEY, USED BY PERMISSION

> Arise and come forth unto me, that ye may thrust your hands into my side, and also that ye may feel the prints of the nails in my hands and in my feet, that ye may know that I am the God of Israel, and the God of the whole earth, and have been slain for the sins of the world.
>
> And it came to pass that the multitude went forth, and thrust their hands into his side, and did feel the prints of the nails in his hands and in his feet; and this they did do, going forth one by one until they had all gone forth, and did see with their eyes and did feel with their hands, and did know of a surety and did bear record, that it was he, of whom it was written by the prophets, that should come.

SUNDAY — THE NEW SABBATH DAY

- **Mark 16:9 "The first day of the week" became the new Sabbath day.** Jesus arose from the dead on Sunday morning (see John 20:1). And thereafter, His disciples assembled to worship on the first day of the week rather than on Saturday (see Acts 20:7). This supernal event, the rising of Christ from the dead, was of such great significance to the entire world that His disciples have, ever since, made it their new Sabbath day.

Elder Bruce R. McConkie said: "Because Jesus came forth from the grave on the first day of the week, to commemorate that day and to keep in remembrance the glorious reality of the resurrection, the ancient Apostles, as guided by the Spirit, changed the Sabbath to Sunday. That this change had divine approval we know from latter-day revelation, in which Deity speaks of 'the Lord's day' . . . (D&C 59:9–17)."[9]

Elder Mark E. Petersen said: ". . . Let us ask ourselves how important the Lord's Atonement is to us. How dear to us is the Lord Jesus Christ? How deeply are we concerned about immortality? Is the resurrection of vital interest to us? We can readily see that observance of the Sabbath is an indication of the depth of our conversion. Our observance or nonobservance of the Sabbath is an unerring measure of our attitude toward the Lord personally and toward His suffering in Gethsemane, His death on the cross, and His resurrection from the dead. It is a sign of whether we are Christians in very deed, or whether our conversion is so shallow that commemoration of His atoning sacrifice means little or nothing to us."[10]

ATTEMPTS TO DISCREDIT THE RESURRECTION

Early Attempts to Discredit the Resurrection

- **John 2:18–21 Jesus prophesied that He would be resurrected.** Very early in His ministry, the Jewish leaders had demanded a sign that He was the promised Messiah (v. 18). Jesus responded with this one: "Destroy this temple, and in three days I will raise it up" (v. 19). They pretended not to understand that "he spake of the temple of his body" (v. 21), and said to Him, "Forty and six years was this temple [of Herod] in building, and wilt thou rear it up in three days?" (v. 20). This was a ruse, because they understood perfectly what He meant, as evidenced by what they said and did after His death.

- **Matthew 27:62–66 The Pharisees and chief priests remember Jesus' prophecy.** Friday, the day of Jesus' death, was "the day of the preparation," so they waited until the next day (Saturday) to make their request to Pilate (v. 62). Note that on this, the second day, Jesus' body still lay in the tomb. To Pilate they said, "Sir, we remember that that deceiver said, while he was yet alive, After three days I will rise again. Command therefore that the sepulchre be made sure until the third day, lest his disciples come by night, and steal him away, and say unto the people, He is risen from the dead: so the last error shall be worse than the first" (vv. 63–64). Pilate agreed, saying, "Ye have a watch: go your way, make it as sure as ye can. So they went, and made the sepulchre sure, sealing the stone, and setting a watch" (vv. 65–66).

- **Matthew 28:11–15 Jewish leaders bribe the soldiers into silence.** The soldiers had run "into the city, and shewed unto the chief priests all the things that were done" when the angels descended (v. 11). And as always, rather than consider what these things might mean, the Pharisees and Sadducees "[took] counsel" and then "gave large money unto the soldiers" to keep silent (v. 12). They instructed the soldiers to say, "His disciples came by night, and stole him away while we slept" (v. 13). And they promised that, if the matter came before Pilate, "we will persuade him, and secure you" (v. 14). "So they took the money, and did as they were taught: and this saying is commonly reported among the Jews until this day" (v. 15).

Modern Doubts about the Resurrection

Studies show that many ministers or leaders of Christian churches today do not believe in a literal resurrection. A survey done by *Redbook* magazine[11] revealed the following information about those who were about to graduate and go into a full-time pastorship of a church or ministry in the United States:

— 56% rejected the virgin birth of Jesus Christ.

— 71% rejected the view of any life after death.
— 54% rejected the bodily resurrection of Jesus Christ.
— 98% rejected the idea that Jesus Christ would ever return to the earth.

To most of these "Christians," resurrection is a figurative concept, and it means something like the spirit rising to a heaven. They teach that we will be judged at the time of our death, with punishments or rewards at that time. The resurrection has no specific purpose in their doctrine. This is one reason why the Book of Mormon is so important as another witness of Jesus Christ.

Elder Boyd K. Packer announced in the October 1982 general conference: "You should know . . . that by recent decision of the Brethren the Book of Mormon will henceforth bear the title 'The Book of Mormon,' with the subtitle 'Another Testament of Jesus Christ.'"[12] This was not a new idea. The title page of the book has declared from the very beginning that testifying of Christ is one of its primary purposes. But the importance of highlighting that purpose has become clear in a world that increasingly doubts the divinity of Jesus Christ.

LATTER-DAY WITNESSES

Modern Witnesses of the Risen Christ

Because Christ had not appeared to any of them for hundreds of years, since the deaths of the Apostles, the Councils of the early Christian church started declaring doctrine by vote rather than revelation. Since revelation had ceased, they reasoned, we would receive no more word of God and would have to rely on what had already been given. This was the same mistake the Pharisees made, worshiping the law and their interpretations of it rather than the revealed word of God that was standing in front of them.

And so it is today, that the Christian world denies that Christ has appeared to any prophet after the days of the meridian Apostles—though they might admit He has appeared to a Saint or two. Meanwhile, the heavens have opened and the resurrected Christ has declared a new and final dispensation of His work. And by these appearances we know that He was indeed resurrected and that He lives.

- **JS–History 1:14–17 Christ appeared to Joseph Smith in a glorious first vision in 1820.** The boy prophet did not expect any such thing when he went into the grove of trees behind his family's farm home. He was simply seeking an answer to prayer—though it was, he tells us, his first vocal prayer (v. 14).

He "kneeled down and began to offer up the desires of my heart to God," when Satan seized upon him, attempting to frighten him away from his purpose (v. 15). "But, exerting all my powers to call upon God to deliver me out of the power of this enemy which had seized upon me, and at the very moment when I was ready to sink into despair and abandon myself to destruction— not to an imaginary ruin, but to the power of some actual being from the unseen world, who had such marvelous power as I had never before felt in any being—just at this moment of great alarm, I saw a pillar of light exactly over my head, above the brightness of the sun, which descended gradually until it fell upon me" (v. 16).

"It no sooner appeared than I found myself delivered from the enemy which held me bound. When the light rested upon me I saw two Personages, whose brightness and glory defy all description, standing above me in the air. One of them spake unto me, calling me by name and said, pointing to the other—*This is My Beloved Son. Hear Him!*" (v. 17).

- **D&C 76:19–24 Christ appeared to Joseph Smith and Sidney Rigdon at Hiram, Ohio**, on February 16, 1832. They were working on a new translation of the Bible and pondering and praying about what

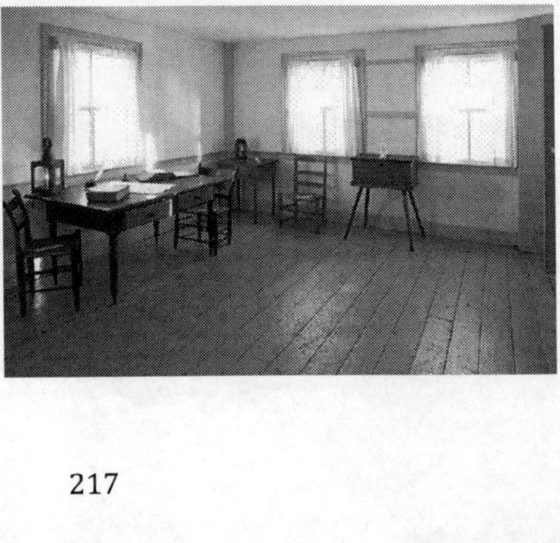

they had received, when "the Lord touched the eyes of our understandings and they were opened, and the glory of the Lord shone round about. And we beheld the glory of the Son, on the right hand of the Father, and received of his fulness; And saw the holy angels, and them who are sanctified before his throne, worshiping God, and the Lamb, who worship him forever and ever" (vv. 19–21).

"And now, after the many testimonies which have been given of him, this is the testimony, last of all, which we give of him: That he lives! For we saw him, even on the right hand of God; and we heard the voice bearing record that he is the Only Begotten of the Father—That by him, and through him, and of him, the worlds are and were created, and the inhabitants thereof are begotten sons and daughters unto God" (vv. 22–24).

- **D&C 110:2–4 Christ appeared to Joseph Smith and Oliver Cowdery in the Kirtland Temple** on April 3, 1836. They declared, "We saw the Lord standing upon the breastwork of the pulpit, before us; and under his feet was a paved work of pure gold, in color like amber. His eyes were as a flame of fire; the hair of his head was white like the pure snow; his countenance shone above the brightness of the sun; and his voice was as the sound of the rushing of great waters, even the voice of Jehovah, saying: I am the first and the last; I am he who liveth, I am he who was slain; I am your advocate with the Father."

- **He has appeared to many other prophets and faithful Saints in the latter days.** The Prophet Joseph Smith said: ". . . God hath not revealed anything to Joseph, but what He will make known unto the Twelve, and even the least Saint may know all things as fast as he is able to bear them, for the day must come when no man need say to his neighbor, Know ye the Lord; for all shall know Him (who remain) from the least to the greatest."[13] The number of people who have seen Christ cannot be listed here, but suffice it to say that there are many since 1820 who have that witness. Chief among these are the Apostles and prophets who have led this Church during the past two centuries. Christ lives, and there are many of us who can bear personal witness to that fact. He has not hidden Himself in some far corner of the universe but continues to direct the affairs of His people and His Church today.

WHAT WE BELIEVE ABOUT THE RESURRECTION

The Resurrection Is Literal

- **Job 14:7–14 "If a man die, shall he live again?"** Job reflected on this question while suffering some of the most difficult adversities ever given to one man. He noticed that "there is hope of a tree, if it be cut down, that it will sprout again, and that the tender branch thereof will not cease. Though the root thereof wax old in the earth, and the stock thereof die in the ground; Yet through the scent of water it will bud, and bring forth boughs like a plant" (vv. 7–9).

  But what about man? Death seems so total and everlasting to those who are left behind. "Man dieth, and wasteth away: yea, man giveth up the ghost, and where is he? As the waters fail from the sea, and the flood decayeth and drieth up: So man lieth down, and riseth not: till the heavens be no more, they shall not awake, nor be raised out of their sleep" (vv. 10–12). "If a man die, shall he live again?" Job asked, and then provided the answer with great testimony:

- **Job 19:25–27 "I know that my redeemer liveth, and . . . in my flesh shall I see God."** Understanding the connection between the Messiah and the resurrection, Job testified, "I know that my redeemer liveth, and that he shall stand at the latter day upon the earth: And though after my [death] worms destroy this body, yet in my flesh shall I see God: Whom I shall see for myself, and mine eyes shall behold, and not another; though my reins [organs] be consumed within me."

B. PICART, 1728

- **Ezekiel 37:1–10 Ezekiel saw a valley full of bones resurrected to life.** He received a vision in which the Lord "carried me out . . . and set me down in the midst of the valley which was full of bones, And caused me to pass by them round about: and, behold, there were very many in the open valley; and, lo, they were very dry. And he said unto me, Son of man, can these bones live? And I answered, O Lord God, thou knowest" (vv. 1–3).

  The Lord then invited Ezekiel to prophesy unto the bones, saying, "O ye dry bones, hear the word of the Lord. . . . Behold, I will cause breath to enter into you, and ye shall live: And I will lay sinews upon you, and will bring up flesh upon you, and cover you with skin, and put breath in you, and ye shall live; and ye shall know that I am the Lord" (vv. 4–6).

  Ezekiel did as he was instructed, and "as I prophesied, there was a noise, and behold a shaking, and the bones came together, bone to his bone. And when I beheld, lo, the sinews and the flesh came up upon them, and the skin covered them above: but there was no breath in them" (vv. 7–8). So the Lord commanded Ezekiel to "breathe upon these slain, that they may live. So I prophesied as he commanded me, and the breath came into them, and they lived, and stood up upon their feet, an exceeding great army" (vv. 9–10).

- **Luke 24:36–43 Jesus demonstrated the tangible nature of a resurrected body.** Despite the attempts of modern theologians to "spiritualize" the resurrection, the Bible tells us otherwise. When Jesus appeared unto the Apostles, they "supposed that they had seen a spirit" (vv. 36–37). But He wanted them to understand the literal and physical nature of a resurrected being, so He invited them to "behold my hands and my feet, that it is I myself: handle me, and see; for a spirit hath not flesh and bones, as ye see me have" (v. 39). Then, He proceeded to eat in front of them so they could understand that the resurrection is literal and physical and not merely spiritual (vv. 42–43). How can any person who claims to believe the Bible think otherwise?

The Resurrection Is Universal

- **1 Corinthians 15:20–22 Just as all men die, all men shall be resurrected.** Paul said that Christ rose from the dead as "the firstfruits of them that slept" (v. 20). And he explained that this was done "since by man came death" and therefore "by man came also the resurrection of the dead. For as in Adam *all die*, even so in Christ shall *all be made alive*" (vv. 21–22; emphasis added). Since the resurrection is as sure and as universal as death itself, it will include the wicked as well as the righteous. The only difference will be the timing of each individual's resurrection and the type of body they will possess as they rise (see 1 Corinthians 15:40–42; D&C 76).

F. COLLANTES, 1630

- **Alma 11:41–45 All people will rise from the dead and be judged of God.** Amulek explained that because the Atonement of Christ will benefit only those who have repented, "the wicked remain as though there had been no redemption made, except it be the loosing of the bands of death; for behold, the day cometh that all shall rise from the dead and stand before God, and be judged according to their works" (v. 41). "The death of Christ shall loose the bands of this temporal death, that all shall be raised from this temporal death" (v. 42).

Amulek then described the resurrection in this way: "The spirit and the body shall be reunited again in its perfect form; both limb and joint shall be restored to its proper frame, even as we now are at this time; and we shall be brought to stand before God, knowing even as we know now, and have a bright recollection of all our guilt" (v. 43). Thus, our bodies will be "perfect" (without defect or deformity) and reconstructed according to our "perfect frame" (genetic code). Thus, I will look like me and you will look like you; each will be a perfected version of the original.

"Now, this restoration shall come to all, both old and young, both bond and free, both male and female, both the wicked and the righteous; and even there shall not so much as a hair of their heads be lost; but every thing shall be restored to its perfect frame, as it is now, or in the body, and shall be brought and be arraigned before the bar of Christ the Son, and God the Father, and the Holy Spirit, which is one Eternal God, to be judged according to their works, whether they be good or whether they be evil" (v. 44). "I say unto you that this mortal body is raised to an immortal body, that is from death, even from the first death unto life, that they can die no more; their spirits uniting with their bodies, never to be divided; thus the whole becoming spiritual and immortal, that they can no more see corruption" (v. 45).

Modern Witnesses of the Resurrection

The Prophet Joseph Smith said:

> Would you think it strange that I relate what I have seen in vision in relation [to] this interesting theme[?] Those who have died in Jesus Christ, may expect to enter into all that fruition of joy when they come forth, which they have pursued here.
>
> So plain was the vision I actually saw men before they had ascended from the tomb as though they were getting up slowly. They take each other by the hand. It was my father and my son, my mother and my daughter, my brother and my

sister. When the voice calls suppose I am laid by the side of my father. What would be the first joy of my heart? Where is my father, my mother, my sister? They are by my side. I embrace them and they me. . . .

> . . . All your losses will be made up to you in the resurrection provided you continue faithful. By the vision of the Almighty I have seen it. . . . God has revealed His Son from the heavens and the doctrine of the resurrection also. We have a knowledge that those we bury here God [will] bring them up again, clothed upon and quickened by the spirit of the Great God.[14]

The Prophet Joseph Smith also said:

> You mourners have occasion to rejoice, . . . for your [loved one] is gone to wait until the resurrection of the dead—until the perfection of the remainder; for at the resurrection your friend will rise in perfect felicity and go to celestial glory, while many must wait myriads of years before they can receive the like blessings; and your expectations and hopes are far above what man can conceive . . . I am authorized to say, by the authority of the Holy Ghost, that you have no occasion to fear; for he is gone to the home of the just. Don't mourn; don't weep. I know it by the testimony of the Holy Ghost that is within me; and you may wait for your friends to come forth to meet you in the morn of the celestial world. . . .
>
> I have a father, brothers, children, and friends who have gone to a world of spirits. They are only absent for a moment. They are in the spirit, and we shall soon meet again. The time will soon arrive when the trumpet shall sound. When we depart, we shall hail our mothers, fathers, friends, and all whom we love, who have fallen asleep in Jesus. . . . It will be an eternity of felicity.[15]

President Gordon B. Hinckley said:

> . . . Death is not final. Though it seems so when its dark shroud overshadows mortal life, to those who accept the Christ and His eternal mission there is light and comfort, there is assurance, there is certainty. . . .
>
> Of all the victories in human history, none is so great, none so universal in its effect, none so everlasting in its consequences

as the victory of the crucified Lord who came forth in the Resurrection that first Easter morning.

We laud the captains and the kings, we praise the nations that are victorious against oppressors. We appropriately build monuments to remember their sacrifices and their triumphs over the forces of oppression. But great and important as are these achievements, none can compare with the victory of the lonely, pain-racked figure on Calvary's cross who triumphed over death and brought the gift of eternal life to all mankind.[16]

Notes

1. For an explanation of this precise date, see John P. Pratt, "The Restoration of Priesthood Keys on Easter 1836, Part 1: Dating the First Easter," *Ensign*, June 1985, 59–68. See also *The Life and Teachings of Jesus and His Apostles* [1979], 137, 190, 198.

2. In Conference Report, Apr. 1996, 90; or *Ensign*, May 1996, 66. In Conference Report, Apr. 1988, 78; or *Ensign,* May 1988, 67.

3. In Conference Report, Apr. 1978, 13; or *Ensign,* May 1978, 10.

4. *Doctrinal New Testament Commentary,* 3 vols. [1965–73], 1:843, 846.

5. In Conference Report, Apr. 1978, 90; or *Ensign*, May 1978, 59.

6. Adapted from S. Kent Brown and Wilfred C. Griggs, "The Postresurrection Ministry," in Robert L. Millet, ed., *Studies in Scripture, Volume 6: Acts to Revelation* [1987], 17–18.

7. Adapted from Larry E. Dahl, "A String of Gospel Pearls," in Robert L. Millet, ed., *Studies in Scripture, Volume 6: Acts to Revelation* [1987], 207–8.

8. *Mormon Doctrine*, 2nd ed. [1966], 639.

9. *Doctrinal New Testament Commentary*, 1:841.

10. In Conference Report, Apr. 1975, 72; or *Ensign*, May 1975, 49.

11. *Redbook*, quoted by Ron Bernier, "A Note from Pastor Ron and the Staff of Into the Light Ministries," http://www. intothelight.org/info. asp (accessed July 12, 2007).

12. In Conference Report, Oct. 1982, 75; or *Ensign,* Nov. 1982, 53.

13. *History of the Church*, 3:380.

14. *An American Prophet's Record: The Diaries and Journals of Joseph Smith*, ed. Scott H. Faulring [1989], 366, 367.

15. *History of the Church*, 6:315, 316.

16. In Conference Report, Apr. 1988, 76, 77; or *Ensign,* May 1988, 66.

CHAPTER 9

CHRIST'S 40-DAY MINISTRY AND ASCENSION

(MATTHEW 28; LUKE 24; JOHN 20–21)

THE FORTY-DAY MINISTRY

After His resurrection, the Lord appeared regularly to the Apostles and instructed them. While we do have scriptural accounts of some of these appearances, we have very little information about what He taught them. For that, we are dependent on slivers of information found in the Gospels and in Acts, and also on the Apocrypha and the writings of the early Christian Fathers—those who were personally familiar with the Apostles and who wrote concerning the Church during the second century (A.D. 100–200). The reason for the sparsity of information seems to be the nature of those teachings. The Lord was instructing them in the higher ordinances and principles of His gospel that were never intended to be widely distributed to the world.

C.H. BLOCH

Keys from the Mount of Transfiguration

- **Matthew 17:9; Mark 9:9 Doctrines that must be withheld until after His resurrection.** The first scriptural indication that some things were not to be discussed until after Christ's resurrection came on the Mount of Transfiguration. As we know, it was on that mount that Peter, James, and John received keys from ancient prophets that they would be expected to exercise on behalf of the Church. But "as they came down from the mountain, Jesus charged them, saying, Tell the vision to no man, until the Son of man be risen again from the dead" (Matthew 17:9). Mark says that "he charged them that they should tell no man what things they had seen, till the Son of man were risen from the dead" (Mark 9:9).

Elder Bruce R. McConkie said:

> Moses and Elijah—two ancient prophets who were translated and taken to heaven without tasting death, so they could return with tangible bodies on this very occasion, an occasion preceding the day of resurrection—appeared on the mountain; and they and Jesus gave the keys of the kingdom to Peter, James, and John.[1] . . . John the Baptist, previously beheaded by Herod, apparently was also present. . . . Peter, James, and John saw in vision the transfiguration of the earth, that is, they saw it renewed and returned to its paradisiacal state—an event that is to take place at the Second Coming when the millennial era is ushered in (see D&C 63:20–21).[2]
>
> . . . It appears that Peter, James, and John received their own endowments while on the mountain.[3] . . . Peter says that while there, they "received from God the Father honour and glory," seemingly bearing out this conclusion. It also appears that it was while on the mount that they received the more sure word of prophecy, it then being revealed to them that they were sealed up unto eternal life (see 2 Peter 1:16–19; D&C 131:5).[4]

Why Did Moses and Elijah Appear?

Members of the Church will recognize immediately that these same ancient prophets appeared to Joseph Smith and Oliver Cowdery in the Kirtland Temple on April 3, 1836. Thus we can see how the Lord establishes His Church in any dispensation. He brings back those ancient prophets who held the appropriate keys of the priesthood and has them bestow them on the leaders of a new dispensation. That was the case in Kirtland and it was also the case on the Mount of Transfiguration. But why send Moses and Elijah?

The Prophet Joseph Smith said: "Elijah was the last prophet that held the [sealing] keys of the priesthood, and who will, before the last dispensation, restore the authority and deliver the [sealing] keys of the priesthood, in order that all the ordinances may be attended to in righteousness. It is true the Savior had authority and power to bestow this blessing; but the sons of Levi were too prejudiced. . . . Why send Elijah? Because he holds the keys of the authority to administer in all the [sealing] ordinances of the priesthood; and without the authority is given, the ordinances could not be administered in righteousness."[5]

President Joseph Fielding Smith explained:

> The keys that Elijah held were the keys of the everlasting priesthood, the keys of the sealing power, which the Lord gave unto him. And that is what he . . . gave to the Prophet Joseph Smith; and that included a ministry of sealing for the living as well as the dead—and it is not confined to the living and it is not confined to the dead, but includes them both. . . .
>
> Elijah's mission was the sealing power. He held the keys by which the parents could be sealed together and children sealed to parents. He bestowed these keys upon the Prophet Joseph Smith. And that applies to the dead as well as the living since the coming of the Lord Jesus Christ.
>
> . . . But what was the nature of his mission to the earth in these latter days? It was to restore power and authority which once was given to men on the earth and which is essential to the complete salvation and exaltation of man in the kingdom of God. In other words, Elijah came to restore to the earth, by conferring on mortal prophets duly commissioned of the Lord, the fulness of the power of priesthood. This priesthood holds the keys of binding and sealing on earth and in heaven of all the ordinances and principles pertaining to the salvation of man, that they may thus become valid in the celestial kingdom of God.[6]

Peter, James, and John received the keys of the gathering from Moses and the sealing keys from Elijah on the Mount of Transfiguration. However, they were expressly forbidden from teaching these doctrines until after the death and resurrection of our Lord. Now, after those great events had occurred, the Lord proceeded to teach the Apostles concerning these and other exalting doctrines. That was the purpose of the 40-day ministry, and we will review in this chapter those things that were most probably taught at that time.

THE RESURRECTED LORD IN GALILEE

"Feed My Sheep"

GUSTAVE DORÉ, 1896

- **John 21:4–7 The resurrected Lord showed Himself again to seven of His Apostles as they were fishing.** Apparently, they had returned to their temporal vocation of fishing. And on this particular morning, "Jesus stood on the shore: but the disciples knew not that it was Jesus" (v. 4). As He had done when He first met them, the Lord inquired whether they had had any success (which they hadn't), and then provided a miracle catch for them, which "they were not able to draw it for the multitude of fishes" (vv. 5–6).

  These two "miracles of the fishes" stand like bookends on the ministry of Jesus Christ. By this means He called His chief disciples and by the same means He announced His presence again on this occasion. They rushed to shore and there Jesus taught them.

  It is interesting that, although they had by now seen Him at least twice before (three times for some of them), they didn't recognize Him at first. Peter declared, "It is the Lord," jumping into the water and swimming to the shore (v. 7). The others came by boat, and when they arrived they found "a fire of coals there, and fish laid thereon, and bread" (v. 9)—apparently prepared by the Lord. None of the disciples dared ask Him, "Who art thou? knowing that it was the Lord" (v. 12). Then they all dined together, presumably including the resurrected Lord (v. 15).

- **John 21:15–17 After eating together, Christ asks Peter to feed His sheep.** He said to Peter, "Simon, son of Jonas, lovest thou me more than these?" (v. 15). He was referring to the fish they had caught and were eating—the temporal vocation of Peter by which he sustained his family. Peter responded, "Yea, Lord; thou knowest that I love thee," whereupon the Lord replied, "Feed my lambs" (v. 15). He said unto Peter a second time, "Simon, son of Jonas, lovest thou me?" and Peter again replied, "Yea, Lord; thou knowest that I love thee," to which the Lord replied, "Feed my sheep" (v. 16).

For a third time, the Lord asked Peter, "Simon, son of Jonas, lovest thou me?" And "Peter was grieved because he said unto him the third time, Lovest thou me?" He protested, "Lord, thou knowest *all* things; thou *knowest* that I love thee," and then the Lord replied again, "Feed my sheep" (v. 17; emphasis added). By now, the point was very clear: Neither he nor the other Apostles were to return to their earthly vocations; they were to devote their full attention to the ministry after He was gone.

Prophecies Concerning the Apostles

- **John 21:18–19 Jesus predicts the manner of Peter's death.** Continuing His admonition to Peter, the Lord observed, "When thou wast young, thou girdedst thyself, and walkedst whither thou wouldest: but when thou shalt be old, thou shalt stretch forth thy hands, and another shall gird thee, and carry thee whither thou wouldest not" (v. 18). His life was no longer his own and because of his efforts to establish and lead the Church after Jesus' departure, he would eventually be taken captive and die for the Lord's sake. The prediction that he would "stretch forth" his hands "signif[ied] by what death he should glorify God"—crucifixion— "and when he had spoken this, he saith unto him, Follow me" (v. 19).

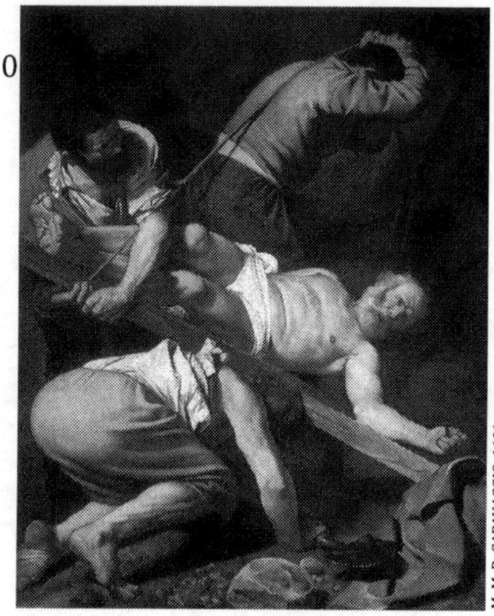

M. M. D. CARAVAGGIO, 1601

Eusebius, one of the Apostolic fathers writing in the 100 quoted the historian Tertullian in reporting that "'Nero was the first that persecuted [the Christians,] . . . when after subduing all the East, he exercised his cruelty against all at Rome. Such is the man of whom we boast, as the leader in our punishment. For he that knows who he was, may know also that there could scarcely be any thing but what was great and good, condemned by Nero.' Thus Nero publicly announcing himself as the chief enemy of God, was led on in his fury to slaughter the Apostles. Paul is therefore said to have been beheaded at Rome and Peter to have been crucified under him."[7]

Eusebius continued: "Peter appears to have preached through Pontus, Galatia, Bithynia, Cappadocia, and Asia to the Jews who were scattered abroad; he finally came to Rome and was crucified with his head downward, having requested of himself to suffer in this way."[8]

- **John 21:20–23 Jesus says John will remain on the earth until He comes again.** Peter then turned and looked at John the Beloved and asked, "Lord, and what shall this man do?" (vv. 20–21). Why Peter should be concerned with John's future is not clear, but the Lord replied, "If I will that he tarry till I come, what is that to thee? follow thou me" (v. 22). And because of this response, "this saying [went] abroad among the brethren, that that disciple should not die" (v. 23). John is quick to point out in this account about himself that "Jesus said not unto him,

He shall not die; but, If I will that he tarry till I come, what is that to thee?" (v. 23), but nevertheless he remains on the earth to this day.

— **D&C 7:1–8 Additional infor-Mation concerning John**. In a "revelation given to Joseph Smith the Prophet and Oliver Cowdery, at Harmony, Pennsylvania, April 1829, when they inquired through the Urim and Thummim as to whether John, the beloved disciple, tarried in the flesh or had died," the Lord provided "a translated version of the record made on parchment by John and hidden up by himself."[9]

G. RENI, 1575–1642

John the Beloved

John wrote, "And the Lord said unto me: John, my beloved, what desirest thou? For if you shall ask what you will, it shall be granted unto you. And I said unto him: Lord, give unto me power over death, that I may live and bring souls unto thee. And the Lord said unto me: Verily, verily, I say unto thee, because thou desirest this thou shalt tarry until I come in my glory, and shalt prophesy before nations, kindreds, tongues and people" (vv. 1–3).

What the Lord said to Peter was, "If I will that he tarry till I come, what is that to thee? For he desired of me that he might bring souls unto me, but thou desiredst that thou mightest speedily come unto me in my kingdom" (v. 4). "I say unto thee, Peter, this was a good desire; but my beloved has desired that he might do more, or a greater work yet among men than what he has before done. Yea, he has undertaken a greater work; therefore I will make him as flaming fire and a ministering angel; he shall minister for those who shall be heirs of salvation who dwell on the earth" (vv. 5–6).

The Lord concluded by saying, "Ye shall both have according to your desires, for ye both joy in that which ye have desired" (v. 8).

In answer to a question as to the meaning of a vision of the little book that John was commanded to eat (see Revelation

10:2, 8–10), the Prophet Joseph Smith said: "It was a mission, and an ordinance, for him [John] to gather the tribes of Israel" (D&C 77:14). At a conference of the Church, held June, 1831, the Prophet Joseph Smith said that "John the Revelator was then among the Ten Tribes of Israel who had been led away by Shalmaneser, king of Assyria, to prepare them for their return from their long dispersion."[10]

Elder Joseph Fielding Smith said:

> A great mission was given unto John because of his desire, and he is even now laboring as "a flaming fire and a ministering angel, for those who are heirs of salvation." In the tenth chapter of Revelation we read that John was given a little book by the angel and commanded to eat it up, which he did, and he said, "It was in my mouth sweet as honey; and as soon as I had eaten it, my belly was bitter." And the angel said by way of interpretation of this act: "Thou must prophesy again before many peoples, and nations, and tongues, and kings." When this mission was given, John was an old man far beyond the allotted years of three score and ten.[11]

Sacred Private Teachings

- **John 20:30–31 John states his reason for writing his gospel.** He did not record everything Jesus said and did, either before or after His resurrection. John said, "And many other signs truly did Jesus in the presence of his disciples, which are not written in this book" (v. 30). However, the things that he did write were for the purpose "that ye might believe that Jesus is the Christ, the Son of God; and that believing ye might have life through his name" (v. 31).

- **John 21:25 Our study of Christ has been only partial at best.** John said in the final chapter of his gospel, "And there are also many other things which Jesus did, the which, if they should be written every one, I suppose that even the world itself could not contain the books that should be written."

- **Luke 24:44–46 Christ "opened . . . their understanding" of the scriptures.** He rehearsed "the words which I spake unto you, while I was yet with you, that all things must be fulfilled, which were written in the law of Moses, and in the prophets, and in the psalms, concerning me" (v. 44). As He reviewed these teachings, He "opened . . . their understanding, that they might understand the scriptures" (v. 45). Doctrine that is not plainly understood benefits few; the Lord, as does Nephi, "glor[ies] in plainness" (2 Nephi 33:6). And at the center of it all was the Atonement: "Thus it is written, and thus it behoved Christ to suffer, and to rise from the dead the third day" (v. 46).

THEBIBLEREVIVAL.COM, #48

- **Acts 1:2–3 Christ taught the disciples for 40 days after His resurrection.** Luke, who is believed to be the author of Acts, reports that "until the day in which he was taken up," the Savior "shewed himself alive after his passion by many infallible proofs, being seen of them forty days, and speaking of the things pertaining to the kingdom of God." There are a number of statements here that need explanation:

  "Passion" comes from the Latin *passus*, "to suffer," and thus Luke is speaking of the Lord's Atonement. "Infallible proofs" come from the Greek "sure signs or tokens"—referring to the appearances of the resurrected Christ, and the special wounds that identify Him. "Forty days" refers to the length of Christ's post-resurrection ministry among His Apostles. And "things pertaining to the kingdom of God" are special, sacred teachings not given to the disciples during the Savior's mortal ministry. These included:

The nature of resurrected beings	(Luke 24:36–43)
The meaning of scriptures not understood	(Luke 24:44–47)
Their role as personal witnesses of the Savior	(Luke 24:48)

Their responsibilities as leaders of the Church	(John 21:1–17)
His visit to the spirits in prison	(1 Peter 3:19; 4:6)
The principle of baptism for the dead	(1 Cor. 15:29)

Teachings Recorded in the Apocrypha

Writings by early (1st and 2nd century) Christian leaders contain many things which a Latter-day Saint would recognize in the restored gospel, but which also raise historical and doctrinal problems. They must be read with great care to separate truth from error.

Dr. Hugh Nibley provides a summary of the most interesting of these teachings:

> . . . The *favorite* theme of the early apocrypha happens to be "the teachings of the Lord to the Apostles after the Resurrection" . . . It begins with the most natural question to ask anyone returning to earth after being away: "Where did you go and what did you see?" The Lord's discourse in reply recalls the journeys to worlds above and below recounted by the prophets and patriarchs of the old Jewish apocrypha. . . . [Christ] goes as a missionary and reports what He has done. The central theme is the Descensus, a mission to the spirits below closely resembling the Lord's earthly calling. He brings the *kerygma* to all, and those who accept it follow Him out of the depths into the light, receive baptism, and hence mount up by degrees to realms of glory . . .
>
> There is a strong emphasis in early Christian literature on the doctrine of the Two Ways, depicting life as a time of probation, a constant confrontation with good and evil and the obligation to choose between them. This is conceived as part of a plan laid down "in the presence of the first angels" at the creation of the world, according to which through Adam's fall the human race would be placed in the position, envied by the angels, of being perfectly free to choose good or evil and thereby fully merit whatever rewards would follow. Satan rebelled against the plan, refused obeisance to Adam, and was cast down upon the earth with his cohorts, to fulfill divine purpose by providing, as "the serpent," the temptation necessary for an effectual testing of human beings. . . .

> What gives substance to this . . . is the imposing body of rites and ordinances that goes with it . . . rites of washing and anointing . . . a symbolic but real and tangible garment, the giving of a name, a garment, and a special mark or sign,[12] seals and garments[13], and anointing[14]. . . . Recent findings indicate unusual emphasis placed on a perfect unity of the sexes in marriage . . . the two becoming one "in the Lord."[15]
>
> [According to William F. Albright[16]], the temple's "rich cosmic symbolism . . . was largely lost in later Israelite and Jewish tradition." . . . As Alfred Jeremias, Sigmund Mowinckel, and others have shown, such elements as its cosmic orientation, . . . the ritual drama of creation, fall, and victory over death, rites of initiation and purification, etc. [have all been lost from original temple symbolism] . . . .[17]

Dr. Nibley also provides a partial summary of prayer circle ordinances that are described in these ancient documents. Keep in mind that *none* of these writings were available to Joseph Smith in his day. The knowledgeable reader will see many familiar things in this list.

> In the book of *2nd Jeu*, considered by Carl Schmidt to be the most instructive of all early Christian texts[:]
>
> The Apostles and their wives all form a circle around the Lord, who says He will lead them through all the secret ordinances that shall give them eternal progression . . . [including] "all ordinances . . . , all knowledge . . . , . . . tokens . . . , supplications (forms of address), [and] degrees [bodily positions]. . . .
>
> ". . . All the Apostles, clothed in their garments, . . . placing foot to foot, made a circle" [with] Jesus standing at the altar . . .
>
> The prayer spoken in the circle differs every time; it is not strictly prescribed. The one leading the prayer expresses himself as the Spirit moves him, and the others . . . repeat each line after him . . .
>
> [The *Pistis Sophia* provides additional details about the prayer circle rites:]
>
> . . . The Lord, having formed the Apostles and their wives in a circle around Him and "taking the place of Adam at the altar, called upon the Father three times in an unknown tongue."
>
> . . . They stood "all in white . . ."

> . . . Jesus prayed in a strange language, beginning with the words *Iaō , aōi, ōia!* which . . . meant "Hear me Father . . ."[18]

Teachings of the Early Christian Fathers

Early Christian letters and texts discovered during the last century also relate what Jesus was said to have taught during those forty days.

For example, early Christian converts were concerned about their friends and family who had never heard the gospel:

> Clement of Alexandria, an early investigator, put this question to Peter: "Shall those be wholly deprived of the kingdom of heaven who died before Christ's coming?"
>
> Peter gives a most significant answer: He assures Clement that the people in question are not damned and never will be, and explains that provision has been made for their salvation, but this, he says, is "as far as we are allowed to declare these things," excusing himself from telling more: "You compel me, O Clement, to touch upon things which we are forbidden to discuss."
>
> Clement later wrote: "It is not right to condemn some without trial, and only give credit for righteousness to others who lived after the coming of the Lord. . . . Certainly one righteous man is not different from another as far as righteousness goes. . . . For God is not the God of the Jew alone but of all men. . . . Those who live righteously before the law are to be counted as faithful and reckoned among the just. . . . God is good and Christ is mighty to save, according to principles of justice and equality, those who turn to Him, whether here or in the next world."
>
> Irenaeus wrote in the second century: "Christ did not come for the sole benefit of those who believed in Him at the time of Tiberius Caesar, nor has the Father a plan for those only who happen to be living today; but it is for all the human family . . . who from the beginning by righteousness pleased God and feared Him in their generations, and dealt justly and religiously with their neighbors, and yearned to see Christ and hear His voice."[19]

THE ASCENSION

An Endowment of Power

- **Luke 24:48–49 A promise of power necessary to bear witness.** Christ told them that their role was to be "witnesses of these things," but they were to "tarry . . . in the city of Jerusalem, until ye be endued with power from on high." *Endued* means "endowed," "clothed," or "invested."

- **Mark 16:17–18 Gifts and signs that will be bestowed upon them.** Mark mentions that these signs will "follow" those who believe in Christ: "In my name shall they cast out devils; they shall speak with new tongues; They shall take up serpents; and if they drink any deadly thing, it shall not hurt them; they shall lay hands on the sick, and they shall recover."

- **Acts 1:4–5 All of this will be bestowed by receiving of the Holy Ghost.** They were not to "depart from Jerusalem, but wait for the promise of the Father, which, saith he, ye have heard of me" (v. 4). That promise was that "ye shall be baptized with the Holy Ghost not many days hence" (v. 5).

PROVIDENCE LITHOGRAPHIC CO., 1901, #34

The outpouring of the Spirit on the Day of Pentecost (just 10 days after Christ's ascension) was a partial fulfillment of this promise. But there was more power with which they had to be "endued" (see Luke 24:49; Acts 1:8).

Elder Bruce R. McConkie said:

> . . . From latter-day revelation we learn that the Lord had something more in mind in issuing this instruction. In this dispensation, after the elders had received the gift of the Holy Ghost and as early as January, 1831, the Lord began to reveal unto them that He had an endowment in store for the faithful

(see D&C 38:22; 43:16) . . . In June, 1833, He said: "I gave unto you a commandment that you should build a house, in the which house I design to endow those whom I have chosen with power from on high . . . even as mine Apostles at Jerusalem" (D&C 95:8–9; 105:11–12, 18, 33).

Thus the Apostles—or any ministers or missionaries in any age—are not fully qualified to go forth, preach the gospel, and build up the kingdom, unless they have the gift of the Holy Ghost and also are endowed with power from on high, meaning [that they] have received certain knowledge, powers, and special blessings, normally given only in the Lord's Temple.[20]

- **Acts 1:6–7 A question about when the Savior would come again.** The question whose answer believers in every age want to know is: *When?* So, "when they therefore were come together, they asked of him, saying, Lord, wilt thou at this time restore again the kingdom to Israel?" (v. 6). "And he said unto them, It is not for you to know the times or the seasons, which the Father hath put in his own power" (v. 7). Like all of us, they would have to wait in faith until the promised return of Christ occurs.

Commissioning the Apostles

PROVIDENCE LITHOGRAPHIC CO., 1905, #38

- **Acts 1:8 "Unto the uttermost part of the earth."** After they have received power from the Holy Ghost, they will become "witnesses unto me both in Jerusalem, and in all Judæa, and in Samaria, and unto the uttermost part of the earth." Theirs was a worldwide ministry, not a local one.

- **Matthew 28:19–20 "Teach all nations, baptizing them."** They were not to restrict their efforts to the children of Israel, but to "teach all nations, baptizing them in the name of the Father, and of the Son, and of the Holy Ghost" (v. 19). They were to look after their converts, "teaching them to observe all things whatsoever I have commanded you" (v. 20). And He promised to be "with you alway[s], even unto the end of the world" (v. 20).

- **Mark 16:15–16 "Preach the gospel to every creature."** Neither the Father nor His Son desire any child of God to be overlooked. Thus, they were to "go ye into all the world, and preach the gospel to every creature" (v. 15). Their work would have eternal consequences in the lives of those who heard them: "He that believeth and is baptized shall be saved; but he that believeth not shall be damned" (v. 16).

  Elder Bruce R. McConkie said:

  > The Apostles of old were sent out to teach, testify, and baptize. They were to teach by the Spirit, testify of the truth, and baptize the repentant souls. They were witnesses. A witness testifies; he has a testimony to bear; he tells what he knows. The gospel is not carried to the world by the teaching process only. Any minister or professor of religion can teach; whether his conclusions are true or false, he can present them and make them seem appealing to some. But only one who knows by personal revelation that certain things are true can testify with converting power.
  >
  > These Apostles were to teach the truths of salvation and then testify that by personal revelation they knew whereof they spoke. They were both teachers and witnesses. For instance, they were to teach that the scriptures said Christ should come and die for the sins of the world; but then they were to bear witness that this man Jesus was the Christ, that He had risen from the dead and that they, His witnesses, had felt the nail marks in His hands and feet, had handled His resurrected body, had walked with Him on the Emmaus road, had seen Him eat fish and an honeycomb, and that they knew by the power of the Holy Ghost that He was the Son of God. They were witnesses.[21]

A Similar Charge in Our Own Day

- **D&C 1:2, 4 "The voice of the Lord is unto all men."** Every child of God will have the opportunity to hear the truth, "and there is none to escape; and there is no eye that shall not see, neither ear that shall not hear, neither heart that shall not be penetrated" (v. 2). "The voice of warning shall be unto all people, by the mouths of my disciples, whom I have chosen in these last days" (v. 4).

President Spencer W. Kimball said:

> It seems to me that the Lord chose His words when He said "every nation," "every land," "uttermost bounds of the earth," "every tongue," "every people," "every soul," "all the world," "many lands." Surely there is significance in these words! . . .
>
> My brethren, I wonder if we are doing all we can. Are we complacent in our approach to teaching all the world? We have been proselyting now 144 years [as of 1974]. Are we prepared to lengthen our stride? To enlarge our vision? Remember, our ally is our God. He is our commander. He made the plans. He gave the commandment. . . .
>
> And as I read the scripture I think of the numerous nations that are still untouched. I know they have curtains, like iron curtains and bamboo curtains. I know how difficult it is because we have made some efforts. Surely the Lord knew what He was doing when He commanded. . . . Somehow, brethren, I feel that when we have done all in our power that the Lord will find a way to open doors. That is my faith. . . . If He commands, certainly He can fulfill. . . .
>
> I believe the Lord can do anything He sets His mind to do. But I can see no good reason why the Lord would open doors that we are not prepared to enter. Why should He break down the Iron Curtain or the Bamboo Curtain or any other curtain if we are still unprepared to enter? I believe we have men who could help the Apostles to open these doors—statesmen, able and trustworthy—but, when we are ready for them. Today [as of 1974] we have 18,600 missionaries. We can send more. Many more![22]

The Prophet Joseph Smith said: "The Standard of Truth has been erected; no unhallowed hand can stop the work from progressing; persecutions may rage, mobs may combine, armies may assemble, calumny may defame, but the truth of God will go forth boldly, nobly, and independent, till it has penetrated every continent, visited every clime, swept every country, and sounded in every ear, till the purposes of God shall be accomplished, and the Great Jehovah shall say the work is done."[23]

Christ Ascends into Heaven

- **Luke 24:50–51 On the Mount of Olives, near Bethany**. When the forty-day ministry came to a close, Christ led His Apostles from Jerusalem over the Mount of Olives toward Bethany, where His ascension to heaven took place. Luke records that "he lifted up his hands, and blessed them" (v. 50), and while He did so "he was parted from them, and carried up into heaven" (v. 51).

G. FUGEL, THE BIBLE AND ITS STORY, 1908

- **Acts 1:9 He was taken up into heaven.** While they watched, "he was taken up; and a cloud received him out of their sight."

- **Mark 16:19 "On the right hand of God."** We are not sure of all things that the disciples saw on this occasion, but Mark records that Christ "was received up into heaven, and sat on the right hand of God."

- **Acts 1:10–11 "Two men stood by them in white."** The Apostles looked earnestly toward heaven for some time, when "two men" appeared and "stood by them in white apparel" (v. 10). And they said unto them, "Ye men of Galilee, why stand ye gazing up into heaven? this same Jesus, which is taken up from you into heaven, shall so come in like manner as ye have seen him go into heaven" (v. 11).

One of the most important things we learn from this event is that Jesus will come again just as He was taken up. He will descend in a cloud of glory from the heavens upon the Mount of Olives at the end of the War of Armageddon. That will usher in the destruction of the wicked, the salvation of His people the Jews, and the beginning of the millennial reign. Until that day, we all look steadfastly toward heaven and pray, "Even so, come, Lord Jesus" (Revelation 22:20).

PROVIDENCE LITHOGRAPHIC CO., 1896, #30

- **3 Nephi 11–28** Shortly after His resurrection, the Lord began His brief ministry among His people in the Western Hemisphere.

THE APOSTLES ASSUME LEADERSHIP OF THE CHURCH

President David O. McKay said:

> The Resurrection is a miracle; however, only in the sense that it is beyond man's comprehension and understanding. To all who accept it as a fact, it was but a manifestation of a uniform law of life. Because man does not understand the law, he calls it a miracle. Some day man's enlightenment may bring this momentous event out of the dusk of mystery into the broad day of understanding.
>
> That the literal resurrection from the grave was a reality to the disciples who knew Christ intimately is a certainty. In their minds there was absolutely no doubt. They were witnesses of the fact. They knew, because their eyes beheld, their ears heard, their hands felt the corporeal presence of the Risen Redeemer.
>
> At Jesus' death, the Apostles were stricken with gloom. When He lay dead their hopes all but died. Their intense grief, the story of Thomas, the moral perplexity of Peter, the evident

preparation for a permanent burial, combine to illustrate the prevalence of a fear that the redemption of Israel had failed.

Notwithstanding the often repeated assurances of Christ that He would return to them after death, the Apostles did not seem fully to comprehend it. At the crucifixion, they were frightened and discouraged. For two and a half years they had been upheld and inspired by Christ's presence. But now He was gone. They were left alone, and they seemed confused, fearful, helpless; only John stood by the cross.

The world would never have been stirred by men with such wavering, doubting, despairing minds as the Apostles possessed on the day of the crucifixion.

What was it that suddenly changed these disciples to confident, fearless, heroic preachers of the Gospel of Jesus Christ? It was the revelation that Christ had risen from the grave. His promises had been kept, His Messianic mission fulfilled. In the words of an eminent writer, "The final and absolute seal of genuineness has been put on all His claims, and the indelible stamp of a divine authority upon all His teachings. The gloom of death had been banished by the glorious light of the presence of their Risen, glorified Lord and Savior."

On the evidence of these unprejudiced, unexpectant, incredulous witnesses, faith in the resurrection has its impregnable foundation.[24]

Notes

1. See *History of the Church*, 3:387.
2. *Doctrinal New Testament Commentary*, 3 vols. [1965–73], 1:400.
3. See *Doctrines of Salvation*, comp. Bruce R. McConkie, 3 vols. [1954–56], 2:165.
4. *Doctrinal New Testament Commentary*, 1:400.
5. *History of the Church*, 4:211.
6. *Doctrines of Salvation*, 2:111–12, 117.

7. *Eusebius' Ecclesiastical History*, translated by C. F. Cruse, complete and unabridged, new updated edition [1998], 63. "*Eusebius, the Bishop of Caesarea* was a 4th-century work giving a chronological account of the development of Early Christianity from the 1st century to the 4th century. . . . Eusebius had access to the library of Caesarea and made use of many ecclesiastical monuments and documents, acts of the martyrs, letters, extracts from earlier Christian writings, lists of bishops, and similar sources, often quoting the originals at great length so that his work contains materials not elsewhere preserved." (http://en.wikipedia.org/wiki/Church_History_(Eusebius)

8. *Eusebius' Ecclesiastical History*, 67.

9. See *History of the Church*, 1:35–36; see also section heading of D&C 7.

10. *History of the Church*, 1:176.

11. *Church History and Modern Revelation*, 4 vols. [1946–49], 1:44–45.

12. *The Odes and Psalms of Solomon* and *The Acts of Thomas.*

13. *The Shepherd of Hermas*, Similitudes.

14. *Apostolic Constitutions VII* and *The Gospel of Philip.*

15. 1 Corinthians 11:11; *Gospel of Thomas* 85:25–35.

16. *Archaeology and the Religion of Israel.*

17. Adapted from *Mormonism and Early Christianity* [1987], edited by Todd M. Compton and Stephen D. Ricks, chapter 2, "Evangelium Quadraginta Dierum: The Forty-day Mission of Christ—The Forgotten Heritage," 10–44.

18. Adapted from *Mormonism and Early Christianity*, chapter 3, "The Early Christian Prayer Circle," 45–99.

19. All quotes taken from Hugh Nibley, *Mormonism and Early Christianity*, chapter 4, "Baptism for the Dead in Ancient Times," 102–3.

20. *Doctrinal New Testament Commentary*, 1:859.

21. *Doctrinal New Testament Commentary*, 1:855.

22. "When the World Will Be Converted," *Ensign*, Oct. 1974, 5, 7.

23. *History of the Church*, 4:540.

24. "Christ the Lord Is Risen," *Instructor*, Apr. 1954, 97.

ABOUT THE AUTHOR

Randal S. Chase spent his childhood years in Nephi, Utah, where his father was a dry land wheat farmer and a businessman. In 1959 their family moved to Salt Lake City and settled in the Holladay area. He served a full-time mission in the Central British (England Central) Mission from 1968 to 1970. He returned home and married Deborah Johnsen in 1971. They are the parents of six children—two daughters and four sons—and an ever-expanding number of grandchildren.

He was called to serve as a bishop at the age of 27 in the Sandy Crescent South Stake area of the Salt Lake Valley. He served six years in that capacity, and has since served as a high councilor, a stake executive secretary and clerk, and in many other stake and ward callings. Regardless of whatever other callings he has received over the years, one was nearly constant: He has taught Gospel Doctrine classes in every ward he has ever lived in as an adult—a total of 35 years.

Dr. Chase was a well-known media personality on Salt Lake City radio stations in the 1970s. He left on-air broadcasting in 1978 to develop and market a computer-based management, sales, and music programming system to radio and television stations in the United States, Canada, South America, and Australia. After the business was sold in 1984, he supported his family as a media and business consultant in the Salt Lake City area.

Having a great desire to teach young people of college age, he determined in the late 1980s to pursue his doctorate, and received his Ph.D. in Communication from the University of Utah in 1997. He has taught communication courses at that institution as well as at Salt Lake Community College and Dixie State University for 21 years. He served as Communication Department chair and is currently a full-time professor at Dixie State University in St. George, Utah.

Concurrently with his academic career, brother Chase has served as a volunteer LDS Institute and Adult Education instructor in the CES system since 1994, both in Salt Lake City and St. George, where he currently teaches a weekly Adult Education class for three stakes in the Washington area. He has also conducted multiple Church History tours and seminars. During these years of gospel teaching, he has developed an extensive library of lesson plans and handouts which are the predecessors to this book.

Dr. Chase has published a twelve-volume series of study guides on the Book of Mormon, Church History, the Old Testament, and the New Testament, titled *Making Precious Things Plain*. These are designed to assist teachers and students of the gospel, as well as those who simply want to study on their own. This book on the Week of Atoning Sacrifice is an outgrowth of those volumes.

41528587R00143

Made in the USA
Charleston, SC
30 April 2015